A Multi Colored Coat

(An autobiography – of sorts)

Joseph J. Cox

Published by Big Picture Books

Modiin, Israel

Hardcover ISBN: 978-1-7332801-5-0

Paperback ISBN: 978-1-7332801-6-7

To my kids. You rock.

CHAPTERS

WHY

"What?!?"

Shocked incredulity. That's what my kids expressed when, one random day, we were driving down the road, discussing school, and I revealed that I was a high school dropout.

I was shocked too.

I have six kids, four of whom were in the car with me. One is 14, the other three 12. Totaled up they are something like 50 years old and – all put together – they hadn't realized that their father was a high school dropout.

Clearly, I was failing as a parent.

We talked, as kids trapped in a car that lacks any video screens and a father who prohibits personal musical devices are occasionally forced to do. They began to understand how I could simultaneously be a high school drop-out, have an undergraduate degree from an Ivy League institution and have a Masters to boot.

I could have written the whole thing off as a tiny little anecdote, but it bugged me. Sure, I guess children ought to know their parents' stories. That sounds all proper and such. But there is a more important principle at stake. People find my stories *fun*. Lots of other people know a smattering of them. So here I am, a father of six, and I'm depriving my children of quite a bit of fun.

That's why I decided to write this book. I'm writing it because people enjoy my stories. But I'm also writing it because my own kids ought to know them.

Unfortunately, for you the reader, I'm not some deeply inspiring person whose life story includes the surmounting of countless obstacles or the development of world-changing science, technology or art. Nobody is going to find the dates and events of my life consequential in that way. There is no critical narrative to follow. This story is more modest than that.

Modest, but still interesting.

Unfortunately, for you the reader (this might get to be a trend), I'm also not somebody who's going to put in all the effort of writing a book just to tell stories. For this reason, I'm going to share what I've learned along the way.

So, that's the plan. I'll intersperse fun and entertaining stories with boring life lessons and hope the stories are just enough to get you through the boring bits. If you are wildly entertained, I'm doing it all wrong. And if you're too bored, there will have been no point in starting. I'm just going to have to try to thread the needle.

One more thing about threading needles. There can sometimes be a fine line between entertainment and destruction. I'll give you an example. A while back my mother wrote a book called *A River Went out of Eden.* I highly recommend it – it's the story of my parents' (and older siblings') lives in north central Idaho. They lived without plumbing and electricity 10 hours from the nearest town (for the three months of the year when you could actually get out). My parents canned and ate bears and mountain lions. They struggled with famine and flood. It is really quite a story. Before her final draft, my mother contacted various people in the book and offered to change their names. After all, she was sharing their stories and she didn't want to hurt anybody. One man by the name (real name) of Mark Houston Haney said, "Use my real name" and so she did.

Now, Mark is a very interesting person. We'll probably touch on his story a little later. For now, let's stay on point. A couple of months later my mother's book ended up in his mailbox. A complimentary copy. He was out. But his wife was home. Mark had been through a lot of wives. This one opened the mailbox, read the book cover to cover, then left a note on the front of it: "I didn't know this about you."

Just like that, she was gone.

My mom felt awful.

Mark didn't mind, though.

As he put it, "I'll just go get me another one."

Given Mark's story, I'm adopting a somewhat different approach than my mother did. Where I can hide identities, I will. Where I can't... well, I'll try not to say things people don't want shared (with an exception for one particular kind of behavior). I know that removes some of the voyeuristic fun. Nonetheless, there's little benefit in sharing terrible stories about people. I'm not trying to make anybody look bad. Some of the people the stories concern are reasonable tough characters. Some are dead.

I don't want an unhappy visit from either type.

Don't worry, though. Many of the people I know have unusual ideas about what would make them 'look bad.'

The stories will *still* be interesting.

ANCIENT HISTORY

I guess any good autobiography starts at the beginning. Of course, the beginning tends to be reasonably boring and purposeless. At birth, people are just packages of potential. They don't mean much. The celebration of life is really only complete with death. I promise you, that idea it isn't as morbid as it seems.

Nonetheless, when it comes to my very early life, I'll only cover the most basic facts. Like most people, I was born. Like most people, I had two biological parents. Like some people, those parents were married. And like a smaller group of people, they had other children.

I guess the only thing that distinguished me at birth was that one of my siblings, Jeremiah Toyam Cox, had died almost exactly a year before I was born.

My middle name is Jeremiah.

I was named after him.

Jeremiah had just turned seven when he'd died. I'm not covering for him when I say that he wasn't responsible for his own death. He hadn't been doing anything stupid. He was the victim of a single act of moderate recklessness.

A single act defined a whole lot of my childhood.

Now I could sit here and talk about death and how I thought about it every day for decades. You might find that depressing, though. I don't want to depress you.

Instead, let's reach back *before* my birth, before Jeremiah. Let's go back a bunch of generations and call *that* the beginning.

Growing up, we knew we were ½ Eastern-European Jew (with some raping Cossack[1] mixed in) and 1/8th Apache, English, Swedish and PWT (Po' White Trash). The PWT were Okie mountain people who just came from the hills. They had completely unknowable origins.

I could go get a genetic test and figure out just how PWT I really am[2]. I won't though. The reason is simple: I don't care

_____

[1] One of my mother's ancestors was raped by Cossacks. The blond offspring of that rape, another of my ancestors, was spared during a violent pogrom. The mob didn't realize she was Jewish.

[2] A sibling did just this and the results *did not* match up with the family stories. If anything, that makes the origins of the stories even *more* interesting. In what circumstances do you claim a rape? How

5

about the truth. The truth isn't what makes you who you are. Sure, some long distant genetics might have an impact, but the *stories* of the people involved are far more important than the truth about who those people actually were. A father who raises you is more of a father than one who was only a sperm donor.

In terms of stories, our family background was well established. We were happy knowing it. And then, the day after my mother died following a horrible struggle with the end stages of cancer, we were going through her papers, and we discovered that there was more to the PWT slice of the family than we'd ever imagined.

Now that 1/8th PWT was important. Growing up, my father proudly demonstrated that PWT was a core part of our identity. We ate PWT foods[1]. We acted like PWT people – us kids were raised on a solid diet of whoopin', swearin' and guns. My father was proud of this. *His* mother, on the other hand, wasn't. My Grannie Annie pretended her husband's mother's family was Norwegian, because nobody liked the Swedes. *She* was an upstanding, upper-middle-class, white woman. Her propriety was such that, despite everybody in my family swearing like sailors, nobody in the family *ever* swore in front of her. She expected more, and so we gave it. I guess that puts expectations right up there with stories. Stories may define the past, but expectations define the future.

---

do you not realize the women who raised you (an Indian) was not your genetic mother (apparently a white woman)?

[1] Including ice cream made from cream skimmed off the top of our illegal non-pasteurized milk. Wow, that ice cream was good!

Speaking of my grandmother, one of my most confusing childhood moments involved her. I was at a friend's house for the Passover Seder. *His* grandmother was there. Over the course of the Seder, I learned that she couldn't sew, cut hair, quilt or even really cook. I always assumed *everybody's* grandmothers could do these things. I was shocked and couldn't really believe she was a grandmother *at all.* For us, practical skills are something you keep picking up – you need to keep picking up – as life goes on. By the time you're old, you ought to be able to do a pretty good variety of things. Building, electrical work, hair cutting[1], sewing, a bit of plumbing. You know the drill. Of course, you don't always do them well. That's part of the PWT magic. One time, my father messed up the venting on our furnace and almost killed the entire family. We were sleeping such long hours. Finally, my parents asked our family doctor (a forensic pathologist) what could be wrong. He knew *exactly* what was happening. He'd had many exposures to the aftereffects of carbon monoxide poisoning. We found the leak and fixed it and stopping taking such long naps.

Getting back to my grandmother... When she was on her death bed (there I go again), she admitted her own mother was Indian[2]. It had been an open secret for years, but she'd finally

---

[1] We even had an old-fashioned barber chair, complete with hydraulics.
[2] An unacceptable term today, but what was used then. I find it no more Euro-centric than 'Native American' given that that names an

fessed up to her roots. Her mother, by the way, was a seriously tough cookie. My grandmother's grandmother (my great-great-grandmother) rode fifteen hundred miles shortly after giving birth. She took my great-grandmother with her. My great-grandmother was laid across the saddle horn of *her* mother's horse and carried from Oklahoma Indian Territory home to Missouri and back again. She grew up with the mark of that horn hollowed into her back. My great-uncle Sylvan (quite a character in his own right) used to say that if Grandmother Tuck hadn't been Indian, she wouldn't have made it. Not as a young woman alone with a baby on a horse through Indian Territory. Not for fifteen hundred miles.

A Gun Crafted by my Great-Uncle Sylvan

There were a bunch of tough cookie stories in that family. I had a great aunt who'd been married something like 6 times. My grandfather was a somewhat difficult character. To give a little color, he went into the World War II as a Lieutenant. He

---

entire continent after an actual European rather than forever capturing the ignorance of the first European explorers.

left with the same rank. That's an impressive lack of upward mobility in a World War. Among his other less desirable attributes, he wasn't the kindest of husbands. He asked that oft-divorced great aunt whether she was afraid of all those ex-husbands lurking around. She looked him straight in the eye and said "Orville, every man's gotta' sleep sometime."

My grandmother reported that he didn't. For weeks.

My grandmother might have been upstanding, but she still kept *some* aspects of that tough-as-nails PWT culture. She made Angel Food Cake and a remarkably light food called "merengue" (they are nothing like store-bought merengues). She knew what it was like to live rough, very rough. And she brooked no nonsense. When I was a teenager, a woman in her neighborhood was raped in her kitchen. The rapist was on the loose. My mother asked my grandmother whether she was worried about being raped in *her* kitchen.

My grandmother looked at my mother incredulously and said, "A woman *can't* be raped in her own kitchen."

"What do you mean?" asked my mom, equally incredulously.

"It's *her kitchen*," said my grandmother, gesturing around, "She's got her knives, she's got her pans, she's got her stove – she *can't* be raped in her kitchen."

That declaration wouldn't have been true for most women, but it was for my grandmother.

The next section, and others formatted like it, are excerpts from another source. In this case, a related story (as told by my mother).

"

In My Mother's Words
Mar 16, 2018

It must have been in 1981. Sylvan had died in 1980, and we had donated many of the things he made to the Idaho Historical Society. Bossman[1] and his mother were invited to attend the dedication of the Buckskin Bill exhibit. Nechama went as well.

I think from the beginning and to the very end, Nechama and Grannie were close.

Nechama and Grannie were walking hand in hand across a city park in downtown Boise. Grannie was explaining that there were two kinds of people in the world. There were the people who remembered the good times and forgot everything else. Then there were the people who remembered the bad times, every single trespass against them, and tended to forget the everything else.

Grandpa Orville remembered the bad things – his sister Olivia stealing fifteen dollars from him when he was a teenager. The other students at Wichita State College who laughed at him because he wore bib overalls. For Grandpa that was real oppression – being laughed at for wearing bib overalls.

Grannie was someone who remembered the good times and wiped-out memories of the bad times. She had, in a sense, trained herself that way.

---

[1] A nickname for my father.

Nechama asked Grannie for the remembrance of a good time? Grannie thought for a minute or so and then gifted her granddaughter with the memory of a perfect moment. "I was about four, I think." Grannie said. "I was walking across a farm field on the way to our uncle and aunt's dug out. I remember holding Sylvan's hand, I remember him talking to me, I remember the sun and flowers. I remember the smell of the cow droppings."

"And…" Nechama asked waiting for rest.

"That was it. It was perfect. It was a perfect moment."[1]

Not every good memory has a back story. Some of the best memories don't have back stories. They just are perfect. Not every good memory has a back story. But I am the sort of person who tends to create back stories. It may have been the day that Grannie's brother Joe was born, and the older children were probably sent to their uncle because dug outs are very small, and no one wanted young children around their mother giving birth. Perhaps it was that day. Perhaps not. I don't know. Perhaps if Sylvan were still alive I could ask him.

Every year in the house on SW Gale, Grannie Annie and Grandpa Orville bought a Christmas tree. Their trees were still rooted in soil and stood in a pot and not on a stand. Every year after Christmas Grannie planted the tree outside in the yard. Grannie knew every tree and the year it was planted and the memories of that year.

Toward the end of their lives, Orville went out one day and cut all those trees down – he cut down most of the other shrubs in the yard as well. He did it he said because the yard needed light. The trees were too big. They were in fact very big. Trees grow very quickly in Oregon.

It broke Grannie's heart…

---

[1] My mother told me that my grandmother confessed this might have been her *only* perfect moment.

On the second day of Rosh Hashana in 1995, Grandpa Orville woke up one morning, visited his wife, got out of bed to get the Sunday paper and dress for their constitutional walk on Fairmount. As he was tying his shoes he fell, spasmed for a minute or so, and died.

Our neighbors the Kinney's came to our door to tell us since we don't answer the phone on Jewish holidays. We drove in.

Of course, Grannie, still in her nighty, was frantic. She called 911 and then she called the family doctors even though she knew Orville had passed.

When we arrived, Dr. Harris and Dr. Shields (good friends as well as doctors) were walking out the door. Dr. Shields turned to Dr. Harris and asked, "What did that man ever do to deserve such an easy death?"

[my mother also tended to protect the guilty. My grandfather hadn't just gotten out of bed. He died in flagrante delicto ***at the age of 82****. All the paramedics could see what had killed him.]*

My grandmother had been raised rough. Her father was a drunk white man, and her mother was a teetotalling Indian. In her world that was how it worked. You either *never* touched drink or you were an alcoholic. There was no wisdom to be found in moderation there. That was it, though. Prior to her parents, there were only anonymous Indians and PWT... disappearing into the mists of time.

Or so we thought.

The document we discovered among my mother's papers was a genealogy. A genealogy for the PWT branch of the family. Apparently one of my ancestors was a signer of the Declaration of Independence. One of his ancestors was Henry the Third – although the final 14 generations from some Lord back to him were a little unclear. The anonymous PWT branch of the family could trace their roots back to Rollo, Count of Rouen, the first Viking ruler of Normandy. He died in the year 930.

My mother's side of the family also claims an illustrious heritage. There's a book, a genealogy of sorts, that claims to trace my mother's family line back to (arguably) the greatest of Talmudic scholar, Rashi[1]. He in turn claimed to trace *his* family line back to Yochanan HaSandlar, then to Gamaliel and from there to King David.

I don't know about the stuff *before* Rashi, but the time *after* Rashi is easier to come to grips with. The reason is simple: within certain families, this sort of tracing just isn't that hard to do. They marry their cousins, almost exclusively, and they pepper in a fair number of famous Rabbis along the way. Without much effort, the family line can be made reasonably clear.

My mother's family was one of those families. Few others had the *yichus* – the family history of documented brilliance – to merit marrying into *their* family. So, they intermarried.

_____

[1] Many people can claim lineage from Rashi. It is quite common. The intervening generations are a little less so.

I'm actually descended, if the stories are to be believed, from *two* of Rashi's daughters (Yocheved and Miriam). Their descendants married each other. I'd guess the PWT and the Rabbis had this in common. While this arrangement produced the occasional stand-out Torah (Bible) genius, it also produced a fair number of psychologically unstable or otherwise damaged children. The rise of the knowledge of genetics might have contributed to my mother's father's decision to marry 'out'. He married a Jewish girl who *wasn't* a cousin. Where his family was famous for its intellectual power, her family wasn't famous at all. But they did have some interesting mystical powers, which we'll get to later.

Amongst the various famous Rabbis there was a less famous Rabbi whose story holds particular appeal. His name was Reb Elinka. His formal name was Rav Eliyahu Schick, the Rodef Tzadik (literally: 'pursuer of justice'). As my mother put it (paraphrasing the Jewish Encyclopedia with a bit of her own commentary):

> *According to one story, when the Tzar's army came to his town to take the little Jewish boys into the army (the assumption was that if you got a Jewish boy at 5 years old or so, you could sever all his ties to family and faith.) They took the boys by force and locked them into a tfissa (jail) in the middle of town.*
>
> *The community came to the Rabbi and asked what they could do. They may have expected guidance in petitioning the Czar or some such activity. Instead, Reb Elinka told them to gather every axe and sledge*

they could lay their hands on. He led his parishioners
down to the tfissa and they chopped it down and freed
the boys.

Now that is an ancestor to be proud of.

The fact is, there were tough cookies on both sides of the family.

Sadly, I haven't carried the tradition forward. I am *not* a tough cookie. I've got some of the brains, but I care more about being considerate and seeing the other guy's (or gal's) perspective.

Then again, nobody's tried to take away my kids.

I find it entertaining how the various branches of the family must have intertwined. I can claim both Rashi and the rulers of the land he lived in (Troyes) were ancestors. The history is actually far darker than that. Rashi, the great Torah sage, died in 1105. A few years earlier, Crusaders had killed thousands of Jews in the Rhineland massacres and burned the Jews of Jerusalem alive in their synagogue. Jews still mourn these massacres on the Ninth of Av. It is probable that *other* ancestors of mine were responsible for those atrocities. In 1131, King Fulk, was crowned the Christian King of Jerusalem. He actually ruled an area almost the size of modern Israel. I'm sure he wasn't a kind man.

All of this makes me wonder... does any of this history actually say anything about me? It does, in one way. My family's history makes it very hard to establish the central fact the contemporary world seems fixated by: identity.

After all, who am I? Am I a European Jew, an American Indian, a Swede, an Englishman, a Crusader, a Cossack or a Hillbilly? In our modern calculus, am I the spawn of the oppressor or the oppressed?

Does my Swedish side owe reparations to my English side, my Christian side to my Jewish side, my hillbilly side to my Indian side? Or perhaps looks are all that matter. Perhaps my mother's blond ancestor (a product of rape) should be considered complicit in the very pogroms that devastated her siblings. After all, she experienced privileges they did not.

I may be blond, blue-eyed and white. But that is as much a symbol of my mother's family's oppression as it is a sign of my grandfather's family's privilege.

All of this is why I don't place too much stock in 'identity.' It is the *stories* that matter. It is the stories we carry forward and the stories we create that define our past and create expectations for our futures. One of *my* best short stories, The Tapestry of Michael Jr., captures this idea particularly well.

As my father's celebration of PWT culture showed (before we had the genealogy), you can be as proud of being low as you can of being high[1].

---

[1] While we lived in the country, we weren't farmers. Instead, as hillbillies we were one full social tier down from farmers. I went to a rodeo as an adult, expecting to kind of fit in. Turns out I wore the wrong kind of boots. Sh-tkickers and cowboy boots speak to two totally different lifestyles.

At the end of her central philosophical work, my mother wrote:

> *Not all of us are Michelangelos and capable of such magnificent measurements of the good, but each of us, as the sum of our choices, is, nevertheless, a measure of the good. Plato and Protagoras; Aristotle and Alexander the Great; Billy the Kid and Susan B. Anthony; Moses and Pharaoh; Martin Luther and Martin Luther King Jr.; Michelangelo and the greengrocer down the street from the Sistine Chapel who lived a quiet life, married, attended church almost every Sunday, and left behind a legacy of kindness and love and grandchildren.*
>
> *Each of us is a measure of the good.*
>
> *On this interpretation, to be human is to choose, and to choose is to measure the good.*

Our human story is complex. I happen to have a better idea of mine than most do. But I wouldn't be at all surprised if there are vast numbers of people descended from emperors and kings, prominent rabbis and great philosophers and (even) priests and monks who (publicly) had no descendants. And I wouldn't be surprised if there are vast numbers also descended from drunk hillbillies, tough native women, abusive husbands and second sons of English gentry.

In all likelihood *your* story is also impossibly complex.

When we boil people down – when we point and say "He is black, she is Ultra-Orthodox, they are Hispanic" we lose so much truth. We aren't simply members of a group and when we think that way, we lose so much goodness and richness and reality.

When I attend shiva calls[1], I consistently ask one question "Tell me one thing, one attribute, one passion, one characteristic, one story, one idea, that would you like to spread from the person who has just passed away." The idea is that I will try to learn from that that thing and share it with others.

As I see it, you live in this world until your impact dissipates from it. The impact of destroyers often totally disappears within generations. We can never know what those they killed might have achieved. But the impact of creators and sustainers can last forever. After all, *between* the couple of rabbis highlighted every few hundred years in my mother's book of Jewish genealogy there are generations of men and women who kept the family close to their values. Who preserved their Judaism. Who kept alive the emphasis on intellectual firepower. Their individual names[2] and their stories are lost, but their impact – today – is far greater than that of King Fuchs or the murderers who gave him his position of power.

---

[1] Visits to the houses of mourners in the week after death.

[2] The names themselves are not lost. Like clockwork names occur and reoccur. My mother's name was Chana. It is a name that repeats again and again throughout her generations. I now have a grandniece named Chana. It is like a mnemonic reminder some core family value and tradition.

18

History has a place, but we don't need names or details to sustain the legacy of our ancestors. And we don't need a legacy to be great in our own time. As much fun as my family history may be, it is just that: *history*. I believe it is what we do with our lives, in the present, that truly matters.

To put it in more contemporary terms...

Identity isn't what you inherit.

Identity is what you *do* with what you inherit.

MODERN PRE-HISTORY

Rodney Thomas Cox

My father grew up as a retarded[1] genius with a serious chip on his shoulder. As was common in those days, my father's school had administered an IQ test. It was necessary for a scientifically prescribed education. As he remembers it, the test was just so incredibly stupid. He couldn't imagine it was *meant* to be that stupid. So, he tried to see the question behind the question. The result was the wonderous score of 68 – more than three standard deviations below average. For those who are not statisticians, if you have 1,000 children only three would have scientifically verified to have been as dumb as my dear old dad.

It took a long time for my father to get over the consequences of that score. For years, his teachers were suspicious of his unusually high scores in normal tests. Particularly in math. He used to have to retake exams, alone, in a room. Even then, they couldn't figure out *how* exactly, he was cheating. Whatever method he had; it was pretty clever for a disabled child.

The funny thing is, even if you were to have met my father in his prime you could have believed the IQ score. He was brilliant, but he also didn't think like those around him. He

---

[1] Politically correct terms constantly shift. 'Retarded' was in play in those days. It literally means 'slow to develop' almost like 'developmentally disabled.'

didn't get what others got. He couldn't explain himself. It was obvious how he could have gotten a 68 on an IQ test.

As a result of this test (and being held back in what passed as special needs classes) my father didn't leap immediately into the upper tiers of the educational universe. The way he saw it, he was just smarter than everybody else but nobody else saw it that way. He probably thought it was only fair if he maneuvered around society's rules in order to square the books.

As a very young man, my father had gone strawberry picking. As a farm hand. He'd watched as the paymasters used little hole punches to make distinct holes in the worker's cards. He'd seen the patterns of shapes they applied each day. Then he went bought himself a hole punch and those same sets of shapes. He sold 'punches' to the other kids, for a slice of the take. It was a good con. It lasted about a day. Another time, apparently when he was around eight, he sold discounted counterfeit tickets to a Roma travelling circus – a block away from the circus itself.

He survived that experience, but barely.

And he learned each time. At first what he learned was that he didn't have what it took to play *those* games. So, he looked for other ways to make it.

He tried his hand at football and ended up playing his first and last game opposite a kid who ended up going pro. It was an unpleasant experience. A flattening one.

My father went to the same High School (around 10 years earlier) as Matt Groening of The Simpson's fame. Matt's first cartoon was 'School is Hell.' They shared that perspective. My dad remembers the rich kids used to toss coins towards the poor kids who'd jump for them. My dad was big, so one day, he figured he'd try his hand at collecting that easy money. But he wasn't one of the poor kids, he was middlin'. When the knives came out, he realized he didn't have what it took to compete there either.

He thought about being a golf hustler, but he was never good enough at golf. He had charisma aplenty, so he thought about being an evangelical preacher. But he couldn't keep a straight face. He had, after all, been kicked out of his own confirmation.

Whatever the process of logic and intuition, my father ended up developing a deep commitment to the ideals of loyalty and trustworthiness. Perhaps it came from seeing how the Roma dealt with one another in face of the big bad world. His was not going to be the path of a con man, even in the guise of a preacher or a golf hustler.

He needed another road.

In the end, he developed an admiration for the great Industrialists of the late 19th century. He was charismatic, mathematically sharp and strategically insightful. He'd been reading the Wall Street Journal since he was 6.

Industrialist seemed to be the card to play.

That's why my father became a student of business history. Before a certain time, he knows the history of all the mergers and tie ups and acquisitions and corporate strategies and whatever else you could think of. Our little lives were filled with business lessons. In our family, you could swear all you wanted. But you could never, ever, say 'synergy.' *That* was a four-letter word.

Some of our business lessons have been passed down through generations. Our great-grandfather was a second son who had an allowance from his family back in England. He moved to Kansas and owned a money-losing farm. *Actually*, farming was beneath him, so he didn't *want* the place to make money. He decided to invest the money he had in currency. It was the 1920s. Figuring the German Mark couldn't keep going down, he invested *everything* he had in it. And he lost everything he had. From a very early age we were taught: "never, ever, speculate in currency."

His own son, my grandfather, went in the opposite direction. He became an insurance salesman. Not a very good insurance salesman[1], but at least he wasn't involved in currency speculation.

After deciding on the path of industrialist, my father ended up going to college at Oregon's not-quite-illustrious Willamette University. *There*, outside the long shadow of a childhood test, he was recognized as a national math scholar. He even won an award from the Dow Jones Foundation itself. It earned him a full-ride scholarship to Carnegie Mellon.

---

[1] My grand*mother* was a very good insurance saleswoman. She made thousands when my grandfather was in the Pacific Theater during World War II. When he got back, he loaned those thousands to a war buddy he knew would never pay him back. It was better not to have the money than to have an uppity wife.

While he was in Pittsburgh, his unconventional analysis of business and social history almost landed him in very hot water. He'd examined the 'business' history of poor Jewish, Italian and other immigrant communities. Kind of like Karl Marx analyzed class history to produce his 'science'. My father's conclusions were a bit different than Marx's though. He deduced that these various communities rose out of poverty through organized crime. Then they got their children out of the business, and they cleaned up nicely.

My father saw the poor black community of Pittsburgh and figured what they really needed was to follow a similar path up and out. Instead of just being customers, employees and victims of organized crime networks, they needed their *own* organized rackets. They needed to run their own numbers and prostitution rackets. They needed their own 'families.' They needed to stop the subservient or disorganized crime and step things up a level.

He apparently met with and presented this argument to a prominent Pastor in the city.

Their meeting didn't go well.

After graduation my father was, for a brief time, a management consultant to a criminal. He worked for the famous Jimmy Hoffa, helping run a legitimate little side business for his organization. The big checks were nice, but my mother managed to convince him it wasn't a wise long-term career choice. He left that world long before Jimmy did.

I'm convinced that what *really* converted my father to a new way of life were the Saints Graham and Dodd. Their concept of value investing inspired him. He believed you could consistently find value; value the market was missing. Tied in with Value investing was the intrinsic concept that there *actually was value*. Not just the transference of money, but the creation of wealth. This sort of wealth creation required what my mother would call mercantile ethics – the most important being trustworthiness and honor. My father ended up doing very well as a value investor, although he was the never the kind of investor whose ideas could scale to the institutional level. His eventual Ph.D. from Columbia University was the first counterproof to the famous Random Walk Hypothesis[1].

Despite his full ride, my father ended up being kicked out of Carnegie Mellon. Not for any dark reason. Well, not *really* dark. He was a Graduate Assistant for a professor who later won a prominent award in economics. My father, at this time, was an economist. At least an economist in training. He realized this professor was picking the years in his models. This means he picked beginning and end dates to make a case that isn't preserved if you shift the years around[2]. For example, you might read in the news today that temperatures have increased X degrees since 1850. Well, the late 1840s were *particularly* cold years. They helped lead to the massive European social unrest in 1848. 1850 was the end of the *Little*

----

[1] Random Walk argues that the direction of any particular stock at any particular time is essentially random. The market prices out any predictability.

[2] One of our other basic lessons as children was that economic models are all bullshit.

Ice Age, which started in 1500. If you use 1850 as a baseline, you're picking your years. It doesn't mean you are wrong, but it does bring the *honesty* of your argument into question. Going back to my dad's case: he realized shifting a month in either direction would have made this economist's grand model fall apart.

Grand models were always falling apart. Growing up, we often discussed the reasons for this sort of failure. Essentially, it came down to this: there are many different kinds of things that fit under the rubric of "model." A model based on a very simple concept – often a scientific concept boiled down to controlled circumstances – is indeed very predictive. The metal ball will roll down the table at just such a speed. But as you pour more real world in, the model becomes more and more speculative. How fast will the feather fall? It depends a lot on many highly complex factors. When you then add elements that *respond* to conditions around them you end up with a seriously difficult model. The speed at which a feather falls when it is attached to a bird is *quite difficult* to determine. As my mother used to put it, we can predict what a pool ball will do when hit with a cue. But try playing pool with kittens instead of balls. Unless you hit them *really* hard, it suddenly isn't so straight-forward.

We *can* use rules of thumbs/principles on a micro scale, but on a macro-scale predictive models tend to be, well, b-llshit. And the fact that you might fit a curve to past data doesn't mean it will fit to future data. Thus, there are no investors who have predictably made billions on the market but there are some investors (my father included) who were *pretty* good at valuing individual small companies or even predicting the failure of individual larger companies.

We've seen more of this reality with the coronavirus. It is a *mutating* virus that responds to surrounding conditions. It is being responded to by communities, scientists and governments that also adapt. Models aren't terribly useful. 'Science', in terms of medical advancement, has done a magnificent job of fighting back. But 'public health', based on large-scale models of what will happen, has been crap. If the virus had a more predictable pattern (say a high death rate) we'd reliably strike back with clumsier tools. The world of modelling would be simplified on both sides. But coronavirus was not simple. In the initial rounds of the virus, those US states that adhered most closely to public health directives also suffered the most deaths. I'm not blaming the public health directives. All I'm saying is that anybody who claims their complex, real-world, model is going to give you overwhelmingly useful and accurate answers is probably far too full of themselves.

Getting back to my father... rather than quietly report this professor's academic fraud, my father decided to print and hand out pamphlets. Nobody could understand them, though. Remember, he was a retarded genius. Nonetheless, his activities drew the ire of the university's administration. They sat him in a room and asked him what he wanted, what he *really* wanted.

The upfront purpose was to pay my father to shut up. But, as my father saw it, the unstated purpose was to blackmail him. There was a small committee of interrogators. At first, my father insisted he couldn't tell them what he wanted. Then he insisted it was too embarrassing. Then he told them he could tell them, but under no circumstances could it leave the room.

My father has a way of speaking more quietly when he really wants you to pay attention. He dragged his interrogators on – getting quieter and quieter until he'd wasted more than a half an hour of their time.

Finally, he told them he'd reveal his innermost desire.

My dad insists the doors to the room moved as those outside were so eager to hear what he had to say. I don't doubt it. I've seen him tell the story; I'm sure he had interrogators on a leash.

Before I tell you what he *really* wanted, there's one more pertinent fact. My dad was 6'4" and massive. When I was 16, he easily picked me up with *one* arm and tossed me 5 feet.

With the audience primed and ready, my massive dad looked down at his belly and said, "I wanna' have a baby."

That was his last day at Carnegie Mellon.

The University actually mailed him his Master's Degree (due to a clerical error). But they also sent a black letter to every school they thought he might apply to for his Ph.D. Wharton had kicked out a very prominent student not *that* long before. That student had gone on to be hugely successful. He badmouthed Wharton at every possibly opportunity.

28

Apparently, the standard policy of the day was to destroy anybody who might make them look bad.

My dad knew about the black letter because it was mailed to Columbia University's School of Business. The dean of that school, Julius Pontecorvo, invited my father to his apartment. He showed him the letter. My dad read it and asked one question, "After reading this letter, how could you possibly admit me?"

The dean, who became a lifelong friend, answered, "After reading that letter, how could we resist?"

That's how my parents ended up meeting at Columbia University.

Chana Berniker Cox

My mother's path to that same school was more conventional. My mother had always tried, desperately, to grasp the conventional. She often failed. The problem was simple: she wasn't as conventional as she hoped she could be. Of course, when she married my dad, she basically gave up any chance at being normal.

I'm going to share my mother's family history in her own words. The following is an email shared with the family about a year before she died.

""

In My Mother's Words

February 27, 2018 (some details are different, these are stories…)

"Go to America and be a good man; I know you will never be a good Jew." These were my grandfather Shmuel Zev Berniker's last words to his youngest son, as that son, my father, was boarding the ship to Canada. Although they did write to each other occasionally, my grandfather and my father never spoke again. In those days there was no money for telephones or long-distance phone calls.

In some ways my father was a good man, but I think in his own way he was also a good Jew.

My grandfather Shmuel Zev was a rabbi descended, as you probably know, from a very long line of rabbis. The Bernikers had *yichus*. He was also a gentle, good, and kind man -- which is saying a good deal for a Berniker. And so, why those last bitter words to my father? And why did my father retell those words and his memory of those words for the rest of his life?

My grandfather had been a teacher and a congregational rabbi in a small town in Poland. I think the name of the town was Loopch, but I have never found it on a map. During WWI, Jews were forcibly moved away from the borders because, as is so often the case, Jews were not trusted. The family was moved to Vilna and, like all Jews in Vilna, they lived in the Ghetto. With the infusion of so many Jews from the villages and smaller towns, there were no jobs for rabbis and although my grandfather continued to teach some students, he could not support his family. His wife Chana Rochel took a job in the munitions factory. My father believed that out of a sense of his own inadequacy as a man and a breadwinner, my grandfather refused to eat meat and fasted every Monday and Thursday for the rest of his life.

The two oldest sons, Chaim and Pinchas, were sent to Yeshiva, earned *smicha*[1] and went off to Cuba to be rabbis. America was closed to immigrants, but Canada was still accepting some Jewish immigrants. From Cuba, the brothers were eventually able to get into Canada where they earned enough money to send back papers which would allow my father's family to come to Canada. Those papers were very difficult to acquire, and my grandfather carried them in the front breast pocket of his coat. The pocket was slit by a thief and the papers were stolen. Eventually the brothers sent another set of papers which allowed my father and his sister Leah to come to Canada. But I am getting ahead of myself.

Unlike my uncles, my father never was sent to Yeshiva. He refused to go. My father was an *apikoros* – Jew who rejected the constraints of religion. An unbeliever or skeptic. He seems to have been a rebel almost from the beginning. When he was about twelve, he walked out beyond the walls of the ghetto and was beaten to a pulp by the locals. Until the day he sailed for Canada, he never left the ghetto again.

When my father was fourteen, he told his father that he did not believe in God. Out of respect for his father, he would continue to go to shul [synagogue] but he did not believe and he would not be a hypocrite. He, with the support of his mother, announced that instead of Yeshiva he would be attending the ORT engineering gymnasium. It was the only engineering school in the world to have ever taught its courses in Yiddish.

My grandfather agreed that if his son did not believe (and in fact refused to believe), he should not be forced to attend services. But my grandfather insisted that his youngest son sit and study *gemora*[2] with him every day. The learning did not continue long but it deeply affected my *apikoros* father for the rest of his life. By the age of fourteen, my grandfather's religion had been stamped into my

---

[1] Rabbinical ordination
[2] Talmud

31

father's soul although, if either of them had been asked, they would probably have denied that.

After my grandmother died, my grandfather (prematurely old and blind), moved to Jerusalem where he lived in Mea Shearim. In a sense, he went to Jerusalem to die. A Jew must be buried in consecrated ground if he is to rise again at the End of Days. A Jewish cemetery in the diaspora is consecrated with a handful of earth from Jerusalem and a fair number of Diaspora Jews lived and died with an amulet containing earth from Jerusalem. But it is always safer to come home and die in Israel. In the end of days, HaShem [G-d] will gather the Jews to him -- beginning with the Jews who have ascended the mountain in Jerusalem. A Jew does not move to Israel, he makes *aliyah*, he ascends the mountain.

Even old and blind, my grandfather continued to learn and teach. He died in 1942 well loved and respected and on his death the rabbis in the city proclaimed a day of mourning. I think of that mourning not as the mourning for one old blind Jewish rabbi. It was a mourning for the millions dying in the Holocaust and for the death of a way of life.

Meanwhile, in Montreal, my father met my mother in night school. She was from a small town in Poland -- the daughter of shoemakers and the cousin of tailors. By conventional Jewish rabbinic standards, he married down. He married way up on the heavenly scale.

On the surface, none of that Montreal Yiddishist community was religious but of course the religion of their parents and grandparents had been stamped into their souls -- perhaps even hidden in their DNA.

As he slowly began to make a decent living after the War, my father continued a committed Yiddishist; even underwriting the publication of Yiddish literature. His children were sent to Yiddish afternoon schools. And he was a committed Zionist supporting

Israel both financially and by encouraging his children to become members of HaShomer Hatzier -- the socialist secular youth organization. All the years I was growing up, our family never attended shul. We didn't celebrate the High Holidays let alone observe the Sabbath. When I joined Bnai Brith as a teenager they asked me whether I was Orthodox, Conservative, or Reform. I said I was none of those things. My family was none of those things. I was a Jew by virtue of my birth, my family, my history. I was not religious. For my father there were only two kinds of Jews -- the orthodox and the "Atheists." Or to use Uncle Sylvan's wording you either got religion or you don't got religion. We didn't have religion.

After the war, when the truth about the Holocaust came out, my father was no longer simply an *apikoros*. Hatred of HaShem had been burned into him. I can remember my father leading a community seder in Yiddish. Yes, we may have seemingly ignored Yom Kippur, but we never ignored Pesach[1]. Every year my father led the second socialist seder where the four questions always began with "Why?" My father had an excellent baritone singing voice I can hear him singing the words he had written for the seder that year. "You gave the Torah to 600,000 Jews at Sinai and 6 million burned out corpses are hurling it back at your feet."[2]

And yet, and yet, about 50 years after my grandfather had moved to Jerusalem my father and his second wife made *aliyah*. About ten years later, after a night discussing Yiddish literature with his friends, my father collapsed and died.

---

[1] Passover

[2] In my own teaching, I often draw parallels between the Exodus and the Holocaust. Millions of Egyptians and Jews died. The Pharaoh of Egypt imagined himself to be G-d and tried to genocide the Jewish people – who were seen as too numerous and somehow too powerful. And, after the Exodus, the Jewish people were brought back to their homeland. Slot in the word Germany for Egypt and the story fits the Holocaust (and the founding of the State of Israel).

He died in the evening. In Jerusalem, no corpse is allowed to remain unburied overnight and so on a cold dark night, the day before Purim, at 9:00 P.M., my father the *apikoras* was buried on the Mount of Olives where he had purchased a gravesite. The family wanted someone to speak about my father at the grave. The man from *chevra kiddisha*, the man who had prepared my father's body for burial, was a very old haredi man. He may even have been the old rabbi from the Sanhedrin in Joseph's story[1]. He ignored my stepmother, saying that he himself would speak at the grave. The family objected. How could this ancient rabbi eulogize my father? He had never even met my father. "Not to worry," the old man said. He knew my father.

And so, on a dark night under the stars that old man stood at the *kever* [grave] and be began to speak. "I have never met this man, Abraham Berniker," he said, "but I know him and I know who he is. Fifty-five years ago, I buried this man's father. Just over there." In fact, my father, the *apikoras*, had bought a grave site just one removed from his own father. And the old man spoke about Shmuel Zev Berniker, about the family, about virtue and kindness, about being a good Jew and about being a good man.

After more than half century my father the *apikoros* had returned to the arms of his ancestors

My father's *yohrzeit* [memorial day] is tomorrow. We will say Kaddish for him.

We are enjoined to raise up the names of the dead upon their inheritance. Avi Yoseph and Lev Abraham are named, in part, for my father, Sammy is named in part for my grandfather as is Zeeva[2]. My father the *apikoros* is the grandfather and the great grandfather of Torah-observant Sabbath-keeping Jews.

---

[1] This is a reference to a short story I wrote: The Secular Kohen.
[2] All grandchildren of my mother.

34

His oldest great grandson, Atniel, made *aliyah* just yesterday.

My great-grandfather, learning Torah

My Grandpa Abe was a die-hard Communist. He was financially and personally committed to the 'movement.' Most of the Rabbi's-son-is-a-Communist stories are told by the Communist side of the equation. After all, people in show biz tend to lean more than a bit left[1].

Sometimes, though, the Rabbis get the last word.

As my mother wrote above, my grandfather was buried right next to his father, on the Mount of Olives. But I remember the key bit a little bit differently. Instead of claiming to never having met my grandfather, the Rabbi got up and started with, "I buried Abe's father here 45 years ago. Tonight, I am burying Abe. I knew Abe as a young man, and I can tell you there's nothing worth sharing after the age of 3."

The man then proceeded to deliver a eulogy for a three-year-old. All for a man who was 81.

My mother sure liked to clean things up.

---

[1] As my mother used to say, after growing up within the Movement, that McCarthy was right about the Communist threat – he just didn't have the right names.

Was he a good man? Was he a good Jew? Despite my mother's words, she certainly didn't think so. I can't judge. What I can do is share some of what happened *after* he was three.

As a big supporter of Israel, my grandfather was closely tied into the Israeli political scene. When Shimon Peres died, my wife and I were driving west on Highway 1 in Israel. The highway *to* Jerusalem was closed because of all the VIPs flying into the country. I called my mom, who was living in Oregon at the time. I was planning to kind of gloat about how I was in the center of it all (unlike those in faraway Oregon). My mom picked up the phone and I said, "Mom, because of Shimon Peres' funeral, we can see all these motorcades of Heads of State heading towards Jerusalem on the other side of the highway."

Without hesitation she responded, "Oh, I remember Shimon. When you and Rebecca were having such a hard time having children, I just kept remembering what a hard time Shimon and his wife were having."

So much for gloating.

I tried to take a stab at unraveling my grandfather's political story. I didn't get very far. A friend of mine with connections in Israel's Secret Service found me a few letters praising him as a man who always came through for the Movement. He may have been in a few photos with Mapam politicians. And my sister, despite there being no citizenship-by-birth in Israel was granted citizenship at birth – which implies some unusual connections.

I know more about other parts of his story. He was a bootlegger as a young man. He was ship's mechanic on a vessel called "The Ganif", which means "The Thief" in Hebrew and Yiddish. It was owned by a Jewish family that later became prominent in the *legal* alcohol trade. They used to make runs up to Saint-Pierre and Miquelon, official French territory off the eastern coast of Canada. They'd buy whatever booze they were buying and then sail back down the coast, staying in international waters while their cargo was off-loaded by smaller vessels making the run into United States waters. Grandpa Abe was apparently proud of his smuggling skills. He once challenged the Chief Customs Officer in Saint-Pierre and Miquelon to a bet. My grandfather bet he could get two packs of cigarettes past customs without said Chief Customs Officer finding them.

My grandfather did hide those cigarettes well. The Chief Customs Officer searched the ship high and low and found nothing. Then, he decided to test the boilers. The cigarettes had been hidden in the boilers.

Grandpa Abe lost the bet.

At some point, Abe lived in Cleveland. I know one story from those days. He and his friends had an Apikoros Club. The thing to remember about a true *apikoros* is that they can't *just* reject Judaism. They have to be knowledgeable about it and *then* reject it. So, he and his friends were hanging out when a young Yeshiva student from the Telshe Yeshiva showed up. He was raising money for the Yeshiva.

These Talmudically trained rejectors-of-G-d asked the young man why he would possibly come to them for money. After all, shouldn't he try the Conservative and Reform Jews first?

The *bochur* (a term for a young Yeshiva student) answered, "Of course, I've gone to the Conservative and the Reform. But without the Telshe Yeshiva there may well be another generation of Conservative Jews and even another generation of Reform Jews. But without the Telshe Yeshiva, there can never be another generation of *apikorsim*."

They gave him money.

Later on, my grandfather became a very successful appliance manufacturer. Literally a Communist factory owner. He'd always insisted he'd give up the factory when the Revolution came. Thankfully, it never did.

Despite growing up in this die-hard Communist household (my mother tells stories of burning books in the basement during the McCarthy Era), my mother was not a Communist. She'd started out as one. She'd been a true believer. Then she'd gone to Communist Youth Camp. At the beginning of the camp, all the kids on the bus were instructed to give *all* their money to the counselors – so everybody would be equal. My mother, a true believer, complied. At the end of the camp, they were dropped off at the same bus stop they'd started at. But they weren't given their money back. *All* the other kids had kept most of their money. They'd only surrendered a token. They promptly paid their fares and boarded buses home.

My mother was stranded across town from her home with no money and (of course) no cell phone.

That's when she realized Communism would never work.

People just weren't made for it.

The story reminds me of a related story involving *my wife's* family. *Her* grandfather also split from the Orthodox world. When World War II came, he was the one who drove from Evanston to Chicago for kosher meat – chickens, specifically. Torah-observant Jews take kosher meat very, very seriously. The animals have to be slaughtered in a particular way, examined in a particular way and then kept segregated from non-kosher meat (as well as anything dairy). Gas was rationed and so his was quite the endeavor on behalf of the community.

On one such voyage, her grandfather noticed the butcher was one chicken short. The butcher said, "Oh, okay." Then he proceeded to take a non-kosher chicken and stamp it with a kosher stamp.

My wife's grandfather was so disgusted that he left Orthodox Judaism and became a key member (and funder) of the local Reform establishment. The family was, as I like to call it, militantly Reform. My mother-in-law ended up marrying a religious man (at 39). One of her two children ended up religious. My wife's grandfather had five daughters who produced ten grandchildren. My wife and her brother (who isn't religious) have more children than the rest of the family combined. Very few of the cousins married Jews[1].

My mother's entire family ended up far from Communism because the *other* Communist Youth held back their money (while the camp counselors kept what they took). The crookedness of the butcher not only drove the family away from Orthodox Judaism, but almost drove them away from Judaism altogether. To me the lesson is clear: when we cheat and we lie, we fundamentally undermine the causes we claim to hold dear.

The ramifications can last for generations.

🎗🎗

In My Mother's Words
March 27, 2018

When I was growing up, Detroit was a safe, vibrant, and prosperous town. By the time I was eight, I was babysitting my four-year-old brain-damaged sister when my parents went out. My parents, always social, were out a great deal. By the time I was 10, my parents did not hesitate to send me on a bus alone. By the time I was twelve, I was shopping alone downtown.

There was a darker side I was less aware of. People in most of Detroit bought and sold houses with language in the deeds that prohibited the sale of the houses to either Jews or blacks. In effect, that meant that our neighborhood was bi-racial, at least when I was going into middle school. It was a world where the only whites the black kids knew were Jewish and the only Christians the Jewish kids

---

[1] There was a great joke going around a few years ago: "What's the difference between Donald Trump and the leaders of major American Jewish organizations? Trump's grandchildren are Jewish."

knew were black. It wasn't an integrated community so much as two communities living, or trying to live, side by side. And, at least in the inner city, the demographic balance was shifting away from the Jews.

Detroit was designed as a concentric city – it was a semicircular plan. Downtown was on the river, major roads led out like spokes from the center, and semicircular roads marked the miles from town.

When I was born, we lived about three miles from downtown. By the time my sister was born we lived in a small flat closer to four miles from downtown. We lived on Elmhurst near Dexter. The big Jewish market, the Dexter Davidson, was still at Four Mile road. The Jews were moving out to Six and Seven Mile road and the Dexter Davidson market moved out with them. By 1959 the Dexter Davidson market was at Ten Mile Road – six miles from the intersection of Dexter and Davidson.

In 1954 my family moved to Windsor, Ontario[1] where my father had a small struggling zinc die casting plant, but Windsor, although in Canada, was part of greater Detroit. I was closer to downtown living in Windsor than I had been living in Detroit.

Not everyone moved from the old neighborhood. My sister-in-law Corky's father had a drug store on Linwood. He and his wife had worked in that store for over thirty years. For the most part, their three children had been raised by grandparents so that the parents could work long days at the drug store. The drug store was what Sam knew, and it was what he did. The store even had a soda fountain.

By 1967 their son Billy, also a pharmacist, had a store farther down the street. Billy had gone to Central High School and I remember

---

[1] They were fleeing McCarthyism. They'd burned their books in the basement before crossing the border.

him as being way cool. His friends were black and he dressed and even walked as if he was black. He had bling coming out of his ears.

Sam, the father, and Billy, the son, were determined to stay in the old neighborhood. Nothing was going to move them.

On the corner outside Sam's drug store, a black kid had set up a newsstand. He was a hardworking kid. Sam was a hardworking man. And the twelve-year-old black kid and the sixty year old Jewish pharmacist became close friends. Sam was always telling the family great things about that kid. Then one day a man came by, picked up a paper, and walked off with it. The kid walked up to a man and said "Mister, you haven't paid for the paper." The man turned on the kid and knifed him to death. Sam saw it all.

I think even Sam knew then that the neighborhood was no place to be. But still Sam didn't move and Billy didn't move.

Then the riots came. In 1967, Bossman and I were already married and living on Salmon River. We were in our alternative universe. We got our news of the outside world every few weeks when Frank Hill airdropped the mail and then we read *Time Magazine* from cover to cover and word by word. It was from *Time* that I learned that the whole block that we had lived in when I was born – on Philadelphia Street – had been burned to the ground. Later, when we came out of the river for supplies, we learned that Sam's drugstore had been overrun. The rioters were after drugs. The young people who swarmed through Sam's drugstore looting and a destroying apologized to him as they ran through. They were the neighborhood kids. They told him it was nothing personal.

Down the street, Billy's drugstore was also destroyed.

As it turned out, Sam owned the drugstore but not the building. He was a renter. He had some savings. Still that store was all he knew. It seemed the work of a lifetime.

Sam and Billy considered opening new drugstores farther out, but then Billy, shaken to the core by what amounted to the destruction of both his livelihood and his mixed-race community, did a little research and came up with another idea. He explained to his father that there was a new kind of business for pharmacists – something called generic drugs. Billy thought that he could maybe manufacture and sell diuretics that had just come off patent.

The father, the son, and the younger son, Jerry, pooled their modest savings and went into manufacturing generic drugs. They left the neighborhood, moved farther out, and set up shop.

The rest, as they say in the movies, is history. Billy was very good at business – big business. Since 1967 Billy built and sold (for hundreds of millions of dollars) several generic drug companies. Some of them were listed on the New York Stock Exchange. Billy was a very rich man when he died in 2017 and he had traded in the bling for philanthropy. In his last years he was most proud of the many millions of dollars he had been able to give to people in need. Billy did a great deal of good with his money

This would be a Horatio Alger story if only Horatio Alger had not been knifed to death outside a drugstore on Linwood Avenue.

Of course, my grandfather was only one of two parents in my mother's life. Where Grandpa Abe came from a family that valued intelligence above all else and who saw themselves saving the world, my mother's mother, Nellie, was something else entirely.

I don't *really* know what, though. My grandmother Nellie died when my mother was 20 and my mother had a tendency to play up the sainthood of the dead. I can say that Eli also thought his mother was a saint. Hearing it from them, my grandfather may have married down within the Jewish intellectual class system – but he married up otherwise. All *I* can share, though, are a few stories told by my mother.

,,

In My Mother's Words

March 9, 2018

I never knew my grandparents. Except for my father's father, who died in Israel when I was about 6 months old, none of my grandparents were even alive when I was born. I don't think any of my grandparents lived to see 60, but I may be wrong about that.

My mother's parents, Niche and Elie Duvid Laznik lived in a two-room house in a Polish town called Chechanov or Chechanova about 60 miles, or was it kilometers, south of Warsaw. One room was my grandfather's shop where he worked as a shoemaker and the other room was where the whole family lived and slept. In the only photograph of my grandparents, you can see his hands – they were the rough scarred hands of a shoemaker.

Niche and Elie Duvid had fourteen children. Six of those children died of the diseases endemic to the poor, and few of the surviving children reached adulthood without being damaged by those same diseases.

Niche and Elie Duvid were probably not happy. Who could be happy losing so many children to poverty? But there was no lack of love and devotion in the Laznik family. I was told by a friend of my mother's that when young people were married in Chechanova, one of the blessings wished on them was that the newlyweds should be as much in love as Niche and Elie Duvid Laznik.

She said the love between Niche and Elie Duvid was a tangible thing—it shined out from them to illuminate their world. I can well believe that. Love shined out from my mother to illuminate her world.

44

Poor Jews in Poland did not send their sick and dying to hospitals. There were communities where the very ill, together with a caretaker from a family, might go to be nursed and to die. Toward the end my grandfather remained ill in Chechanova while my grandmother was dying of cancer in another town alone; except for my mother who nursed her.

It is my mother who told me this story.

One day a postcard came in the mail. It said that her father, Elie Duvid, had just died and the family was sitting *shiva*[1]. My grandmother asked my mother to read the postcard and my mother, wanting only somehow to spare or delay the pain, fabricated a message about some other family news.

Her mother lay back on the bed and said "No, my Nechele that is not what the letter says. It says that my Elie Duvid is *nifter* [deceased]. I know because he came to me last night and held out his hand. He asked me to come to him. I was only waiting for him to call."

A few hours later my grandmother stopped breathing. Within twenty-four hours of my grandfather Elie Duvid's death my grandmother died.

My mother's parents loved each other. Their love was legendary.

May their remembrance be for a blessing.

May all our children and grandchildren be blessed by at least the touch of such a love in their own marriages.

My grandmother seemed to have that same gift as my mother's grandmother. Once, a cousin of hers died in Chile.

---

[1] A seven-day mourning ritual where you remain at home and are visited by guests who visit to talk about the deceased.

The next morning, before the news had travelled through conventional means, she got up and told the family about it. She too had been visited in a dream.

Even my own mother had a related experience. In the final days before her cancer took her, she started speaking in a language we'd never heard before. Along with stating again and again that "G-d is so far away", she kept referring to a place. It was a place we'd never heard of: "Kosp of the Osp". She was referring to it in a thick accent. She kept repeating and repeating it. Just now, while writing this paragraph, I tried (once again) to find the place. I *might* have succeeded. There was a Jewish community in the city of Khust on the Hustets river. While reading shtetlroutes.eu, I found this:

> *The most respected among the 19th-century rabbinic scholars was Rabbi Moshe Schick (1807–1879), who in 1861 established a yeshiva in Khust – the largest one in Eastern Europe at that time... Moshe Schick (Maharam Schick, 1807–1879), born in Birkenhain (now, Brezová in Slovakia), was one of the most prominent 19th century European rabbis and one of the leaders of the rising Orthodox Judaism...*

Schick was the name of one of the families my mother's father is descended from. Rabbi Eliyahu Schick was the ancestor who rescued the children. Considering their level of intermarriage, it is quite possible my mother was related to

46

Rabbi Moshe Schick as well. It is also quite possible, although odd, that my mother would be referring to this city we'd never heard of on her deathbed.

My mother really wasn't big into this history. She didn't study or fixate on lineage. Sure, we knew the *yichus* (or lineage) was there in some vague sense. We used to joke that it provided us with a kind of particularly obnoxious kind of brains. Nonetheless, one thing my mother had kept from her Communist father was an active disdain for *Yichus* as a marker of anything of importance.

Nonetheless, she was fixated on Kosp of the Osp.

It could have been random neurons firing[1] or, perhaps, there was more going on in her final days than I could grasp.

Speaking of neurons firing, my parents didn't place a whole lot of stock in psychiatry or related fields. But a psychoanalyst is responsible for my existence. Within a week of my grandmother dying, my college-aged mother learned that she'd be unable to have children. Distraught about the loss of the past *and* the future, my mother turned (for the first and only time) to psychiatry for help. The story I've heard is that she was referred to none other than Anna Freud, probably through the Slifkins (who we'll get to soon). If so, she must have been

---

[1] She desperately wanted to keep her mind; pain be damned. It was so core to her identity. Her last cogent sentence, well after the Kost on the Osp started, was in reference to morphine: "My mouth may want it, my throat may want it, my body may want it, but *I* do not want it."

visiting New York at the time. My mother laid out what was distressing her and waited for Anna to counsel her.

The doctor only had four words to offer: "get a second opinion."

"

In My Mother's Words
Mar 20, 2018

Cancer runs in my mother's family just as schizophrenia runs in my father's. My mother feared cancer and she feared pain-killing drugs. She had been the one to administer morphine to her own mother when her mother was dying. My mother told me that every day she was torn between administering too much morphine and killing her mother, in doing so, or too little morphine and increasing her mother's unendurable pain.

My mother had been so ill so many times that she was in dread of addiction. Better the pain than the drugs. But she had a toleration for pain that passed all understanding – or at least all my understanding.

They removed tumor after tumor from my mother's body. None of them were malignant.

Some years later, my mother died of a cerebral thrombosis. When I was cleaning out her handbag after her death, I came across a letter she had written in pencil -- on an aerogram – on an aerogram. An aerogram was a thin light weight piece of paper which could be folded into an envelope. If there was no additional paper in the "envelope" the postal rate was low for overseas mail. I don't know why my mother used an aerogram. It was not a letter meant to be mailed overseas. It was not a letter meant to be mailed at all. She must just have had an aerograph in hand. It was addressed to me and to my brother. My mother had written the letter in the hospital the morning of one of her tumor surgeries – perhaps when the surgery itself was considered life-threatening. There were enough life-threatening surgeries in my mother's life. In the letter, she had told us that how very much she loved us and whatever happened in the course of the surgery, that she had lived a good life, that her husband had been a good husband and that he was still young and should remarry. Whatever happened, she asked my brother and me to take care of my sister Nina. That was our charge. Take care of Nina.

My mother's last will and testament to her children was written in pencil on an aerogram which she probably carried around in that handbag for years. It was mailed from Olam Habah [the world to come].

Even when she was facing death, my mother, even when she was facing death, was determined to protect her children from many of the truths about her own marriage. Young children do not need the truth. They often need to be protected from the truth. I was protected.

My mother was the best of mothers.

My mother's family, on both sides, was almost entirely spared from the Holocaust. You've already heard her father's story. One of her mother's uncles had been shamed because (despite being the son of a shoemaker) he'd shown up at a wedding without shoes. He proceeded to leave Europe for the United States and then he paid for over 30 of his relatives to do the same. He found places for them in the US, Canada, Chile and Peru. Only one brother stayed behind – the older brother who could afford shoes.

Only that brother and his family were murdered.

49

Despite the fact that her family was no longer in Europe, my mother was deeply impacted by the Holocaust. Right after the war, her mother took in some survivors. My mother was supposed to be asleep one night, but she'd wandered downstairs. While there, she'd heard a story from a woman who had faced Sophie's choice. She'd been forced to choose between her children. The experience of secretly watching that woman tell her story had left my mother scarred for life. She only ever told me that story once. She was in her 70s.

We rarely talked about the Holocaust, but it was always there.

Unlike her father (and mine, for that matter), my mother's reaction to antisemitism or any other kind of overwhelming social dogma was to hide. She learned this as young child. At home, they knew about the Crusades (as any European Jewish family would). The Crusades were a story of rampaging Christians slaughtering Jewish communities. At school, though, the Crusades were held up as a model. My mother learned to give the school the answers they wanted while keeping what she believed to herself. Considering the Communist history of the family, it was probably something they were pretty good at. She kept up this approach for the rest of her life. She became a University Professor in the Pacific Northwest. Nonetheless, it wasn't until she retired that she 'came out' as a conservative and Tea Party activist.

Mom and Dad

Like my father, my mother pursued math as an undergraduate. He went to Willamette University in Salem,

Oregon. She went to Reed, only a few miles from his home in Portland, Oregon. They never met in Oregon. Eventually, they both ended up at Colombia University. My mother was pursuing her Ph.D. in the History of the Philosophy of Science. My father pursued his Ph.D. in Operations Research.

My father was not a normal student. Despite pursuing a Ph.D. at the Columbia school of Business (basically, as strait-laced of an environment as you could find at Columbia in the 60s), he wore jeans and a bearskin hat his uncle had shot. He loved to show people the bullet hole. My mother, in her own way, wasn't quite normal either.

The two of them actually met in line for off-campus housing. My father was in front of my mother. The landlord was renting places out to the students in the line. When it was my father's turn, he proceeded to insist on a number of changes to the standard contract. The landlord was upset but agreed to the changes. When it was my mom's turn, she essentially said – in a twist on *Harry met Sally* – "I'll have what he had."

Later, when she wanted to break her lease, she went back to my father. He reassured her, given the contract changes, that the landlord would prefer breaking the lease to trying to maintain it.

The rest of the story is a little vague. My father's memories tend to have a little color added to them. My father ended up camped out on her doorstep, then eventually convincing her to let him move in with her. They weren't dating. In fact, she made a big point of dating others. My father used to pick up the phone and try to scare those dates off.

My mother (second from front) as a young woman

He was generally successful.

At one point, she refused to go on a date with him and so he picked her up (she was only 5'4"), threw her over his shoulder and walked down Broadway with her kicking and screaming. Times were different then.

Nobody got in his way.

My father was not very successful on the dating scene. He tended to scare the hell out of people, women in particular. For reasons he couldn't understand, his dates would routinely burst into tears. As I understand it, he did fine with their fathers; the daughters were another matter entirely. In my mom's case, it was a little different. Despite the kicking and screaming, my mother was never afraid of him. But her father was. Grandpa Abe offered to let my dad take over his business, so long as he left my mother alone.

The simple fact was that my mother was exactly what my father wanted. As he put it, he had a checklist, and she was the only woman he'd ever met who fit the checklist.

He wasn't letting her go.

As she put it, "I just thought, eventually, he'd go away."

He never did.

The simple fact was that that was exactly what she wanted too[1].

One day, about a year into their relationship, friends of theirs (New York Supreme Court Justice Morrie Slifkin and his wife Rozie) took them aside and explained that it was time for them to get married. The Slifkins had a gorgeous home on the Hudson. Morrie was apparently the first TV justice (although the NYTimes article that refers to it is behind a paywall and I don't feel like paying to confirm this). According to my father, he was also a contributor to the legendary Glass-Steagal Act. For her part, Rozie was friends with everybody who was anybody – particularly artists. I visited her many years later and she showed me her collection of paper plates. All the artists who'd visited her, including a number of very famous people (Pollock, Picasso etc... etc...), had painted or sketched on her paper plates. It was quite an unusual and personal artistic treasure trove. Both of the Slifkins were also extremely active in a wide variety of charitable ventures.

---

[1] Her later romance novels played off a similar dynamic.

The Slifkins basically announced that my parents were getting married *that* weekend. My father wasn't Jewish, though. To make matters more complex, he wouldn't convert. He wasn't going to do a paper conversion for the purposes of marriage. In those days, even Reform Rabbis weren't cool with intermarriage. The Slifkins were the Slifkins, though. They browbeat some unlucky fellow into performing the honors and a few days after telling my parents it was time to get married, they were indeed married.

For me, the best marriage stories reveal character.

My wife's parents have a wonderfully revealing story. My father-in-law had been given my mother-in-law's number when he was 39 and she was 30. He didn't call; he was busy. He was given her number again when he was 47 and she was 38. He took three months to call, the holidays were busy (and he was a shul secretary). When he finally did call and set up a date, he was three hours late for the date itself. He wasn't sure what they'd do, so he decided to have dinner by himself first (and he doesn't eat quickly). She wasn't impressed. My father-in-law carried a raincoat around everywhere, just in case it rained (to be fair, it can rain any time in Melbourne). He left it in her apartment by accident. Then he went back to get it and, somehow, the rest was history. Well, not quite. Not long after, she was travelling back to visit family in Chicago, and he asked her to get her parents' Ketubah (Jewish wedding contract). The standard way of demonstrating a person is Jewish is through their parents' marriage contract. Coming from a militantly Reform family, she wasn't even sure her parents had a

Ketubah. She asked him why he needed it. He told her. He needed it so to provide evidence that she was Jewish. Otherwise, the two of them couldn't get married.

That was how he proposed.

I have a friend, we'll call her Shoshana, with an even more revealing story. One of her family members was a Russian immigrant into New York. She found New York boring and wanted to go someplace more exciting. New Orleans was supposed to fit the bill. So, she got on a ship to New Orleans. Another relative, meanwhile, was an inveterate gambler in New Orleans. He'd gotten himself into real trouble and his father had agreed to bail him out for the last time. There was a condition, through: they were going to go down to the docks and the desperate young man was going to marry the first Jewish woman who came off the boat. That was, of course, exactly what happened.

My parent's story didn't end with the shotgun wedding. My mother's father was disgusted that my mother had married a goy. And my father's father was disgusted that his son had married a Jew. He always made a point of sharing his anti-Semitism with us, his grandkids. It was wonderful. But time does heal many types of wounds. By the time I came along, both my mother's father and my father's parents were a part of our lives. Even though my father had converted.

Of course, my parents did more than meet at Columbia. Growing up we heard about my mother defending her thesis.

My big (and only) sister apparently spent the time eating sugar cubes in the waiting area. She'd never encountered sugar cubes before. My mother's lesson from the thesis process was this: "If you don't know, say so." Nothing was worse than being walked into a corner because you tried to bullsh-t your way to an answer in front of somebody who knew better than you. In my own professional life that has morphed into a rule with regulators: never make a decision during a meeting. If what you decided before can stand, then explain it. But if you need to change something, only do it after some 'offline' consideration. You don't want to walk yourself into a bad corner.

For his part, my father had a number of memorable exams. At one point, he flunked an accounting exam that had only one question: "What is the purpose of accounting?"

My father, ever succinct, wrote a one sentence answer: "To minimize taxes."

At another point he disagreed with one of those 'big-system' economists. He sat an exam and wrote what he really believed about the questions being asked. After failing, he was graciously given the opportunity to retake the exam. My mother convinced him to tell the Professor exactly what he wanted to hear. My father proceeded to answer the questions with memorized excerpts from the Professor's own book. Thankfully, the Professor didn't realize he was being mocked and my dad passed with flying colors.

99

In My Mother's Words

Apr 11, 2018

Buckskin [my great uncle, featured prominently in *The River Went out of Eden*], delighted in hats and in bizarre clothing. He made a Viking fur outfit and wore it with a Viking horned helmet. He had coonskin hats and leather hats and army helmets – medieval army helmets. He liked hats.

Buckskin made Rodney a spectacular black bear hat. It seemed about 18" high and it was more or less conical – not more or less canonical. Rodney would make a big show of taking the hat off, sticking his finger through a hole – the bullet hole – which Buckskin had left almost in the center of the hat.

Yes, the bear had been shot and yes it was quite dead but, like Atniel's Pookie[1], the bear was dead before this story began. It had died while attacking our chickens. If you must cry, cry for the chickens. They were the underdogs.

It was a spectacular hat and Rodney got a lot of mileage by wearing it at Carnegie Mellon and at Columbia. Bossman was kicked out of Carnegie Mellon because of his "attitude." The hat was certainly an expression of that attitude.

In New York, however, that same hat was received with wonder and admiration.

Rodney was commuting in from Long Island where he lived briefly with a minister friend of his. He was saving rent. The train stop was on the east side of Harlem, and he would walk westward on 125th to get to Columbia. Every day more and more black kids would follow

---

[1] A hat my nephew made from roadkill and then sold to an Israeli guy he ran into on the street who *had* to have it.

in his wake. Both Rodney and the hat were accustomed to getting attention, but there were so many kids after a while that he began looking like the pied piper of Harlem.

Finally, one day, one of the more intrepid kids pulled close and then yelled back to his friends, "It's a fake. The dude didn't grow it. It's a wig." In Harlem in the mid-1960s, a big white guy with very pale skin and blue eyes who had grown a long black Afro was something worth seeing.

When told, Buckskin was absolutely delighted with the success of his hat in the streets of Harlem.

The black kids and the school administrators were not the only people who noticed the hat. One evening my dad and Rodney were at Idyllwild (or was it Kennedy Airport by 1966?) waiting for my brother to come in from Israel on El Al.

An earlier flight had landed, and a number of Chassidim had filed off. As they passed Rodney and my dad they bowed slightly toward Rodney. Rodney, being Rodney, bowed back in greeting. What did he know? But my father understood. Somehow, he convinced Rodney to store the bear hat, together with my father's standard Russian sheepskin hat, in a locker until my brother arrived.

After that we noticed other people in New York acknowledging Rodney or at least the hat with deference. Apparently, Buckskin's bearskin hat, (complete with bullet hole) was a very impressive *shtreimel*. It didn't look like a *shtreimel* to me but what did I know from *shtreimels*?

Rodney stopped wearing the bearskin hat – at least in New York. He always wore one of the ten-gallon cowboy hats which attracted more than enough attention on the New York subways. Once a very nice solidly middle class somewhat academic looking woman walked up to us, smiled, and said "And the Emperor wears no clothes."

58

She had a point.

My father knew about the deeper significance of hats. Once my father picked us up outside the Detroit Airport. We left Jeremiah, who may have been about four, in the car, while we went back in to collect the luggage. When we came out my father was wearing a "hat" made of an origami folded newspaper on his head. My father and my son were chatting together.

I must have looked the question. Why was my father wearing a newspaper hat at the Detroit airport? My father, the *apikoros*, explained that Jeremiah had come into the car and happened to look up at his bare head and then quickly looked down again. That's all it took.

Later my father told us the story about a friend of his – a distinguished Yiddish poet living in Jerusalem. The poet, who is the true source of this story, was getting on an elevator in Jerusalem. There was a boy – around 10 or 12 – on the elevator. The boy was clearly Haredi and the poet was clearly not. The boy looked at the poet's head and then looked back down again. The poet started a conversation in Yiddish, of course. Both the poet and the boy were far more comfortable in Yiddish than Hebrew.

"So, what are you looking at, young man?" The poet asked.

The kid was feisty as kids often are and rose to the bait.

"I was looking at you. Why aren't you wearing a hat? As often in Yiddish the word "*hittel*" was in the diminutive – why wasn't the poet wearing a *hittel*. A *hittel* could be anything from a yamulka. a Charedi black hat, or even a ten-gallon cowboy hat.

The poet answered "The whole *himmel* (heaven/sky) is my *hittel*."

The kid shot back, "The whole *himmel* is too big a *hittel* for such a small head as yours."

Jeremiah was only four and he was not feisty, and he hadn't said anything. He was only a little disappointed. And so my father, the apikoros, folded the newspaper into a *hittel*.

My mother, experienced at telling people what they wanted to hear, was well on her way to a flourishing academic career when my father somehow convinced her to change tack. Somehow (and I've read their letters and still don't understand it) he convinced her to move to rural Idaho.

When I talk about rural Idaho, I don't mean some small town in amongst the potato fields. I mean a plot of land with nothing on it but an 8' by 12' shack that had no electricity or running water. A plot of land located at the bottom of the second deepest river canyon in the US (behind Hells Canyon on the Snake River). And a plot of land 10 hours from the nearest town.

My mother wrote *A River Went out of Eden* about their time there, which I've already referred to. I highly recommend it. People really enjoy it. She wrote about being pregnant in the wilderness, about starvation, about flood, about building a house, about canning bears and about so much more.

Rather than rehash it, I'll just share what *wasn't* in the book. First, my parents became Torah-observant Jews in the wilderness. They were only there for eight years (not 40). Nonetheless, it was enough. The causes were two-fold. First, they couldn't keep track of the date. There were no phones and there was no community. Marking a mark on the wall didn't work, not for extended periods. It was too easy to get confused about by whom and when the wall had been marked. They started to read the weekly Torah portion so they could agree on the seventh day. It was a large and memorable event. From there, they could keep track of all the rest of the days. Torah reading, in English, was a key part of my growing up. We'd sit on my dad's lap and 'read.' At first, he would hold our fingers and point at the words, and we'd repeat after him. There was a special emphasis on clear pronunciation and elucidation. Then, bit by bit, we began to actually read. It was old-school, sure, but it worked. With coronavirus, I started doing the same thing with my children. I seem to be unable to suppress such classic phrases as "look at the words, young lady!" or "Stop lollygogging around and get over here!"

The second thing they did was get a copy of the *Kitzur Shulchan Aruch*. This is a compendium of Jewish Law. When its source document (the Shulchan Aruch) was written, it was very controversial. The Talmud recorded arguments and discussions. The idea was that, even as you wrote things down, you'd maintain some oral aspect to the law. It wouldn't just be stated. The Shulchan Aruch just stated it: "The law was x." My parents didn't get the Kitzur Shulchan Aruch, which was a summary of the Shulchan Aruch, out of some religious drive. They were living in a pre-modern wilderness. They needed a guide to truly rustic living. They turned to the Shulchan Aruch as a practical matter. It laid down rules for life in a time before technology. That's why they didn't use the Shulchan Aruch the way most people do. Specifically, they ignored all the "spiritual" laws. They only cared about the practical laws: how far your outhouse should be from the house, when and what to wash, etc... etc... Basically, all the stuff Torah-observant Jews ignore today.

One day, my parents read: "Be careful not to drink water that has been left uncovered."

The next paragraph says:

> *It is forbidden to place any food or drink underneath a bed even if it is covered, because an evil spirit abides over them. In villages some people keep potatoes and other foods underneath the beds; —they should be warned against this.*

Reading this, my parents figured this was one of the irrelevant 'spiritual' laws.

After all, it concerned evil spirits.

The next morning my mother happily poured water from a beaten copper jug into everyone's glasses. Then she looked into the jug and found a dead rat.

That law became the first law they kept that they hadn't understood *a priori*. From there, they added more and more laws. Keeping kosher was hard (as it tends to be when bears and SPAM are major sources of protein) but they made inroads, bit by bit. My father ended up converting – I believe it was three times in total: Reform, Conservative and Orthodox.

This religious road was extremely unusual. Our Judaism started at two ends of Jewish tradition. The Chumash (or Five Books of Moses) were at one end. The Kitzur Shulchan Aruch was at the other. Everything in between was missing. Where other kids learned Mishna and Talmud, we didn't. We were practicing Orthodox Jews who basically ignored the bulk of Jewish thought.

The effects were odd. For example, we had some very strange traditions. Most prominently, we used to send away our goat before Yom Kippur. It was a weird modern version of Azazel (the scapegoat). This tradition had been abandoned thousands of years earlier. We didn't know that. Interestingly, the goat always came back. Perhaps it represented our people. Despite being driven away from our home, we always dreamed of returning. Until, eventually, we actually managed to make it happen. Or perhaps it just represented the nature of my family's sins...

More critically, we *read* things differently than other people did. My mother had literally been bred to have a Talmudic brain. Her family had married and intermarried with one another with a singular purpose: to produce children who would excel at a particular kind of textual analysis. But the Talmud wasn't a part of her life. So, she applied that same intelligence to the Five Books of Moses themselves, while kind of glossing over all the commentaries. She was never much of a Torah scholar (Plato and Aristotle were more her thing), but her intellectual perspective and approach was passed down to us. My Torah analysis, which we'll get to eventually, was informed by this sort of stunted Torah education. I live a Halachic life – that Shulchan Aruch connection. But my Torah study is weird. Even today I read the Talmud and find myself seeing Roman legal and scientific influences miscoloring our understanding of our foundational document. It's why I don't study Talmud. I'm far happier being a poorly-educated Torah-observant Jew who has weird ideas about symbolism than a perfectly educated Jew who can't help but knowledgably criticize Roman and Platonic influences on Jewish belief.

What else wasn't in my mother's book? There are gaps I haven't been able to fill in about their time in other places (aside from specific stories). I know my father was an investor in mining stocks. He believed strongly in very hands-on and deep research. At one point he spent some time in Australia. He's told two stories about his time there. In one, a mining operator was trying to get on his good side. Being a mining operator, the obvious answer was plying my father with prostitutes. My father didn't bite, so to speak. They tried to figure out what was wrong and then realized their error: the prostitutes weren't Jewish! So, they found some desperate young religious woman (a young mother, no less) and hired *her*. My dad, understanding she must have been in some sort of extreme position, invited her in, paid her a little extra cash and after sufficient time to convince the miners that he'd been satisfied, sent her on her way.

My father's last day in Australia involved a library. He was doing research and another fellow in the library asked him about one of Australia's larger mining companies. My dad explained that if he were the other company's bankers, he'd call their loans. Turns out the guy *was* their banker. He called their loans the next day, leading to one of the larger Australian bankruptcies of the time. My father was advised to leave.

He didn't come back to Australia until just before my wedding.

After my mother's death, I discovered my parents spent far more time in Israel than I'd known. My mother's letters are littered with references to their time in Israel, but I'd had no idea about it. All I knew was that my sister was born there. It turns out my parents not only spent time here, they owned a house on Yegi'a Kapayim Street in Ramat Hasharon.

In death, all sorts of random details tend to pop out.

The book also doesn't talk about *names*. All my older siblings had Nez Perce names. That was the name the French gave the tribe that lives in the area; their actual name is Nimiipuu. The little nook in the river had been a place of refuge for thousands of years. Native Americans had run there, Chinese had run there, and my parents had, in their way, run there. The little nook in the river still has ancient remains from those tiny native settlements. It also had perfectly constructed water runs built by Chinese refugees panning gold. I've seen them. Almost a hundred years after they were built, the little rocks that formed their base and sides still intersected and interlocked in a near perfect display of workmanship.

My older siblings were all given names that belonged to that place. Nimiipuu names. The eldest was Jeremiah *Toyam* Cox[1].

---

[1] His initials were JC because my father was a convert from Christianity and thought this was funny. I was born a year after he died, so I took on the JC initials.

Toyam meant "On Top of the Mountain." Jeremiah's full name thus meant: "Appointed by G-d, on top of the mountain."

The second was Nechama *Sulynn* Cox. The Hebrew Nechama means "comfort." *Sulynn* means "bend in the river." She was named after the place they lived: "Comfortable Bend in the River."

The third was Isaiah *Watas* Cox. *Watas* means "land." Isaiah means "G-d Saves". So, "G-d Saves the Land."

Of course, my family wasn't Nimipuu. So, while I know the meanings of their Hebrew names, I can accept that my brothers were actually named "Wart" and "Snotface" while my sister was named "Ms. Gullible."

Such things have been known to happen.

The final thing that isn't in the book is the answer to the question: *why?* Why did my parents try to build a life in the Idaho wilderness? The best I can offer is that they didn't really fit in the normal world, particularly my father. The normal world didn't embrace them. So instead of trying to fit in, they decided to define their own world.

Ultimately, they failed.

My parents left Idaho immediately after my oldest brother, Jeremiah, died.

As my surviving older brother once put it: "G-d had brought them plague and starvation and flood. But they didn't leave. It was only when He took their firstborn that they finally rejoined the world."

\-\-

That was a great place to leave this chapter, I know. But before we move on to me, I need to share a caveat. I'm not as interesting as many of those people who came before me. But the influence of their stories is deep. The death of my brother is, of course, particularly important.

The story of Abraham in the Bible describes his early life.

> *Now these are the generations of Terach. Terach begot Abram, Nachor, and Haran; and Haran begot Lot. And Haran died in the presence of his father Terach in the land of his nativity, in Ur Kasdim. And Terach... went forth with them from Ur Kasdim, to go into the land of Canaan*[1]

When I read those verses, I see a cause and effect. My parents left Idaho because their son died there. Likewise, Terach left Ur Kasdim *because* his son died there.

Later on...

> *And [G-d] brought him forth abroad, and said: 'Look now toward heaven, and count the stars, if thou be able to count them'; and [G-d] said unto him: 'So shall thy seed be.' And he believed in the LORD; and He counted it to him for righteousness.*

---

[1] I always liked that old-style King James Translation. After all, it was how I learned to read – sitting on my father's knee.

And He said unto him: 'I am the LORD that brought thee out of Ur Kasdim, to give thee this land to inherit it.'

And he said: 'O Lord GOD, whereby shall I know that I shall inherit it?'

Avraham goes from belief to disbelief in an instant. I believe the reason is that G-d claims he brought Avram out of Ur Kasdim. It was not Avram, but Avram's father who left Ur Kasdim – due to the death of his son.

For G-d to claim *He* took Avram out of Ur Kasdim is for G-d to take *credit* for the death of Avram's brother. Of course, Avram cannot quite accept that.

So, he says, "How shall I know?"

This concept of a G-d who takes life for purposes *we* often consider unworthy is a constant challenge in Torah. We see it, or its corollary, again and again. Rather than whitewashing this reality, the Torah embraces it.

Understanding the Torah requires understanding its answers to this most fundamental of riddles.

We'll get there, eventually.

CAMP COX

At one of my recent Torah classes, one of the participants made the following statement: "People like to fit in, they like to be one of the crowd."

I'd heard that before. I just can't imagine applying it to myself or to my family.

In my family, fitting in was a cardinal sin. It was an abandonment of what was really important in service to popularity. It was an abandonment of Virtue.

In fact, the only way to stay on track was to completely ignore social conventions. By demonstrating your rejection of those conventions, you demonstrated your Virtue and your dedication to Truth.

That perspective, of course, had consequences.

The Property

I grew up in a house in rural Oregon. Unlike my parents' house in Idaho, it was only 35 minutes from downtown Portland. We had running water from a well and electric power from the city (most of the time).

It had all the accoutrements of a proper house. But the neighborhood was still tough. Sometime before we'd moved in, there'd been a string of robberies in the area. The locals had worked out who was responsible. They went to the police. The police didn't do anything. So, the neighbors banded together and burned the robber's house down.

The robberies stopped.

The neighborhood wasn't exactly welcoming to new folk. Perhaps thinking they could intimidate my parents, the neighbors apparently set up a shooting range which lined up uncomfortably well with the position of our new house. My dad and Mark Houston Haney put rifles over their shoulders and paid the neighbors a visit. The shooting range was adjusted. About a decade later, those same neighbors tried to claim half the house on the basis of a surveying error. The place was resurveyed and the property line was moved six inches over, into what had been their land.

Basically, the area had two sorts of folk. The mountain folk, such as they were, and the few very rich folk who came and built mansions on the hill. My parents didn't fit into either group. Nonetheless, they established themselves in that place.

My mom designed our house, modifying what she found in a blueprint catalog. It had a two-story entry way which was basically an atrium. That entryway had a massive Oriental rug hung on a massive wall above the stairs. It also had, as any atrium must, a small tree.

The house was located at one of the highest points in the Portland area. It was, my father liked to point out, at 1608 feet of elevation. When I look at it on Google, though, it is only at 1500 feet)[1].

A scant 2 miles away, the elevation is only 50 feet above sea level. This suggests, in theory, that my parents' house should have had a magnificent view.

It didn't.

The problem was simple: my father was always geologically aware. Oregon has a history of infrequent, but massive, earthquakes. He also had an affinity for a certain kind of geological dome – something that would yield water and oil. And so instead of building near the edge of the hillside (literally across the street), he built at the high point. It was years before I realized just how close we were to one of the most magnificent views I've ever encountered – anywhere in the world.

I'm sure there's some lesson in there about awareness and the broad vistas of reality available to you if you only make the effort to find them. I'll work it out, someday.

My parents built the house on that land with their own hands, of course. As my mother used to argue, with a decent Liberal Arts education you should be able to learn how to do anything. That included building houses. My father was proud of how inexpensively he managed so much of the project. The whole thing cost $70,000 to build (in 1978). He didn't build it

---

[1] My father has a tendency to see a reality that's a little more exciting than, well, reality.

for $70,000 due to his own skills at discount shopping, though.

The reason he built it so cheaply was because of the community he was a part of.

As a friend told me years later, when my father first showed up at Congregation Kesser Israel, the community didn't know what to make of him. He was a mountain man; a massive, hugely-bearded, wild-eyed mountain of a man.

It is hard to get a picture (and my dad doesn't like photos), so I'll borrow one from legend. In our house, we used to sing *John Brown's Body*. If you don't know the song, it starts with this:

> *John Brown's Body lies a moldering in the*
> *grave, moldering in the grave. John Brown's*
> *Body lies a moldering in the grave, moldering*
> *in the grave. But his soul goes marching on.*

I didn't know what John Brown looked like. I didn't know what he'd done. But years later, I came across a picture of him online and I read his biography. Today, I could almost swear that my father is the reincarnation of John Brown... *His soul goes marching on.*

It isn't just looks (although they have exactly the same eyes), it was attitude and outlook and expectations. The two men share a detachment from reality, an inability to plan, a fundamental charisma, and a deep (although often misunderstood) sense of honor and justice.

They also tend to scare the crap out of those around them.

Rodney Cox, née John Brown

So, this reincarnation of John Brown, only not in the nice suit, shows up at Congregation Kesser Israel. And nobody knows what to do with him. And then he stumbles and mumbles his way through the mourners' Kaddish. I can imagine him, saying that first Kaddish, being wracked by sobs and shaking with regret and sadness.

The community took him in. He built that house for $70,000 because this man found him marble from a bank building being demolished and that man found him leftover lumber from another project. And a third man found flooring, at a nice discount. And so on.

The community took care of my family as they literally built a new life.

I don't know all the details of what they did, but in the week after my mother died my father was remarking at how naïve he was not to recognize that the prices he'd paid were completely absurd. He wasn't just getting the opportunity to buy leftovers from projects and demolitions – the community was giving him charity. He would have been too proud to accept it if he'd known. But years later... he knew.

And he couldn't help but marvel at their kindness.

House upon the Hill

We grew up in a house in the woods at the top of a hill not far from a city. We grew up as Torah-observant Jews, albeit not living a normal Orthodox life. For one thing, there was no community anywhere close to where we lived. My father couldn't stand living in a city. Kesser Israel and Shaarei Torah, the two communities we were affiliated with, were 20 miles away. We often went in for daily services, but almost never for Shabbat services. Instead, for Shabbat, we made our own little community.

Our Shabbat dinners were always filled with interesting people. Some were Jews, many were not. Some we'd known for years and others my father had picked up just hours before. My parents counted among their friends: world-famous authors (Jean Auel), a former senior official under the Shah, a preacher with millions of Latin American followers (he came along after I left), a woman who seemed more connected to tofu and the stars than happenings on earth and even the families of international fugitives. There were also all manner of perfectly ordinary people: my guitar teacher, the student counselor at my high school, other professors at my mother's college, computer geeks.

The regulars at these meals, and the drop ins, formed what became known as Camp Cox. An eclectic mix of pretty random people who would come up for a unique cultural experience. It was not only an Orthodox Shabbat dinner; it was a *hillbilly* Orthodox Shabbat dinner. There was a competition to see who could bang the table the loudest at grace. There were arguments – across all ages – about politics and values. Time and again, my father trying to 'get a rise' out of my mother's liberal friends. He almost always succeeded. I'll leave the exact words out of it, but he had a few catch phrases that could result in immediate violence in today's day and age. My mother, for her part, tried to carry on intellectual and well-thought-out arguments and discussions in amongst it all. She didn't always succeed.

But us kids were exposed to all of it.

And when my mother's students came? Things were turned up a notch. We meant to (and succeeded at) overwhelming their bourgeois expectations.

The more we could shock them, the prouder we were.

After dinner, what guests remained would retire to the living room where my mother used to read the *Tzena U'rena* in Yiddish. It was a sort of "Woman's Torah" which mixed the stories of the Torah with interpretations meant for women. She had no problem with the Yiddish words (it was her first language, after all), but the Hebrew ones tripped her up every time. The next morning, we'd pray together, sometime before noon. We'd pretend we had a proper minyan (prayer group), just substituting a stand-in for G-d's name in those the parts that required a minyan. One of us would be the chazan and we'd be expected to do a decent job. It was a good way to learn, with minimal pressure. Davening was broken up with a fair amount of talk but eventually we got to the Torah reading – the Jewish highlight of the week.

As I covered before, that was when we learned how to read.

Aside from the Shabbat guests, there were also the people who *lived* with us. It was never more than 1 or 2 at a time, but they were there, nonetheless.

Some stayed a few days, many for a few months and one for years. The first of these troubled youth was the son of our family doctor. He (the Doctor, not the son) was a forensic pathologist. I will admit he was an odd choice for a family doctor. Then again, my father sat in on an autopsy while I was being born; in order to calm his nerves. This kid lived with my parents in Idaho, just after they were married. He lived in a dugout (literally a hole underground). He came in a troubled youth and after a summer of torching spiders with his lighter, left and became a successful airline pilot. More kids followed. Dozens of them. The vast majority left better than they arrived.

The therapeutic process, if you want to call it that, started with a simple ingredient: My father would convince these kids that their lives could have meaning. As he used to say, "If you don't change the world, then you've wasted your life." My father is charismatic. He'd convince these kids, often for the first time in their lives, that *they could matter*.

One of my cousins, our longest-term resident, shared his experience of my father's touch. He was doing his freshman year of high school, for the fourth time. As he told it, the first year he'd kind of been trying. The second, he'd been hanging out with friends. The third had just been to do drugs. And the fourth was because there was nothing better to do. He had dropped several hundred hits of acid, which does things to your mind. He was upstairs at his mom's house when my dad showed up. My dad called him downstairs, and he was ignored. Then, my dad *called* him downstairs. He came, unhappily.

He was being forced and he didn't like being forced.

My father looked him in the eye and said something to the effect, "Get off your -ss and stop wasting your f-cking life."

It worked. Our cousin, who had no belief in himself, suddenly had just a little.

He came back home with my dad. At least in principle he was interested in change.

That started the second stage of the process.

Here, my parents worked as a team. My mother managed the details – ensuring the kids showed up at school, having us little kids drill them on SAT words, tracking performance, feeding them. My dad managed other things. Most often this involved, well, *overcoming* their resistance.

My father fundamentally believed that boys needed physical interaction and labor – especially when coming off drugs. It was a great way to stop them from overthinking things. He also believed that everybody, absolutely everybody, needed to *make* things. Some people would just never understand the rewards of making things until they'd been *made* to make things. I never noticed it, but that same cousin told me my father used to start his day with something tangible and simple: fixing a fence, replacing a light bulb. Something to get those *creation* juices flowing.

Faced with an expectation to do what the family did, my cousin resisted right out of the gate. Resistance was just his thing. Shortly after he arrived, my parents decided we were going to the movies. My cousin didn't want to go. As we drove into town, he literally shredded his suit (he'd been wearing it for Shabbat). By the time we arrived at the theater, it was in tatters. To add to the spectacle, he was loudly protesting. Nonetheless, my father made him walk into the theater. He made him watch the movie.

Over his first summer with us, that cousin dug our mikvah (ritual bath). By hand[1]. Oh, and he also passed his GEDs[2].

For all of his worldly exposure, my cousin had some gaps in his experiences. I remember we were filling the truck up with gas and my brother asked him to stop filling (we didn't have enough cash for a full tank). My cousin yanked the spigot out without stopping the flow. He poured gas all over his right pant leg. We ended up cutting it off and burning it in a parking lot before getting ice cream at Haagen Dazs. He was only wearing a half a pair of pants[3].

Of course, we didn't only teach those kids, we learned from them. That particular cousin had a cardplayer's way of looking

---

[1] See benefits of physical labor (above).

[2] That man is in his early 50s now. He graduated high school. He still struggles with addiction issues, but today he serves as an anchor of his community. He helps others with problems like his own realize that they can be more than simply addicts.

[3] He ended up sewing those pants together with a half of another pair. It was the 80s; it kind of worked.

at things. On the simplest level, he taught me that what matters is the odds, not the outcome. In other words, if you play a hand well and lose, you're fine. Likewise, if you play it badly and win, you shouldn't feel too good. This lesson has always been part of my life. You never know what's going to happen. You just have to know you've played the odds and try to be comfortable with whatever the outcome happens to be.

What that cousin excelled at, more than anything, was argument. He'd inherited the capability from my mother's side of the family. Despite the acid, he was a master at intellectual Judo. I'll share just two examples.

My cousin hung out with a lot of people who had anti-Semitic conspiracy theories thoroughly baked into their brains. When people would claim the Holocaust never happened, he'd happily agree. They'd say it was a hoax and he'd agree. And then he'd say, "While we're at it, World War II never happened." That'd get their backs up and they'd point out, correctly, that their grandfathers had fought in the War. My cousin would just shrug. For those who were particularly dim, he'd add, "Well, my grandfather survived the Holocaust."

The other great argument concerned the popular conspiracy that Jews control the world. We've all encountered this. I've dealt with it in my own way, but my cousin's was the cleverest of all. He'd ask the theorist which countries the Jews controlled. After all, there weren't enough of them to control *every* country. An old familiar list would be rattled off: England, America, maybe Canada. Some might even go so far as to say Western Europe.

"Hmm..." my cousin would say, "It seems like we're doing a pretty good job. After all, would you rather live in one of the countries we don't control?"

When not playing mental Judo, my cousin had a bullheaded sense of humor about him. One time, when Kurt Waldheim was President, he was arrested in Austria. He kept asking the cops in the station why they had a picture of a Nazi on the wall. He was liberally beaten, but it was worth it. He thought it was funny.

Another time, on a dare, he was crossing the US-Canadian Border. The Border agent asked: "Do you have any illegal drugs?" My cousin answered, "Whaddya' need?" That didn't work out well either.

As the saying goes: you might have rights on one side of the border, and you might have rights on the other side of the border, but you have no rights in the middle.

As you might imagine, with these kids around, drugs were a constant part of our lives. On one level, there was practical knowledge to be gained. For example, no matter how great the trip, never, ever, forget about time. The temptation will be there, but if you do that, you might never wake up again. Another practical tidbit was to always have your friends take something new *first*. Today, I apply that to corona medications.

There was one other critical rule: If you're tripping and the person you're tripping with sees the same thing as you – you ain't trippin'. We learned this from my cousin's experience with a friend. They were both on an acid trip when they got back to the friend's house. They both saw flames on the wall, a common enough trip. But then they realized they were *both* seeing the flames. They deduced that it was a real fire. My cousin's friend's dad had fallen asleep with a cigarette on the couch and their house was burning down. There's your practical advice of the day: If you see the same trip as somebody else, you ain't trippin'.

For all our exposure, we never saw or took drugs. So many of those kids were recovering addicts. We saw what drugs did. We saw how they tried, and sometimes failed, to recover something of their lives. We saw how everything about the existence resolved around trying to dig out from their past mistakes.

Yes, the drugs sometimes provided wonderful stories (my cousin's description of his friends' most exciting acid trips are indeed legendary). But the stories never came close to being worth the price paid to experience them. None of us kids ever had *any* doubt about the impacts of drugs. None of us ever dabbled in them.

My drug policy, if I ever actually had a chance to influence policy, would be this: make it all legal. Legal drugs offer lots of advantages, including regulated dosing and purity. But before people can use drugs or alcohol, require them to get a license. Licenses can't be hard to get (or people will just get drugs illegally). All you'd need to do to get your license is spend 40 hours in a drug-rehab facility or Narcotics/Alcoholics Anonymous meetings focused on the particular drug you want to get a license for[1]. Get to know the effects before you decided to condemn yourself to the life of an addict.

Even with this exposure, people will still decide to use. Many people *want* to destroy themselves and it isn't as if the effects of heroin, meth or fentanyl are a secret. Dealing with those underlying issues is a much broader question. A much more important question. Drug policy, one way or another, won't fix the fundamental problems that drive people to destroy themselves.

The resident kids weren't all like my cousin. Some were downright scary. My parents went into town once, leaving my brother in charge of the house. He was 16. Another cousin, one of the failures, was 18. He thought (given his age) that he should be in charge. Not only that; my parents had set the alarm on the house. That older cousin was both locked in and not the top dog. Driven by *something,* the cousin pulled a knife on my brother. My older brother *relishes* combat. He reached into the closet next to him and retrieved one of the 30+ guns we had sitting around the house. The knife was politely dispensed with. That cousin then came up to our room (we were the little kids). He asked my little brother for the alarm code. He knew my brother could set the alarm. My little brother, brilliant little kid that he was, answered, "I only know how to set it – I don't know how to disarm it."

---

[1] I've been told that AA meetings are far more interesting than NA meetings. Drug addicts all have basically the same story and similar perspectives on the world. Alcoholics are a more diverse bunch.

That, of course, was b-llshit. We all knew how to disarm the system.

"How? What's the combination?" asked the dangerous 18-year-old addict.

"You press 0 and then *Arm*," said my brother. It was completely useless. The kid ended up going out a second-story window and breaking a few tiles getting down from the roof. He then walked for miles and miles to get into town and do whatever he felt so compelled to do.

The resident with the shortest stay of all was the grandson of a Chassidic Rebbe. We knew a lot of those kids. He just showed up one Shabbat night with no car and no visible means of transport. He was thousands of miles from home. He had literally crossed an international border in search of guidance from my father. He stayed just the one night. I think he was feeling utterly constrained by the realities of his world. But he was *also* unprepared for the realities of ours. He borrowed my little brother's bike to go into town and then proceeded to try and ride it straight down the side of the mountain – through the forest. We never found the bike again. We ended up speaking with his family and helping him find a halfway reality. He was a good kid; he just needed a little help.

It was easy enough to separate the successes and the failures. You could almost do it before they even showed up. Despite all their moaning and complaining and resistance, the successes *wanted* to be there. They believed in my father's vision. The failures didn't and nothing my parents could have done would have helped them.

83

Of course, not everybody who came was there because they needed that kind of help. One young man, we'll call him Alex, was an Army Ranger. He was the son of one of my parents' friends. His parachute had been shot out during the invasion of Panama. CNN had announced the invasion before it'd happened and said the airport was a target. Noriega's forces had a chance to get ready. They shot out Alex's parachute. He'd hit the runway and been left for dead. Alex never stopped hating CNN... After they'd scraped him off the runway, the doctors weren't sure that Alex would ever walk again. He did. He was permitted to rejoin the regular army, but not the Rangers. As the US Army in the '80s was such a pathetic institution, he resigned. Alex explained to us once that America tank parades were always single file because the tank drivers couldn't be trusted not to hit each other if they drove in dual columns (like the Soviets did). He had no respect for, and didn't want to be a part of, the regular Army.

He came by our house, I imagine, to hang out and recuperate. I remember air gun competitions that Alex always won. His arms were massive. Apparently, the kids in synagogue were in awe when he put on tefillin. My dad used to claim Alex was his bodyguard. I think Alex enjoyed the role. There were no actual threats, but there were some good stories. One time, my father was on the phone with a particularly aggressive business counterparty. I believe this was in the early 90s and they were Russian. One of our cats had been violently attacking the others. My father, off-handedly, had remarked the day before that that particular cat had to go. My dad was on the phone with this counterparty when a shot rang out. The guys on the phone asked what it was. My father looked around, realized what had happened and said, "My bodyguard just shot my cat."

It changed the tenor of the conversation.

Apparently in a positive way.

Another time, a cat had got into the mud closet in the middle of the night. Alex had come downstairs, gun drawn, to deal with the intruder. Then he realized that my mother would be very upset if he put holes in the walls. So, upon reaching the kitchen, he decided to use a knife instead of a gun. The problem was, he couldn't remember which knives were *milchik* (for dairy products) and which were *fleishik* (for meat products). He didn't want to use a *milchik* knife and render it non-Kosher as a result of stabbing an intruder[1].

Thankfully, he worked out the intruder was a cat.

No knife, of either type, needed to be sullied.

My mother's efforts to help kids extended beyond our home. My mother spent a few years on the Citizen's Review Board – a group that reviewed social services cases and rendered official opinions about what social services *should* do in individual cases. The work was both rewarding and deeply frustrating. I remember her telling us about a kid who came before the board. He was a football player and good enough to go to college on a full ride. The problem was that his SAT scores were too low. Despite his talent, he couldn't go to

---

[1] He didn't know it'd be rendered non-kosher even if it was *fleishik*.

college. He'd been assessed as having anger management problems and so the State had spent thousands and thousands of dollars on counseling. My mother knew that what the kid *really* needed was $500 to pay for Princeton Review, bump his scores up a bit and get on with his life. But that wasn't an option. Only counseling. The State effectively told itself that counseling was what would speak to the fundamental issues at hand. Of course, it was doing nothing of the sort. If you were a highly talented person who couldn't progress in life because you sucked at some other (not even tangentially related) skill, wouldn't you be angry?

Sometimes, you must be *flexible* in order to really make a difference.

In later years, my mother dedicated quite a bit of effort to pushing back on the Common Core. Neither she nor I believed in the effectiveness of education that tried to skip simple skill-development while surreptitiously drilling home particular social values.

My mother never won these battles. Then again, she never stopped fighting them either.

My father's efforts also extended beyond our home, on occasion. People just knew he was somebody who could help. Once, a business associate of my father's called. His manic-depressive son was suicidal. The kid was on suicide watch in a rubber room. My dad went into the room with him late one night and came out the next morning.

"He won't kill himself," my dad stated definitively.

"How do you know?" asked his associate.

"Because he has a mission in life," said my father.

"What mission?" asked the young man's father, genuinely confused.

"He wants to kill me more than he wants to die."

Sometimes, you must be *flexible* in order to really make a difference.

I later got a Bar Mitzvah present from that same family. It was large and in a brown cardboard box. My dad was worried it was a bomb. We threw it off the deck, just to see if it would blow up. It didn't. It was no bomb. It was a beautiful coffee table book of photos and poetry from astronauts looking down on our marble of life. It was a beautiful coffee table book with a sizeable dent marking where it had hit that same marble of life.

Jewish Country Life

Elijah's Cup

Jewish tradition has it that Eliyahu (Elijah) visits every Passover Seder. We pour a special cup of wine for him and invite him in. Of course, he never drinks the wine. Figuring he's on a tight schedule, my parents always left the wine outside. The fun part would come the next morning.

Our animals, who *all* lived outside, would *sometimes* try out a little of the wine. Once, a cat drank some of the wine. Now, I know, our cats shouldn't have had access to wine. But you have to keep things in context. While alcohol is quite poisonous for cats, so are owls. Living outside in the country came with some risks. Thankfully, the cat only drank a little. It was fine, in the long term. In the short term, the effect of a drunk cat was *deeply* off-putting. Cats are meant to be graceful. Something seems fundamentally wrong with the world when they aren't.

The most spectacular drinker wasn't a cat, though. It was a chicken. Not that chickens are all that smart to begin with. One Shabbat night, I was out on the deck, and I saw one of the chickens (a sober one). It was watching the goings on in the living room. You know, all the guests, the light – my mom reading the Tzena U'rena.

It wanted to get in.

It proceeded to walk straight into the glass door.

"Buuk."

It stumbled back, went back to where it had started, and then decided to trot into the room.

"BUUK!"

It hit harder, shook itself off, examined the glass through each eye and then went back to the starting line.

This time, it just *ran* at the glass.

"BUUUUCK!" it smashed into the window.

I could swear the bird was concussed as it stumbled away.

The point is, a sober chicken ain't too clever.

A drunk chicken, through is something truly amazing to behold.

Sometimes it seems like sober chickens can barely walk. But the drunk chicken was like a caricature of a completely plastered human being. Legs akimbo, tripping over itself, weaving from side to side.

I know I'm a horrible person, but the drunk chicken was very entertaining. It too survived (I think an owl ended up getting it). I hope it didn't have too much of a hangover.

The Pool of Blood

For the most part, our chickens provided us with eggs. In Idaho, my parents slaughtered a rooster for Passover Seder, but they couldn't eat it. They knew it too well. It was the same in Oregon. We could slaughter them, but we just couldn't eat them. For a few years, we did slaughter some of the chickens for Kaporot[1]. One time, a recently slaughtered chicken got dropped and proceeded to run (as headless chickens are wont to do). Only instead of running randomly around, it was heading straight for the pool.

A headless chicken pumping blood out of its neck would have been less than desirable in the family swimming pool. I guess it would have had the last laugh – if it had only remained capable of laughing.

"Stop that chicken!" shouted my dad.

I was closest to the chicken, but I didn't want to stop it.

I remember running behind the bird and weighing my options: seriously pissed dad and bloody pool I'd probably have to clean vs. tackling a headless chicken pumping blood out of what had been its neck only moments before. I wasn't quite willing to make the final tackle, but I was building up to

---

[1] A sort of process of symbolic atonement before Yom Kippur.

89

it. My older brother was also running for the bird. I don't think he had my reservations.

Then, at the last moment, the bird veered right, and I was rescued from actually having to make a choice. It keeled over on the grass, only a few feet from the blue chlorinated waters.

I did end up bringing one of those chickens' pre-eggs (oocytes?) to my third-grade class for show-and-tell.

That was fun.

The Fantastic Fox

The chicken didn't end up with the last laugh. But other animals did. My father's favorite animal revenge story involved a chicken farmer in Idaho. He was pretty successful and had bought himself a tip-top trailer home – in the story, it was worth $80,000. Quite the trailer home, especially in those days. He'd put it up on blocks. He was living the high life. The trailer was his pride and joy. But he had a nemesis: a fox that kept killing his chickens. It took him months, but he finally trapped the fox. Having bested his tormentor, he didn't want to just kill it, though. He wanted it to suffer in style. So, he wrapped dynamite around the animal and then lit a fuse. He wanted the fox to experience the mirage of safety before it was blown to smithereens.

The fox had other ideas, though.

Freshly lit, it headed right under the farmer's brand new, top-of-the-line, trailer home.

There was nothing the farmer could do as his pride and joy was blown to smithereens by a particularly fantastic fox.

In addition to the cats and the chickens we had many, many dogs. People would routinely abandon unwanted dogs near our house. We had a three-legged dog who ran away from a neighbor (who lived about 3 miles away). We had Guido Savachini, a truly brutal (and massive) dog. Guido murdered a kitten by staring at it until the poor little thing had a heart attack and just keeled over from fright. I watched the whole thing.

Our neighbors had had a brutal dog too. A Doberman Pinscher. I hate and fear that breed (my brother says it was a pit bull, but my visceral fear says otherwise). One day, it came into our property, and it killed one of our goats. Another day, it came back and tore the ear off another of the goats. My 5'4" mother ran out with a *broom* and chased it away, screaming her face off. The dog was a danger to us, no doubt. My parents informed the neighbors that if the dog came onto our property again, it would die. Those were the rules. You can look them up in the Bible if you want.

It came by once again and my dad shot it. The dog made it home before it died.

The neighbors were mad, but they knew we were right.

For his part, Guido had a tendency to stray onto *their* property. Once he stole an entire deer carcass from them. They insisted, correctly, that the dog had to go. They had history, law and country ethics on their side. My dad loved the dog, but the dog had to die. It was our responsibility.

One day, when my dad was out of town, my mom brought the dog out to the woods behind the house. It was my job to shoot it. I had the shotgun. I lifted it. I sighted on the dog. But I chickened out. I just couldn't pull the trigger. My mom kept insisting that I do it, but I couldn't. She wasn't willing to either (that and the shotgun probably would've knocked her over). We ended up driving the dog someplace else. I don't know what happened with the dog or what it later did, but whatever it was, it was the wrong choice. I should have pulled that trigger. It was my responsibility, and I didn't live up to it.

The best dog we had was named Cardiac. He was an Oregon Health Sciences University practice dog. He'd apparently had dozens of heart surgeries and multiple transplants. He was an amazingly happy dog, for the three months prior to his death (by a presumed heart attack). When he first got out of the van, he saw the stairs to the house and rushed them. However, he'd never encountered stairs before. He plowed right into them, face first. Undeterred, and smiling like nobody's business, he got back up, figured out the stairs and rushed up them. We all knew he wasn't going to be around for long, but he was such a happy dog. It was a simple delight to have him around.

My Little Pony

At one point, we had a pony. The pony was also a miscreant. He liked to sneak away to the proper horse farm down the road and do things that proper horse farmers don't like mutt ponies doing. I was always scared of riding him, and with good reason. He *loved* to mess with his riders. I was easy to kick off, but his tricks extended far beyond bucking an undesired passenger. One of his favorites was to let you get on nicely and then be very peaceful. Moments later he'd take off for a low-hanging branch and sweep you off his back. I hated that pony. My dad probably thought it was funny. Eventually, to protect the chastity of the horse farm's mare's, my parents built an electric fence around the property. I electrocuted myself on that fence more than a few times. In the end, it didn't keep that pony in – or me. Not long after, facing a patrimony lawsuit, we sold the pony to the farm for $1.

I imagine he became dog food.

Lamb Chop

My least favorite animal was a sheep. He went by the name Lamb Chop. He was given to us by friends – the same ones who described my father as the Kaddish-saying mountain man. They had a tendency to pass off animals who outgrew their digs in town. They tried to pass off an alligator once, but my mom nixed that on the first day the thing was in her bathtub.

Lamb Chop, was a true terror. Being a ram, he loved nothing more than, well, ramming into things. And nothing was more fun than ramming into my little brother[1] and I. We *feared* that sheep. I still remember getting home in our giant blue Buick. Everybody else would get out and walk into the house, unmolested because they were far bigger than Lamb Chop was. My little brother and I would take up our positions

---

[1] He was 18 months younger than me and virtually the same size.

on opposite sides of the car. Inside the doors, of course. We'd haggle and fight about who had to sit closest to the house. I was never really sure which seat was better. Lamb Chop tended to wait on the house side of the car. On the other hand, if you got out on the other side, Lamb Chop would have more time to catch you.

As we argued, Lamb Chop would wait patiently. Like a shark from Jaws. Eventually, we'd count down and then open our doors and dash for the house. We had to manage the gravel driveway, then the stairs and then the porch. Lamb Chop would pummel us the whole way. He'd knock us over and slam us into the railings. He'd do whatever he could get away with before we got inside. He was gonna' get one of us, we knew that. The key was for him to get the *other* one of us.

I'm just thankful he'd been dehorned.

As usual, my father thought the whole thing was hilarious. My mother was less impressed. Eventually, she got my father to give Lamb Chop away to a proper sheep farmer. As the legend goes, that sheep farmer had a female sheep who still had her horns.

She tamed him on the very first truck ride to their new home.

Goat Heaven

The last kind of animal we had were goats. I loved those goats. Unlike chickens, goats are clever. Well, except with ropes; goats are real idiots when it comes to ropes. We used to tether our goats so that they'd eat a particular section of the lawn.

94

The goats would proceed to wrap themselves up in knots. It took about 20 minutes. We'd sit by the window and when the goats couldn't move anymore, we'd come out and untie them. Rinse and repeat.

I'm sure somebody has some more clever tether that avoids this, but we weren't that clever.

Hillbillies, remember?

Our two goats were named Zoom and Gali Gali (after the traditional Zionist labor song). Zoom was the one killed by the neighbor's dog. Gali Gali had one ear (again, the neighbor's dog) and tended to get trapped – and not just by ropes. I can't imagine, today, how a goat gets trapped. But I do remember going under the deck to rescue the animal.

On occasion, I got more involved with the health of those goats than I wanted to.

When we first moved to Oregon, the house my parents built had two major problems. One was that the chimney leaked something crazy. The second was that they couldn't get anything to grow in the clay at the top of my father's beautiful dome. In other words, our 'yard' was hard, dead and brown. It was the second of these issues that, indirectly, led to the most disgusting task of my life.

Both the chimney and the lawn issues were addressed, in a way, by the explosion of Mount Saint Helens. The ash from the explosion (which was only 50 miles away) not only destroyed my favorite toy truck (which had been left outside) and required us to wear masks for weeks, it sealed the cracks in the chimney and provided some sort of necessary nutrition to our clay yard.

Given the possibility of growing *something*, my parents planted clover. It grew *wonderfully* and soon covered the little patch designated as 'the lawn.' I remember searching it for four-leafed mutants.

The problem was: goats eat everything.

That and: clover is deadly to goats.

One thing led to another and one of the goats ate the clover and got desperately ill. Goats can't vomit and so after consulting with a vet it was determined that emergency action was required. We had to stomach pump the goat.

Our equipment: a garden hose.

And me.

Let me rephrase, we had to siphon the goat's stomach contents. In case you are unfamiliar with siphoning, it involves sucking one end of a hose until a liquid flow is established. By then holding one end of the hose lower than the bottom of the receptacle, said receptacle can be emptied of its contents. That receptacle could be a car's gas tank[1] or it could be a goat's stomach.

I was the only kid who was capable of the siphoning operation (and who could possibly be convinced to perform it). My older brother could 'delegate' to me, and my younger

---

[1] I had to do that once, when we didn't have enough money to buy gas for the car we drove, but had gas left over in another, non-functioning, vehicle. It didn't work, though, the gas tank was protected against siphoning. All I got was a lungful of petroleum fumes.

brother wasn't about to be dragooned into such a job. He would have just sat there, in dumb (but very wise) protest.

I would have loved to have had my older brother do it, but I lacked the authority to (literally) tell him to go suck it. Anybody with an older brother could understand.

I took a couple of big inhalations. I tried. But it was just *too* nasty. I almost vomited myself. I managed to pass off the hose which went to my older brother and then, I believe, to my father. It was my dad who ultimately saved the goat's life.

Gali Gali, who my older brother loved, died in the dead of a particularly cold winter. We'd opened the garage so the animals could shelter there, but Gali Gali hadn't come. Gali Gali was discovered during my older brother's birthday party. My dad wasn't around. I remember how distraught my older brother was as the assembled attendees at his birthday party watched him try to dig a goat-sized grave in the frozen earth.

I guess we buried the animal after it warmed up.

It Came from the Sky

Aside from all the animals we did have, there were a few animals that weren't ours that also had a pretty big impact. I encountered the first when I was probably in 4th or 5th grade. I was carrying a 5-gallon bucket of feed down to the chicken coop (I remember how heavy those buckets were, especially when filled with water). I got close to the coop when I saw that there was something wrong. There was a bird in the coop and the darned thing seems *bigger* than I was. I dropped the bucket and *ran* back to the house. My father wasn't impressed (and he didn't believe me). He just thought I didn't want to feed the chickens. I managed to convince him to walk back to the coop and, low and behold, there was a massive owl inside. It had flown in through a hole in the top of the coop and gotten trapped. It had beheaded a bunch of chickens, the rest seemed to be cowering in the corners (it was like a pastoral version of an African dictatorship). My dad maneuvered behind the bird and, as we all watched, convinced it to fly out of the coop. Wow, that thing was majestic as it spread it wings and took off.

I *know* intellectually that it must have been much smaller than I was. But I can still *swear* that it was bigger.

Over the next few weeks, a few of our cats went missing. Among them was the much beloved Momma Cat and the not-so-pleasant City Bitch.

Ultimately, it wasn't the drinking that did them in.

Imaginary Animals

The other critical animals were largely imaginary. The most important of these were the cougars and the bears. When new residents arrived, my dad would explain that they shouldn't try to run away because the cougars and bears might eat them. These were city kids. They also tended to be drug addicts. They had no idea whether there were *really* cougars and bears. They wouldn't have admitted it, but they believed my father just enough not to head into the woods by themselves. Many remained reluctant even after they'd spent some time with us and realized *we* weren't worried about the cougars and the bears. There were *eventually* cougars. There are now. I don't let my own little kids go into the woods alone. My mom said she actually saw a bear once, and she would know. But none of the animals every gave us kids a hard time.

Guns

One thing we were worried about, when we were rampaging through the woods, was the hunters. We always wore bright, or even reflective, clothes into the woods. My mother was adamant about that. She was really worried about us being shot.

Guns, of course, were a part of our lives. Some readers might identify with this, particularly those with a more "country" bent. If you grew up this way, I hope I don't bore you too much with the next few paragraphs.

I first went shooting when I was six. My kids first went shooting when they were five. This was *completely* normal and even recommended.

The reasoning was simple.

If you were going to have guns around (and everybody did) it was best to teach younger kids that touching them was tantamount to a death sentence and *then*, when they were old enough to overcome that resistance, to take them out and let them fire a few rounds.

Just for context, using CDC data, 601 children six and under died from gun injuries in the United States from 1999 to 2019. This excludes others intentionally murdering those children (which has nothing to do with gun safety) but includes accidental discharge of weapons by others and intentional discharge of weapons by those children themselves. That works out to 30 children a year or a 0.0001% chance of death by firearms. For comparison, 11,699 children drowned over that same time period (584 a year). Death by drowning is almost 20 times more common, despite the widespread prevalence of guns in homes in the United States.

Six is a critical age for having kids fire those first few rounds – firearms are not very dangerous to younger children but can be for older children. Part of this is simply that if they aren't chambered, many types of guns are impossible for kids to fire. Most *adult women* find it difficult to chamber a large-caliber semi-automatic handgun.

What did exposure accomplish?

First, it robbed the weapons of their mystique and their sense of being a forbidden fruit. But it also *scared* most kids. Their desire to play with guns, for whatever reason, would be severely curtailed. There was one final benefit. *Some* kids weren't scared. Some kids *loved* shooting. If you encountered one of those, you'd raise the caliber in the hope of inspiring fear. If that didn't work, then your family needed a whole new approach to gun safety. One of my sons *loved* shooting. He was five. He loved the .22. He loved the 9mm pistol. He even loved the AK-47. We acquired gun locks.

Growing up, we didn't go shooting down at some range somewhere. We went shooting at an abandoned rail line in the woods below our house. These old rail tracks were used for logging before trucks were practical. The berms were beautiful. We had strict range rules. One of them was that you had to announce yourself (and be acknowledged) before you could approach the range. One day, I announced myself but didn't wait for acknowledgement.

I violated a range rule.

My parents took drastic action.

The family doctor, the forensic pathologist, was invited up. He brought with him a slideshow of about 20 cases he'd worked where accidental deaths had been caused by failure to adhere to range rules. I *still* remember some of the bodies and some of the stories.

I was six.

I never broke range rules again.

Purple Potatoes

Near the house, we had about a half-acre of land we used for tiny-scale farming. We had corn, peas, a variety of herbs, rhubarb, cucumbers... you know, all the usual suspects. Corn was awesome. It grew so quickly, it got so tall, and it tasted *so* sweet right after it was picked (before the sugars turned to starches). The most unusual of our crops were the purple potatoes. They were Peruvian and they'd be brought into the US in a diplomatic pouch specifically for the benefit of a restaurant in San Francisco. The potatoes were purple all the way through. At the time, no other potatoes in the country were like that. The restaurant ended up going under, but my great uncle got his hands on their stock of potatoes. He proceeded to grow them on the river in Idaho. Then, *we* inherited them. We weren't great farmers and our collection of potatoes steadily dwindled. In a last gasp attempt to rescue the breed (at least in the US), we handed our remaining stock of a few hundred potatoes to our neighbors. A few years later, they began to appear locally, in chips. Now, purple potatoes are a routine part of the American diet. It's kind of fun how little individual actions can spread and have such a wide impact – albeit a small one. It isn't often that you get to know your own part in it.

Education

Life wasn't all animals, Shabbat dinners, long-term guests and farming. We weren't *just* some backwoods family.

Let's start with Idaho. Sure, my parents lived in the backwoods. And sure, they had no plumbing or electricity (at least initially). And, sure, they looked like mountain folk. And yet, while in the Idaho wilderness, they were each completing their Ph.Ds. at Columbia University.

There was more to the story than people assumed.

Initially, when float boaters or dudes would come down the river, they didn't know what to think about my parents. The Forest Service tried to convince each band of float boaters that they were the first civilized people to explore the River of No Return. Invariably, given the expectations of the day, my parents were categorized as Noble Savages. It wasn't a label they particularly embraced. At first, my parents would try to convince the float boaters that they were educated people. Then, they realized it was hopeless and they changed gears.

My father found a particular joy in their new approach to presumptuous strangers.

For example, some Mayor from some small town in upstate New York would ask "Have you ever been to the big city?"

My dad, who had recently spent years in New York City, would answer "I went to Boise once as a boy."

Sometimes he'd call it "the big smoke" just for color.

My favorite example of this genre involved people who asked my dad whether he could read. "Naaaw," my dad would drawl, "I tried to learn once, but I couldn't figure out whether to look at the white part of the page or the black part." Even with a line like that, people wouldn't realize he was making fun of the person asking the question.

For my part, I grew up *primarily* on a hilltop in Oregon. But my family wasn't just a collection of hillbilly Jews. We were homeschooled, which meant we weren't tethered to one place. Aside from Oregon, we *also* spent time in New York, London and Israel. My parents bought a flat in London in the mid-80s (prices were great then). I knew (and know) my way around both London and New York. We went to the London theater all the time. I still remember seeing *Memorandum*, long before the Berlin Wall fell (and Vaclav Havel went from being a persecuted playwright to the President of Czechoslovakia). I also remember seeing *Hamlet, Improvised*. Twice. It was hilarious. One time, Hamlet died from toothpaste. That was my suggestion.

The point was, we lived on a hilltop, but that didn't mean we didn't see other parts of the world as well. When we did travel, we never did the touristy things. Instead, our father would take us to see stock exchanges and banks. These weren't vacations. Our father hated vacations. You *always* had to have a good reason for going where you were going. It was like toys. If we wanted our parents to buy them, they had to serve a purpose. If they did serve a purpose, then our parents would have bent and heaven and earth to get what we needed.

My mother, though, was not like my father. She always wanted a *real* vacation. A *normal* vacation, like any *normal* family would enjoy. After years of trying, my mom convinced my father to take us all on just such a vacation. Just for a weekend. We got a friend's recommendation (from the same family with the sheep and the alligator) and we were off to the Breitenbush Hot Springs and Resort for Shabbat. My mom was very excited. The place seemed to have everything. It was in the mountains, the food was very strictly vegetarian (which was enough for our level of kashrut at the time), it seemed beautiful, and it came highly recommended.

My mom was going to show my dad the value of a good vacation.

It didn't quite work out.

We showed up just before Shabbat – with no time to go anyplace else. This was it, all in. We drove through the gates and my parents discovered, to their horror, that they'd brought their children to a nudist colony just in time for the Sabbath.

We stayed in the cabin, although my big brother snuck out – he was an adolescent boy. Just to cap things off, we all suffered food poisoning from the vegetarian (but not hygienically prepared) victuals.

It was the last vacation we ever went on.

While we certainly spent a lot of time in big cities (and a little time in nudist colonies) we also frequented other locales. My father was an investor in junior mining companies who decided to try to develop mineral properties himself. My mother worked with my father. She was the grounded and organized manager who balanced his charismatic, big picture view. The company offices were in Calgary, Alberta and I spent quite a bit of time there. I helped deliver packages.

As I used to say: "Child labor: better hours, no pay."

My little brother and I were even the subject of a photo on the Calgary Herald. It was front page and above the fold. The caption said something like: "Joseph Cox and Benjamin Cox enjoy cooling off in Eau Claire Park during record heat wave."

I remember sitting in that park, trying to be polite to the family that was showing us the city for the day. I was wondering why I was wasting my time there.

Even then I didn't like vacations.

The offices were in Calgary, but the properties were in the Canadian Arctic (what is now called Nunavut). My parents went to the Arctic many times. I remember the one time I went with them. It was around Halloween. I was a little kid. I remember the prop plane flying north, I guess from Yellowknife. I remember the trees getting smaller and smaller and then disappearing. I remember the bathrooms – giant garbage bins you sat on top of and pooped in because the ground was frozen solid and there was neither plumbing nor digging. Those *really* stank[1]. I remember shirtless kids in a place that was – to this southerner – quite cold. I remember watching skidoos on the water. I was fascinated by the idea that they didn't just fall in. I remember all the doors always being open, because propane was provided free of charge by the government in a successful effort to promote town-dwelling. I also remember Inuktituk – the written and spoken language (the orientation of letters tells you vowel sounds!).

Most of all, I remember Halloween night. Now I was a *tough* kid. I was particularly proud of not being a *cold* kid. I ran fast, in all sorts of ways, and I just wasn't normally cold. When I was, I never wanted to admit it. I was too tough. That night, I had been properly bundled up by my parents. But I was *still* cold. After a long struggle, I finally turned to my dad and said, "Dad, I'm chilly."

He just laughed.

It was 40 below zero, on both scales, *before wind chill*. It was freaking freezing. It was so cold there you couldn't wear contacts because they'd freeze to your eyes. My dad was even sued by the city of Yellowknife because he tripped and shattered the sidewalk.

It was very, very cold.

Once we got to the party, it warmed right up (free propane does that). The costumes were like nothing else I've ever seen. These people took Halloween seriously. I remember finding a

---

[1] A few years ago, I told an Ethiopian guide (who was trying to find my family the best bathrooms in Addis Ababa) about them. He was blown away by the very idea of above-ground plastic bins for toilets.

guy who looked like he was just hair. And I remember poking him, trying to find his face. My parents were mortified, but he didn't say anything. The Inuit – at least in those days – never publicly displayed anger.

The stories of the north, especially the stories my mother shared, had a fundamental impact on my life. My parents would often repeat the advice to shed all your clothes, one by one, if being pursued by the polar bear. Apparently, the bears will investigate each article of clothing – being curious. Then when they find you naked and prone in the snow, they'll assume you're dead and leave you alone. As my father used to claim, "polars are like humans, they hunt for sport."

For me, this sort of practical advice ranks up with keeping track of time while on an acid trip.

But we had other nuggets of practical wisdom as well.

For example, never leave a peanut butter sandwich in a helicopter in the North. Somebody did that once and the polar bears smelled it from miles away and thrashed the helicopter. Also, it is extremely rude to turn down still-beating caribou heart. My mother had been offered such a heart as an honor. It was far from being kosher. My mother had to claim she was fasting and was eating no food whatsoever. The Inuit, supposedly these remote people, knew all about fasting. They'd seen TV reports about somebody who had fasted for 30 days. They were fascinated to see such behavior for themselves. For the remainder of her trip, my mother could never be seen eating. It would have meant a massive dishonor.

My parents built a runway in the north, out of permafrost and gravel. It was big enough, barely, for C-130s. My mother spent a fair amount of time there, including with a man named Simeonie Irqittuq who took her on a three-day canoeing trip in the dark. I can't remember the reason why she took that trip, but she wrote about it (and her respect for Simeonie) at the end of her magnum opus, *Reflections on the Logic of the Good*. I also remember that Simeonie committed suicide in his 40s. My mother was devasted, but suicide was an acceptable thing in Inuit society. It was tied to an ancient need to *never* be a drag on society. Survival was so fragile that if you didn't think you were pulling your weight, then it was time to end your life. A few years later, a large number of teenagers in Hall Beach committed suicide. It wasn't all at once, but over the course of a summer. By the end of that summer, something like 15 kids died. They inhaled that free propane and then smoked. Hard as heck for us southerners to understand, but there you go.

My mother had real friends in Hall Beach. Women she shared something critical with: they had all experienced outsiders who would come in, ask inappropriate questions and then believe everything you told them. Anthropologists were fascinated by the Inuit. They are considered the only culture that never shows anger. My mother, who was no anthropologist, insisted that this didn't mean they were never angry.

If you're curious about her perspective on the Arctic, check out *Inungilak*. It shares, through fiction, some of what my mother learned. She also talks about her experience, and her respect for Inuit knowledge. She even has a story about a woman fleeing a polar bear.

I heard all these stories, but that one trip just brought them more to life.

Being in the iron ore business, my parents spent time in many other places. One particularly touching story involved a trip to Salt Lake City for an iron ore conference. At that time, my parents were happy to eat 'kosher ingredient' foods and so they had breakfast in their hotel. It was, at the time, the best hotel in Salt Lake City. They were confused, though. All of the waitstaff had developmental disabilities. When they asked about it later, a local explained that rather than hiding away such people they preferred to celebrate them. They made sure all their most important visitors saw them and knew they were a treasured part of Mormon society. It was, and is, a beautiful concept.

As our parents spent so much time travelling, a significant amount of my child-rearing involved not only my siblings, but a very wise man named Robert. Robert took great care of us. He read us the Hobbit, he told us great stories about his own childhood, he taught us important songs ("back-to-back, they faced each other" and "Battle of New Orleans") and he passed on a few kernels of parenting wisdom. For example, he used to threaten that if I didn't blow my nose, he'd "cut off my ears and feed them to the chickens." I was scared of the chickens; this was an effective threat.

Then one day I realized he couldn't possibly go through with it.

When he asked me to blow my nose, I defiantly said "No!"

I expected him to slowly escalate until I called his bluff. He didn't. He just grabbed a knife, grabbed my ear and moved in to cut it off.

I *freaked* out, surrendered, and blew my nose.

I asked him about it later and he said that sometimes you need to escalate quickly in order to keep children on their toes. My own children think I learned that lesson a little too well (they're probably right).

My parents built our house so that it formed a complete track on the basement and ground floors. You could go around and around and around the house. Oregon gets a little wet and we lived off in the middle of nowhere, so we used that 'track' as a roller-skating rink and as a tricycle racetrack. The tricycle racetrack was in the basement. We'd get a whole head of steam up, go up on two wheels, the whole bit. When we got going too fast, Robert used to say: "If you crash and spill your guts and blood and brains all over the floor, you've got to clean it up."

We slowed down.

He explained the psychology of this as well: we really couldn't conceive of the level of pain we'd experience if we crashed. But we understood bleeding and cleaning up and we hated it. We slowed down.

Robert's father was named Masil because *his* parents really wanted a girl. Like a character out of "Boy named Sue", he grew up to be an extremely tough character. He went by Mace. He even won some sort of national honor after being shot three times by a purse snatcher (and then shooting back and killing the guy). Robert's brother, meanwhile, gave me my first smoke (at 6) and the two of them hung me over the second-story banister head down. The smoke was okay but being suspended from my feet and being told it was dangerous to wriggle was not fun. It was less fun when my older *brother* (who was much smaller than them) tried the same trick off the front porch.

As involved as Robert was in *our* lives, we were almost completely unaware of his. He asked for the day off once and my mom asked why. He said it was his son's birthday. We didn't even know he had a son and asked which birthday. The guy was raising us, and it turned out we didn't even know he had a *seven-year-old boy*. He was very private, in his way.

His kids, not surprisingly, are very impressive people.

I digress. I don't feel bad, though; this whole book is a digression.

Now that I've got the basic background down, let's get into the proper educatin' part of things. For secular studies, up until the 3rd grade, I was conventionally home schooled. We used a curriculum my parents had started using in Idaho: the Calvert School. We had a schoolroom in the basement. It had a proper blackboard and desks and even an old-time phone for decoration. Very little of our education actually involved that school room. My parents weren't terribly hands-on about homeschooling. Or anything for that matter[1]. Instead of a heavy dose of parentally driven education, there was a curriculum delivered by the Calvert School (initially developed for diplomats' children and the like). We were expected to work our own way through it. We worked anywhere in the house (my favorite spot was laying down over the heating vents in the living room).

When my parents would walk by, we'd want to be seen to be working – of course. But school took no more than 90 minutes a day. We weren't the kinds of kids to finish up, show our lessons to our parents and get on with things. Instead, we procrastinated while *pretending* to be doing our schoolwork. Instead of *actually* working, we were reading magazines tucked in between the pages of our books. We'd slip them under the books if we heard our parents were nearby. Of course, the only magazines my parents had around were things like Forbes, Aviation Week, the Economist and the like.

I didn't realize, until my younger brother's wedding, that that had been the plan all along. My parents *wanted* us to feel like we were getting away with something when actually we were learning exactly the way they wanted us to. I've never

---

[1] They discovered I needed glasses when they brought me to a Trail Blazers game and asked me how I liked it. I said TV was better, because you could see the players. In truth, I could make out where the players were (barely), but the ball was completely undetectable. This was in the old (and small) Memorial Coliseum. To *confirm* I had terrible eyesight they didn't bring me to an optometrist. Instead, they brought me to another game and asked what the score was. I could see the score itself, but everything else was a blur. My eyesight problems confirmed, I got to see an optometrist.

managed (or even tried) that sort of duplicity with my own kids, but it was very effective when used on me.

To keep us busy, my parents had a rule. If we said we were bored then we had to work. Most often that meant cleaning. It also involved yard work (imagine mowing three acres of poorly maintained yard with a push mower) or forest work (like cutting unwanted plants over a 5-acre area). Sometimes, it involved chopping wood. I was too small to cut down trees or even to chainsaw them afterwards. When times were lean and we needed firewood, we did a fair amount of that. At one point, we cut down all the trees near the house in order to have a firebreak (and raise some cash). That year we planted thousands of new trees, almost all sequoias and cedars. One time my father cut down a particularly large tree. Only, instead of falling properly, it just kind of slid off the stump and buried itself in the ground – still standing. *That* was dangerous. A bit of wind or a poorly considered cut and that whole tree would tumble. We had to get a *real* logger up to the house to fix that particular problem.

All in all, it was best not to be bored. So, we found things to do. I played guitar and wrote. My younger brother hunted berries in the woods and made jam. He also collected rocks (most of his adult life has involved working in the mining industry).

Whatever it was, we were rarely bored. We couldn't afford to be if we wanted to avoid real work.

The one thing that was absolutely verboten in our house was TV. We had TVs. My antisemitic grandfather was convinced we were being raised in a cult. He gave us the TV as his way of ensuring we were exposed to the rest of the world. He didn't really understand that between the long-term residents, the Shabbat guests, the magazines and the travel we were probably *more exposed to the world than he was.* Nonetheless, every year, he'd give us his TV from the last year. He liked new TVs. But we weren't allowed to watch the TVs he gave us.

There were exceptions to the no-watching rule. Specifically: if there was a war, if the Olympics were on, or if the Trailblazers were in the Conference Finals (or better), then we were allowed to watch the TV. But just TV related to those topics.

My dad caught us watching a sitcom once. He warned us that if he caught us again, he'd shoot the TV. Five minutes later, he caught us again. The TV was carried outside and then executed (by shotgun to the back). It wasn't nearly as exciting as I'd hoped (shooting in the glass would have been more fun but more dangerous). Nonetheless, the TV was dead.

I was educated strictly within the Calvert system through the 2nd grade. During that time, for religious studies, my father taught us. It was kind of a blind leading the blind situation. My dad couldn't read Hebrew. Nonetheless, we learned Shema and a few other things. I remember really concentrating on "Shema Yisrael" ("Hear O'Israel") and then hearing a voice. Everybody insisted they hadn't spoken, and I felt foolish.

Maybe I was foolish, maybe I wasn't. Either way, even at the time I couldn't understand what the voice had said.

I achieved my highest academic success in the second grade. Every 20 lessons, we sent off our material to be graded. A teacher in Baltimore would review and then return our tests and assignments. It was part of how our work was accredited.

I'd written a poem for an English assignment and my "teacher" had sent it back. I had to redo the assignment. She'd suspected me of plagiarism. I was *so* mad, but my parents managed to convince me it was actually the highest form of praise. My mom kept it and I collected it after her death. I've pasted it above – complete with the grader's comments.

For those who don't enjoy a second-grader's scrawl, here is the poem and the commentary:

The Branch

The bold branch floated in the cold water
like one stranger among many friends
By rolling about, he tries to get out, out from
the rushing water
The water replies, by throwing him up, up
into the sky's [hey, I was in second grade!]
He shoots threw the air [ditto!] with hopeless
care, as the water shoots down
And then he stops and starts to drop to the
ravine below
The branch the poor branch plummets to the
cold gray water.

'Teacher's note': I didn't realize you'd meant this for poetry when I started to correct it. Did you write it? Retest.

For me, this poem isn't only important because I was accused of plagiarism. It was important because, on some level, I could empathize with a stick.

For third grade, I went to school. My siblings went to the same school. I learned later that we went because my mother was involved in the school management; it looked bad that her own children didn't attend. That year wasn't a resounding success. I did fine academically, but I was a precocious punk. In my family, "precocious" wasn't a good thing. We used to read the Calvert School magazine and learn about these people sailing around the world with their little overachievers getting educated on their boat (or similar stories). It always made us (parents and children alike) feel so inadequate.

My mother would comfort herself with something her father used to say about precocious children: "Check back when they're 30."

There was a deep wisdom involved in that simple comment.

In our family, "precocious" meant more than being a talented youngster. It also meant being horrible from a behavioral perspective. I scored well on both fronts. While I sat in the third-grade classroom, I was doing fifth, sixth and seventh grade subject matter (homeschool has its benefits). I was a terror otherwise. I organized a gang and got into fights. I considered it honorable because we only attacked older and bigger kids. I once leveled a smaller eighth grader (smaller than normal, not than me). He hadn't done anything to me, I just relished the challenge. His much, much bigger seventh-grade brother (the biggest kid in the school and the undisputed bully of the place) picked me up by my neck in a poorly applied chokehold. I swung my head back and broke his nose. I was the hero of the little kids (except his sister, who was in my class).

The school was aghast.

My parents were called in.

Predictably, they thought it was funny as hell. Only my mother had the common sense not to admit it to the Principal[1].

The final straw *might* have been the chicken oocyte I brought in for show and tell and then left in the teacher's fridge for three months.

I doubt it, though.

The fact was, I was out of control. I had been diagnosed as hyperactive and my parents had been told to put me on various drugs to address the problem. They never trusted the concept of drugging children for behavioral problems. My sister ended up coming up with a working solution. They'd let me stay up as late at night as I wanted. Then they'd wake me up at 6:30 every morning. The strategy was simple: keep Joseph tired and you'll maintain some sort of control. I'm very thankful for my sister's advice. People just see a lack of focus with kids like me. Even though we aren't focusing on the task at hand, we *are* learning from all those things other folk consider distractions.

My sister's intervention helped, but it didn't solve things. As much as my teachers might have been impressed by my brains,

----

[1] The ambiguity in that sentence is intentional.

my behavior did a fair amount to even things out. I even broke a kid's tooth once. I'm sure he didn't deserve it.

When it came time to reenroll, I wasn't welcomed back.

Despite it all, my teacher in 3rd grade ended up leaving to become a private tutor for just me and my brother. We added a few more kids later on, but it started with us two. Mrs. Shaff was incredible. She referred to me as the apple of her eye and I imagined that to be something exclusive. But she'd been a teacher since 1947. She'd had lots of beloved pupils.

One time she took us to the beginning of a murder trial. I think it was a bail hearing. I could only think poorly of the young man on trial. Who would want to associate with such a possible killer? After we left, Mrs. Shaff explained who he was.

He'd been, not that many years earlier, her favorite pupil.

At first, I was jealous.

Then I asked, "Is he guilty?"

"I don't know," she'd said, "But I love him anyway."

That really confused me. How was she loyal to a guy who'd possibly murdered somebody else? How could she be loyal and still think he could be guilty?

Only while writing this did I notice that that trial had another effect. Thinking back, I realize Mrs. Shaff meant it as a warning. Beverly Shaff would still love me, no matter what. But even her favorite students could end up doing horrible things. I was no exception.

I don't remember ever behaving badly around Mrs. Shaff.

Like my grandmother, she expected more from us.

I ended up dedicating my first book to her.

Most of our education with Mrs. Shaff was like the murder trial. We'd do a little schoolwork – often in the loft of her condominium. We'd play at picking stocks and tracking them. Or writing essays and learning about structure and form (something this book is intentionally lacking). But most of all, we'd drive around in her old, square, Volvo sedan. We'd just go look at things. The first long-distance power transmission (from a dam in Oregon City to Portland). Ideas and hopes people had for places like Salem, Oregon City or Longview. The largest and smallest city parks in the United States. The murder trial. I guess the way she figured it, we didn't need much book learning. But we needed a lot of *other* learning. There ended up being as many as five or six of us in that group. A second teacher was hired. I don't remember her name, but I do remember she had more of a focus on traditional academics. She did not see eye to eye with Mrs. Shaff.

At the time, I agreed with the other teacher 100%.

Now... well, now I've learned better. Kids need the basic skills, no doubt. But once they have them – at an age-appropriate level – they need to begin to grasp something more nebulous: wisdom.

When talking about those years, I keep saying "we learned." The *we* included my younger brother. He was only eighteen months younger than I. He had a very hard time with school. He was, and is, brilliant. But he was far more intuitive than academic (like my "mentally retarded" father). One day, my parents pushed him very, very hard[1], – they were testing whether he was being lazy or faking. He was good at being lazy and avoiding work, but that wasn't the case with his learning. He just had real learning difficulties – combined with a brilliance that was a whole lot harder to measure than my own intelligence. To give just one example: my brother only learned how to read when he was 8. When it came time for college applications and they asked for the list of books he'd read during high school, we stopped listing them at around 1300. He couldn't read words, based on the letters. He could, however, vacuum sentences based on the words. I'm not a fast reader. I remember struggling for weeks through the Grapes of Wrath. He borrowed it for a night and returned it the next morning.

Just like that, he was done.

He's never stopped vacuuming up the written word.

As an aside (from an aside, from an aside), our family moved out West during the same time period as the Grapes of Wrath. But they did it differently. My grandmother was hired as a nanny for a family of loan sharks. They taught her how to behave like a lady. If you're a mobster who wants to play at "class," your nanny has to be able to play the role. Sure, they hired a half-Indian/half-PWT girl, but they educated her well. Even at 80, she properly folded herself into the seat of a car.

---

[1] Although they only meant the best for him, that day really shook me up.

My grandmother took care of the mobster's kids as they drove from Oklahoma to California and back in their limousine.

They fit the stereotype of evil bankers and she helped them do it. The class she was taught may have only been pretension for them, but it became reality for her.

She exuded it, and spread it, for the rest of her life.

Mrs. Shaff did a pretty good job of working to each of our strengths. We ended up with a setup where we did religious education in the mornings and secular education in the afternoons. A rabbi was bought in to Portland to teach us; a gentle and wonderful man named Rabbi Chatan. He was a Chabad Chassid. We'd learn the Five Books of Moses with him, as well as davening and other things. We never achieved the levels of education expected of Chabad kids. Not even close. So much of what we did was focused on very basic textual analysis: identifying roots, identifying grammar, doing translation and some really limited interpretation. I was good at these things. My brother wasn't. He was good at other things. But the Rabbi couldn't do two tracks at once. In the end, going as slowly as we did was very good for me. That sort of baseline textual analysis has proved critical to my own Torah understanding.

My real interest as a kid was in being a writer, like my mother. I had a brief time when I also pursued guitar but when

I realized I'd never be very good (much less world-class), I gave it up. I saw no point in continuing.

Writing was different.

I remember being a *really* little kid when my parents held a book warming party. I'm pretty sure it was a party for a friend and not my mother because my mother didn't have parties for her books – not in the 1980s. My mom wrote schlokies then and she was a bit embarrassed by them. My mom's real name was Chana, but she wrote under the moniker *Eleanor Anne Cox*. The schlokies were bodice busters *without* the bodice busting. Basically, they were period pieces in which she explored ideas about politics and life that most readers would never sense within the texts themselves. They were the kinds of things that sold at supermarkets. You know, in the romance area that used to be near the checkout. They sold pretty well. Like a hundred thousand copies well. Eventually, she had a falling out with her agent[1] because my dad was such a pain to deal with. Just imagine the guy who negotiated the student-apartment lease getting between the publishing house, the agent and the author.

The agent' ultimatum was clear: lose the husband or lose the agent.

The husband won and the schlokies ended.

My mom had always been working on other books, though. Books on philosophy like *Reflections on the Logic of the Good*

------

[11] Also, Jean Auel's agent – Jean helped her get the agent in the first place. I've tried but failed to continue the relationship with the agent's daughter.

and *The River Went out of Eden*. And her best fiction book, *Inungilak*. This final book, although it fell well within the agent's purview, was never published. Possibly, it was due to the fall out. Just as likely, it was due to how unrealistic the book seemed. After all, it was the early 80s and my mom was talking about how weak the Soviet Union actually was. I eventually self-published *Inungilak* some 30 years later.

Anyway, this book warming party was almost certainly for a very particular friend. She'd recently published a massive tome of a book and my parents were doing their best to support it. They'd even bought 10 copies at her launch; just in case nobody else would. All of it was totally unnecessary. The author was Jean Auel, and the book was the *Clan of the Cave Bears*. It was on the best seller list for eight months and sold millions of copies worldwide. Its success was not exceeded until 1997 with the publication of *Harry Potter and the Philosopher's Stone*. It was *that* big.

My parents' gesture ended up being a pretty cute one.

The book launched in May 1980. I was three and a half.

The party was the most important party of my life.

There was a large group of literary-minded people around. They were in the living room. I remember hiding behind my mother. I was shy. My mother told me, "Don't be shy." I don't know what went through my head, but I *decided* not to be shy. And I began to tell a story. It wasn't anything original, it was a take on a story I'd heard my mother working on for *Inungilak*.

A story about a polar bear chasing me and how I managed to escape.

The room was riveted. Some people said some very nice things to me. I decided, then and there, that I wanted to be an author.

I wrote a couple decent things and a bunch of terrible ones. I wasn't very good at capturing people in my stories, so inanimate objects did tend to feature rather heavily.

I tried to write my first proper book at 8. About 50 pages in, my older brother read it and told me it was hackneyed and boring. He was cruel, but right. I distinctly remember overusing the phrase "blood coursed through his veins." I tossed out the book. I tried again when I was around 12. This was going to be a book set in Chile, during Incan times. Somebody was going to be washed up on shore. I remember doing research at the library in London. I remember friends thinking I wasn't serious. I guess I wasn't.

I wrote a few chapters, but never got any further.

But I didn't stop trying.

Writing, throughout my life, has been what I've identified as my key capability. And my key passion. I've never made any money at it. Nonetheless, my writing is the reason I'm married to my wife and have the chance to share what I've learned with a community. My storytelling, albeit in other mediums, has been key to my professional success. I may not make any money *as an author*; but being a writer has paid off in spades.

After elementary school was complete, I was enrolled in a prestigious Oregon high school. The kind of place where kids' parents would show up in exotic cars – on occasion. My father wouldn't let us to go to public school. His own experience, labelled as a retarded child and facing the difficulties he faced, ruled it out. For her part, my mother was very reluctant to send us to a private school. Particularly *that* school.

On the micro-level, she was right. The school was terrible. My grades were terrible. It wasn't that I wasn't working hard, or that my work wasn't good.

No, there were a range of other factors.

On the most benign level, the teacher's liked to see themselves as parents. It was one of these all-encompassing touchy feely (sometimes too touchy feely) kind of places. It didn't help that the faculty's own children hadn't been as successful as my older siblings. My older sister, with learning disabilities of her own, had gone to Columbia University (Barnard College) and my brother had gone to Princeton. Their kids hadn't. I was the third kid in the batch and the relationships were strained.

Second, they saw me playing basketball at school during recesses. They had no idea how hard I worked when I got home. I did great in math and science. You couldn't 'adjust' scores in those subjects. But in the soft subjects I didn't do well. Again, and again my evaluations read: "his work is excellent, but he doesn't apply himself, so..." I was a B-student.

To be fair, some of my "doesn't apply himself" issue had to do with some adjustment issues. I wasn't a normal kid. It was a point of pride, really. I also had never gone to school (except the 3rd grade). I'd do things like stand up and yawn in math class or argue with my English teacher about the Bible. He thought he knew the Old Testament better than I did. Even in those days, that wasn't true. But I didn't really understand how school was done.

My lack of 'schooling' also got me in trouble in part because I really didn't understand the rules. As I understood it, the goal of school was to *really* learn the material. I considered it cheating to study for a test. You either knew the material or you didn't. I did reasonably poorly on a test and my teacher asked me about it. Proudly I responded, "It wasn't bad, considering I didn't study."

What I was saying was: "I did quite well, considering I didn't cheat like the rest of the class did."

What he heard was: "This kid is proud he didn't apply himself."

In time, I did adjust to school. But, even then, politics remained a problem.

I single-handedly published (and wrote some of the articles for) a fortnightly unofficial newspaper called *Read the Disclaimer*. The place, like most very rich high schools (and certainly those in Portland, Oregon) was extremely liberal. They did a survey of student opinions about the election between Bill Clinton and Bush Sr. The entire student body,

127

with the exception of (I think) 3 students (who declined to answer), were unanimously in support of Bill Clinton. *I* even declined to answer, which I regret.

My unofficial paper existed, as per the disclaimer,

> *...not to offend, but to spark controversy. Without people saying: 'I take this side and I will argue for it,' no creative airing of our differences can exist... I want to create an environment that is conducive to more than one or two opinions... I will not publish personal attacks.*

Apparently, I failed at encouraging discussion. One issue was actually gathered up as soon as I'd distributed it and burned in the student lounge. I was almost as angry as I'd been about the 2nd grade poem. But, again, my parents informed me that it probably meant I was doing something right.

I still have some of those old issues. Looking back, I published some offensive things; things I would never write, think or even *publish* now (I did have contributors I didn't agree with). I was willing to shock, even when I shouldn't have done so. Quite simply, I didn't have the sensitivity and maturity I do now. My focus was on bucking overwhelming and monolithic peer opinions. I was perfectly willing to publish a variety of viewpoints, including those that dominated the school. I truly wanted *different* perspectives. But, even then, exclusion (rather than engagement) dominated some areas of political "discourse."

People want to hear those ideas they agree with. Trying to expose people to other perspectives is very hard to do.

It turned out that the school had fundamental issues of its own – issues far greater than what I faced. They were later sued for extensive sexual assault and harassment of students by teachers. Generations of assault. I had one teacher, a perfectly nice guy, who couldn't stop commenting on how beautiful my eye lashes were. He even took me and a few other kids to a showing of the *Rocky Horror Picture Show*. All that was fine, but I believe there was a subtext I was intentionally ignoring. He was a very nice guy, and he never really did anything untoward towards me. I doubt he ever did towards anybody.

Nonetheless, if he had, the culture of the school would have ignored it.

Years later, the school had its own version of a Truth and Reconciliation Commission – after one of my English teachers fled the country.

From the short accounts I've read, "eyelashes" was never accused of anything.

I legally can't go into the details, but I never finished high school. I dropped out. It had nothing to do with the widespread sexual assault – although the culture that allowed it might have played a part.

To this day, I have no diploma and no GED.

Like everybody, I have high school regrets. Not many, but a few. Once I freaked a girl out. I just didn't understand social conventions. Another time, I insulted a girl who didn't deserve it. I and the group of loser boys I was a part of were just picking on somebody to try and put ourselves *somewhere* other than at the bottom the food chain. It was cruel and to this day it is the thing I regret more than any other. I came across an old yearbook and looked the woman up. She's done very well for herself.

I sent an apology, but I never expect a reply. I don't really deserve one.

Of course, there were fun things too. Sometimes, I used to drive an old beater of a Ford F250 to school. It was huge and red and lacked a functioning muffler. The highlight of that truck's career probably happened when one of my classmates was being picked up by his father. The kid's dad had a Lamborghini or Ferrari or some such super car. It was the same color as my truck. He was parked right in front of me, at student pickup. He revved his engine. It was loud and throaty and impressive. He was showing off. So, I stuck my truck in neutral and I did the same. My truck, my 1976 Ford F250 was *even louder* and throatier.

I thought it was funny.

He probably didn't.

There was one other aspect of my high school career that I'm not particularly proud of: my brief foray into academic fraud. My cousin, the one who'd done freshman year of high school four times, had learning disabilities. He could talk ad nauseum, but he couldn't *write*. He could also think his way through a problem perfectly well, but he couldn't put it down on paper.

I used to help him with his college homework. He'd dictate and I'd write. He had two classes that I helped with. One was about media; the other was basic computer science. In both cases, my cousin would dictate, and I'd type. I'd help him structure things, just a bit. I'd talk it over with him and we'd come to a consensus about what was actually going on on the page. It was working pretty well until he came home one day with a rather embarrassing tale. Apparently, he'd had to explain to his professor how he'd misspelled his own name on an assignment.

That wasn't terribly good.

The ultimate joke was on us though. That cousin went to college for a year and a half. He pretended to go for three. He'd come home and tell us all about his day at school, a day he'd never had. That was *impressive* academic fraud. I asked him how he pulled it off and he said it was simple: "Just talk endlessly about whatever you're lying about, and people will never suspect a thing."

I've never mastered his skill at fabrication. I never want to.

In the end, on the macro-level, my mother was wrong about the high school. I developed such a chip on my shoulder – particularly about the liberal arts – that when I went to college, I pursued precisely those subjects I was *worst* at in high

school. Although I never spoke to those teachers again, I was –
in my own mind – trying to prove them wrong.

Religion

I promised to spread out the serious stuff. Well, here's a major
helping of it all in one concentrated batch: I grew up in a house
of death.

My eldest brother, Jeremiah, had died the year before I was
born. My family was shattered by that. Yes, my parents stayed
together but I can't imagine that was easy. The missing brother
was a constant and massive part of our lives. One of my
siblings, by the age of 12, was writing incredible and incredibly
dark poetry. I found some once and read it and was just
stunned both by how good it was and by how much it tore at
the soul.

I didn't suffer the first-hand experience of Jeremiah's death.
I didn't suffer the debilitating loss of a brother or a son. I
experienced it all second-hand. I had just enough distance to
think about what had occurred without being overwhelmed by
it. Even so, when my mother died decades later, I choked up
when I noted at her funeral that she was buried near her son[1]. I
could handle the death of my mother. I never really got there
with the death of the brother I never knew.

---

[1] The occasion, otherwise, literally put the 'fun' in 'funeral.' It was
immensely entertaining. Among other things, my mother was a
playwright and so, with hours to set things up, we cast her funeral as
a play. She had a starring, but non-speaking, role. She would have
loved it.

As a child, I didn't really understand how G-d could have taken Jeremiah. I remember blowing out the candles on my birthday cake and wishing for one thing only – that Jeremiah could come back. I remember my mother telling me that it didn't work that way. But what were miracles for except for things to work out differently?

I was about six, a pretty normal age, when I began to understand what death really was. I used to sleep at the foot of my sister's bed, on the floor, relying on her for the comfort necessary to come to grips with the most basic and common part of our human existence. I remember her telling me that we just had to do the best we could with our lives.

At least I think she was the one who said it.

Growing up in that house I understood that life was ephemeral. It could be taken in an instant[1]. I also understood that you had to make the most of it that you could.

There's a Jewish holiday called Rosh Hashana. On it, we analyze what we're doing with our lives, and we ask whether we're doing the most we could. For me, every day was Rosh Hashana from when I first encountered death as a six-year-old until I was in my forties. I was constantly asking: "am I using the tools that I have well?"

I was constantly reassessing and readjusting.

---

[1] Although I do have a real health issue, it is not life-threatening. Just awe-inspiringly painful. Nonetheless, I'm a hypochondriac with a proclivity towards mortal illnesses. My fear that death is right around the corner is a *major* spur to the volume of writing I do.

I was probably around eight when I started to think about philosophy and theology. The initial ideas were simple. The only person I could *know* was real was myself. I got it into my logical head that I couldn't prove that everything and everybody else was not simply a simulation. If so, then the whole world was a test of how *I* would perform. I knew it wasn't true. I could *sense* that others were real and that they suffered real pain and experienced real joy. I couldn't *prove* it, though. I didn't really square the two realities until much later.

Like most kids, I thought I'd be an incredibly impactful person. But it didn't come from dreams of fame or sporting accomplishment. I imagined I'd be three things: a businessman, a writer and a thinker. In a way, although not in the spectacular way I envisioned, I've become all three.

But those wasn't really my ultimate goals.

My ultimate goal, informed by that early experience of death, was to die as a man of G-d.

I wrote some pretty dark fiction as a kid.

All that said, as a kid, I certainly didn't begin to live up to that goal. I was out of control. Aside from the fights, my greatest problem was my fits. I'd hyperventilate and I'd throw these momentous fits. My father, a huge man, used to sit on me to hold me down. Some of these fits were provoked (a certain sibling enjoyed setting me off), but others were not. My father used to throw me in the swimming pool to calm me down. I had these fits *all the time*.

Then, one day, my little brother had one. I must have been in my early teens. I saw him and I was so deeply embarrassed for *myself* that I vowed I'd never do it again. I've lost control here and there (my anger regulation is far from perfect), but I've never since had a *real* fit.

When I was a teenager, I took the notion of control to an extreme. I basically thought that if I let my passions take the lead, I'd be right back where I'd been before. And so, I tamped down *everything*. Joy was limited right alongside anger. I was trying to live the ideal and that involved total self-management. Somebody told me that even Moses farted in front of G-d. I disagreed. I believed a man of G-d would need more control. I know it sounds ridiculous, but I didn't fart outside of a bathroom for years.

I locked myself down and I wouldn't really begin to open up again until after I left home.

Business

The other critical axis of my childhood was the business. It didn't only involve my parents travelling. There was a fully functioning office in the basement. Robert administered it. We grew up answering phones, "Hello, Borealis." We drove back and forth to Calgary. It was a constant in our lives. We even had a business-festival of sorts four times a year. It was called the Quarterly Reports. We'd all set up around the dining room table and fold, stuff, label and seal the regular reports required for a public company. I learned a fair amount about process optimization (and motivating people during repetitive and boring activities) doing that particular activity. Continuous improvement and pride in individual and group metrics were effective motivators.

I was a baby, in diapers, when my father got into a dispute with a banker. My father, who really didn't know *how* to change a diaper, ended up changing *my* diaper on the man's desk. He made a terrible mess in the process. I was a tool of negotiations[1]. I don't think I succeeded.

The "business" was a constant part of our lives. It was a difficult part as well. The optimism my father had for the kids we brought in extended to the rest of the world. He always saw a different, better, reality. He always thought we were weeks away from everything coming together. The lack of business success left many people embittered towards my father. They'd invest, taken in by his charisma and his belief, and then nothing would come of it. We never were mere weeks away from taking flight.

My father cared deeply about a certain kind of honor. "Fiduciary duty" was a critical term in my childhood. The ventures may not have taken off, but they also never went away. The ventures were also more than the pipe dreams of some get rich quick scheme. Major mineral explorations were launched, mining camps were established. Real work was

---

[1] In the 80s, we worked with a Russian man named Ilya. He had friends who could go back and forth to the USSR. I remember us buying cameras and electronics for his Soviet friends. Apparently, such things could be traded for extravagant benefits within the USSR. One time, the President of a Central Asian Republic even came by to meet with Ilya at our offices.

being done. My mother was responsible for managing a lot of it. But things just didn't work out. The full picture just never came together.

I suppose you can analyze why something doesn't happen until the cows come home. I know the reasons my father gave. Perhaps there was a lack of market understanding, perhaps there was an expectation that stars would align... I can't really say. Sometimes, things just don't work out.

That's why, as a child, I experienced both wealth and poverty. Sometimes we were rich, sometimes we were broke. When times were bad, there was constant pressure from creditors.

At one point, my younger brother was paying the mortgage by trading baseball cards. He was a natural. I remember repeated assessments of the house. We'd clean it up to get a good valuation for a mortgage and we'd trash it if a creditor was assessing it; we didn't want them thinking it was worth foreclosing on.

Dodging process servers (people who deliver paperwork initiating lawsuits) was a regular part of our lives. I remember one of my brothers and I were alone in the house. A man came to the door, claiming to be a Deputy. But we couldn't see him. We were probably around 10 or 12 years old. We wouldn't open the door. He *could* have been a process server. He threatened to come in anyway. My brother had positioned himself at the second floor, overlooking the entrance to the house from an internal balcony. He had a 50-round Ruger 10-22. We told the man that if he broke in, we'd kill him.

We meant it.

He ended up leaving. It turned out he actually was a Deputy and my brother and I had threatened to kill a cop. All that said, the cop – having no warrant – had no right to break into the house.

My cousin used to say that we were the only white people he knew who were scared of cops. I guess it was the PWT in us. The feds, the wolves (bankers and creditors) and the cops were only sources of trouble and we *never* wanted anything to do with any of them. We were *scared* of all of them[1].

Whenever we were dealing with the big bad wolf, we acted like the gloves were off in our interactions. We were little guys and so we had to punch harder to counterbalance our disadvantages.

At one point, a major bank was foreclosing on the old house in Idaho. It couldn't be avoided. We couldn't possibly pay the mortgage. There was a homeowners' association, though. There were ten plots of land and one real house. My father ended up having the homeowners' association allocate its own debts on the basis of the value of the plots of land. The house was worth more than the empty plots and so the bank ended up with debts that exceeded the value of the home they'd foreclosed on. The bank wasn't happy. Then again, they had the lion's share of the homeowners' association assets *and* liabilities. It was fair, in a way. They ended up suing us, civilly,

---

[1] Our relationships with all three have improved dramatically. It is far more productive to work with people and systems than to helplessly battle against them. The fights just rob you of so much productive vigor.

for racketeering. You know, like we were mobsters. As owners of plots of land, my younger brother (15) and I (16) were probably the two youngest racketeering defendants in the history of the United States. My dad thought it was funny. My mom didn't. The judge ended up throwing it out.

Another time my parents bought an early laptop from Epson. It was a piece of junk. When Epson wouldn't take it back, they went to the store and stomped it into pieces in front of all the other customers.

Then there was the Buick. It was diesel and a true lemon. In the first six months it had to be repaired numerous times. Again, the dealership wouldn't take it back. My parents ended up parking this almost brand-new car in front of the dealership and then *torching* it. The only thing more embarrassing than having one of your cars torched in front of your dealership is suing one of your own customers for torching one of your cars in front of your dealership. The publicity would have been devastating. The dealership never did anything about it, and we never bought another Buick.

As my mother used to say, you can have blood or money – but never both.

Despite it all, we were never *really* poor. Sure, we were broke, but we always had food to eat, and we always believed that *somehow* we would still have food in the future. The business had some very hard times, but bankruptcy was never declared, no matter how lean times were. Debts were settled and the companies my father formed *still* exist. We are *still* building them. But we don't expect everything to happen in a week. We have a large and professional team methodically developing a product. Those original shareholders (or their heirs) remain significant owners. We never walked away from them, and I hope we never will. After all, fiduciary duty is a critical concept.

My older brother and I, who work together, are still trying to honor the commitments our father made.

The whole situation tends to remind me of the Mongolian destruction of Baghdad. Every Muslim in Baghdad was killed. Nonetheless, Baghdad is not a Mongolian city. Sometimes, if you just refuse to admit defeat, you will end up achieving victory.

The experience of those hard times didn't leave me untouched. I don't have a fear of poverty, though. I've managed to get by some pretty lean times. What I have a fear of is debt. I am willing to work my tail off to honor the commitments of others – whether they be bosses or family members (or both). But I am *desperately* afraid of dishonoring commitments of my own – and thus desperately afraid of *making* commitments of my own[1].

---

[1] We lived almost a year and a half in Israel with 6 kids (in a neighborhood without good public transportation) without a car. I wasn't willing to take out a loan.

When we meet others, my brother introduces me as the brains and himself as the balls. He's got plenty of brains, but he's right about who has the balls[1]. I'll never be a CEO. I'll always be a Biblical-style Joseph, consulting in the courts of others[2].

I couldn't handle it any other way.

Attitude

If I were to try to define my upbringing with one word it would be this: attitude.

At my older brother's wedding the Rabbi praised the union of "East Coast Jewish Royalty and *another kind of Royalty.*" We wouldn't have had it any other way. We were religious hillbilly Jews who were just as proud of our lack of money and manners as we were of our educations and lineages.

At my older sister's wedding (held at the house because we really couldn't afford anyplace else), we thought we were having a mighty fine shindig. But some of the Persian in-laws were deeply unimpressed. I imagine something about having them sleep in a hayloft may have disturbed them.

The fact was, by anybody *else's* measure, we weren't royalty. I remember, in my first proper year of college, tearing up and throwing pieces of challah as we did in my father's house. One

---

[1] He too has learned from the past. It is no longer us against the world. Increasingly, we are a part of that world.

[2] I've worked in over a dozen companies, wearing many different hats. I've acquired a pretty good appreciation of what makes things tick.

of the other students at the table called me a dog. I challenged him, asking him why I ought to do what everybody did. He said, "When in Rome, do as the Romans do."

I don't know if I answered right away but my comeback ever since has been: "If when in Rome you do as the Romans do, you'll never be anything better than a second-class Roman."

I've never been a Roman. We identified as strongly with men named Mountain[1] as we did with folk named Cohen. We moved in all these different circles – from London to the Arctic to the backwoods of Idaho. Everywhere we went, we were outsiders. But we also, almost always, had a toe on the inside as well.

Yes, we were proud of being free of peer and social pressure (and thus able to pursue virtue and truth). But we could also relate to many different kinds of people. We could relate to them, and we could find things to admire within them.

Today, I don't respect people for their money, their education or even their success. I *know* you can find something to honor in people whether they are rich or poor, brilliant or simple. You can find something to honor whether they've been successes or failures.

---

[1] Mountain was huge. He once got a job at a sawmill. In the middle of the building was metal ring welded to the frame of the mill itself. When new 'tough' guys were hired, the workers would challenge them to lift and move the ring. They'd tug and pull and get nowhere. Everybody would mock their failure. It was a great fun. Then they challenged Mountain. He grabbed the ring and pulled, and the *entire building* began to torque. Nobody every mocked Mountain.

142

I *know* this and I like to think it enriched my experience of the world *after* I left home.

LEAVING HOME

The Ivy League

I was 16 years old and playing cribbage with my cousin. We were in my parent's living room, as we often were. Cribbage is a good game for conversation. It doesn't require too much thought. So, my cousin and I would often play. Our games would normally last until one or two in the morning. We'd talk (although he probably did most of the talking). It was only on very rare occasions that we'd play all night.

This was one of those times. As my cousin sat across from me, as we steadily pegged our way around the board (time and again), he was the one talking. He was telling me that he was going to kill himself.

Why?

Because I was leaving.

He understood I had to leave, he knew it was for the best, he *wanted* me to leave. But he'd kill himself, nonetheless. My being around was the reason for his being around.

Looking back, I realize that if somebody is telling you they'll kill themselves they probably won't. But I didn't know that, then. So, I spent the entire night, the night before I left home, talking my cousin down. After I left, he realized my brother was *also* a good guy to hang out with too. So, he's still with us.

The cause of that late night talk was, again, my sister. After being kicked out of high school, my sister suggested that I *not* enroll in another high school. Instead, I ought to start attending college.

In my family, when it came to education, money was no object. Education was important, but not because it raised future potential earnings. Education was important because it changed *who* you were. That's what made it priceless. It enriched you in a way that went beyond money.

Because finance wasn't the reason for college, the cost of college wasn't really a factor. I wasn't eligible for anything but the most basic student grants (it wasn't because we had paid off all the earlier loans given to one of my siblings). I didn't really have the money for college. Despite this, the lesson was clear: do anything you can to get an education, sort everything else out afterwards.

That's why "college" didn't mean community college or local college. We were all expected to go far from home to the best possible schools we could get into. Ideally, East Coast schools. Our parents preferred the ethos of those schools to the top-tier West Coast schools. My sister went to Barnard, my older brother to Princeton. My younger brother went to Brandeis.

My parents raised us so that, if we chose, we could be completely independent by the age of 15. Going far away, in case you missed the cut-off, was a good way to reinforce things.

Independence and enrichment were the point of education. The goal was never erasure and reinvention. Many communities (like Chassidic Jews or Native Americans) legitimately fear that going to University will fundamentally alter the children they know. They will go, they will learn, and they will no longer be real members of the community. Oftentimes, the community and its values are more important than anything college could offer. Increasingly, many religious Christians feel the same way.

My parents didn't expect college to reinvent who we were. We had a good strong grounding; we'd had plenty of practice relishing our differences and we'd had early childhoods exposed to a wide variety of ideas. College wasn't going to erase us. We already knew most of the arguments against any identities that might need defending (from religious Judaism to conservative culture). My parents knew we could integrate what we would learn, instead of being integrated by it.

The first University I attended was Harvard. It was a rolling admissions summer program, so my having gone shed no light on my intelligence or capabilities. Pretty much anybody could get in, they just had to apply early enough. The Harvard experience had a big impact on me, though. Part of it was educational. I was an A- student there, unlike in High School. At the end of the summer term, I asked my Russian History professor for a recommendation. He asked me why I needed it. When I said, "to get into college," he was genuinely confused. He'd thought I was a graduate student. That acknowledgement was important. Sure, I believed my parents when they told me my high school was off its rocker. But outside validation sure helps.

My work in that Russian History class resulted in another milestone. While my father always praised our work as world-class, my mother *never gave unqualified* approval. The best positive feedback I ever got from her was "that was good for a college student" or "that was good for your age." She was angry about my grades in High School (angry with the school that is). But she wasn't that impressed with my work in and of itself. The term paper I turned in for that Russian history class was the first work I'd ever done where my mother simply said, "That was excellent." I hadn't even realized that kind of feedback was missing.

The other impact was social. It was at Harvard that I had my first girlfriend. Our relationship wasn't long. There were good reasons for that (not least of which was that she dumped me at the end of the summer). She helped me a lot though. First, she tried to translate the very old Russian state chronicles stored deep in the Harvard stacks. Second, and more importantly, she gave me two very good pieces of advice:

1. She told me that I should try to stick out for *good* reasons, not just for the purpose of sticking out in and of itself.

2. She told me I had to learn to let my positive emotions out, even as I tried to control the negative ones.

If she happens to be reading this, I want to thank her. I internalized what she said, as best as I could at the time.

After Harvard, my sister had me come down to Columbia. She was going to enroll me as a "Visiting High School student." The most important part of the process of becoming a "Visiting High School student" was documenting why I felt it was necessary to "visit" Columbia. Basically, I had to say what Columbia would provide what my high school wouldn't. I dutifully filled out the papers and then showed up for my interview.

The interviewer invited me in. He was sitting behind a big desk in a densely cluttered room in Lewisohn Hall. I sat down in the chair opposite him. He asked me the key question: "Why leave beautiful Oregon to come here?"

I gave him a bullsh-t and political answer. Something along the lines of "there are courses here that I can take that aren't available at my high school."

Before I even had a chance to complete that formulaic answer, the man stood up and walked out. He had a phone call or something. A few minutes later he came back and asked me the same question. I gave the same answer. We were interrupted again. He came in a third time and asked the question a third time.

This time I simply said, "High school sucked."

"Good," he said, "That's what I needed to hear."

He approved my paperwork. I was in.

After one semester, I discovered I'd only been admitted for one semester. I went back to Lewisohn Hall to seek admission for a second semester, but nobody seemed to have heard of the Visiting High School student program. They sent me upstairs and the people upstairs sent me downstairs. Then I was sent upstairs again. Sensing a potentially less than helpful pattern, I sought out my sister. She knew how to solve the problem. Sure, I needed paperwork signed, but I was *already* in the system. Apparently, in those days it was a sport to see what kind of signature you could get away with on your course registration. So, as we sat outside the School of General Studies my sister, aka George Washington, admitted me for a second semester.

I was only a part-time student while I was at Columbia. I was limited to two classes a semester. I learned how to take notes, for the first and last time, in Classical Greek History. Everybody else was doing it so I figured I ought to as well. It didn't work for me. I learned better writing 3 words on a page over the course of an hour than writing 300. I also gained an appreciation for *why* art might seem so entirely unnatural in Medieval Architecture. I'd always assumed it reflected a lack of skill, technique or technology. It hadn't occurred to me that the flat, unshaded, medieval visions were capturing a concept of heaven – one so perfect it had no dimensions or darkness. Putting myself in that alien perspective was enlightening.

The most valuable course was Honors Math. Naturally, that was the course suggested by my sister. All the best math students at Columbia took it. I wasn't one of them. There were about 50 students at the beginning of the course. Of those 50, 2 had never taken calculus. Me, and a religious Jewish girl who was straight-out brilliant. By the end of two semesters, something like seven students remained. Most were doing pretty well. I wasn't. I finished that second semester with a C+. I survived, but barely. My sister did better than I did. She was one of the four who survived her round of the full two-year course.

I survived. But I did more than that. This was the kind of course where you spent three weeks just defining what a number was. Through its logical discipline, the course taught me how to form a mathematically rigorous argument.

While I was struggling in Honors Math, I found myself thinking that doing normal Calculus would help. I went down to the basement of Earl Hall and audited the Calculus course. I figured it'd be easy. But after two weeks, I was understanding *nothing*. The professor kept talking about "the srope of the Rhine" and I had no idea what that was, and I was too proud to ask (plus, I wasn't actually enrolled). Finally, one of other students raised their hands and asked. The professor looked at him like he was an idiot, drew a horizontal and vertical line on the blackboard and then drew a line at a diagonal.

"The SROPE OF THE RHINE" he almost yelled, "What's wrong with you?"

He was talking about the "slope of the line." I figured if I couldn't get the 'slope of the line' in a Calculus course then I'd never get anything else either. I stopped attending.

On the social side, Beth Samuels had the single greatest impact on me. It wasn't that I knew her well. But I knew her, a bit. In conversation - at least at the time - she came across as a valley girl. Her intonation and diction gave away none of her brilliance. In a New York environment surrounded by hard-nosed driven students, she was a refreshing break from the norm. What struck me about Beth is that her personality changed, fundamentally, when she prayed. She became intense, driven and concentrated. I didn't see her pray often, but on those few occasions where I caught a glimpse, I felt ashamed - like I should not be witnessing something so personal. I never met her again after that year, but Beth went on to educate Jews in the Ukraine, serve as an auxiliary Police Officer in New York, teach Torah, earn a Doctorate in Mathematics from Yale, get married and have a daughter.

She died at age of 32.

The greatest impact Columbia had on my theology came from a single event on one particular Shabbat. A large number of developmentally disabled children had been invited to join the students for Shabbat. I wasn't a real student, but I came for some of these events. The Rabbi leading the occasion spoke about needing to break out of our everyday mold: the father who reads the newspaper every morning and that sort of thing. I didn't really sympathize with that. But then he shared a word of Torah that stuck with me. It is quite a common one. He spoke of a great Rabbi who would always stand when a developmentally disabled person entered the room. The reasoning was simple: G-d gives us the capabilities we need to complete our souls; the disabled person had so few conventional capabilities that they clearly had few tasks remaining in that process.

I wasn't sure I bought into the concept of reincarnation at the heart of this idea, but the thought behind it bubbled away inside of me. It resulted, a year later, in my first coherent theological ideas.

I was not a social success at Columbia. I hung around the edges of rooms hoping others would notice me. They rarely ever did. I had a passing very light friendship with Beth and a few others, but I really didn't fit in. It was obnoxious but I felt like the people around me were simply far too shallow. Beth and the genius math girl were exceptions.

The simple reality was that I hadn't yet learned how to appreciate how much the others had to offer.

That year at Columbia I lived in married housing, across the street from the coffee shop in Seinfeld. I wasn't married, my sister was. The housing was subsidized, and I worked as a babysitter. I ate very cheaply and walked almost everywhere. My parents paid my rent, but I had to cover everything else. Babysitting covered food, barely. Tuition was another matter. While it was only the School of General Studies (and it was *much* cheaper than normal attendance) it was a challenge to get it paid off. It was eventually covered by my parents, but before long, educational debts were going to become a serious issue for me.

In their way, they'd be a defining one.

While at Columbia, I applied to numerous schools for regular college. I got into two: U. Penn and U. Chicago. I didn't get in because I'd shown great academic prowess. I'd been an excellent student at Harvard and Columbia, but my record beforehand was poor. My SATs were also far from noteworthy. The fact was, I only got into these schools because I was 1/8th Native American. I felt bad about that, depriving some white kid of his proper spot. But I did very well in college, significantly better than most of the white kids. I belonged there, on a purely academic basis.

When it came to choosing schools, I respected Chicago more, educationally. And they wanted me. They had a recruiter take me to dinner and make a personal pitch. I was willing to go through quite a bit in the name of education. But the place was simply *too* depressing. Half the people told me they wanted to transfer or kill themselves. The other half told me the first half didn't really mean it because they hadn't gone through with either option yet. I showed up at Penn during Spring Fling, which is as much fun as it sounds. I went to Penn.

My major at Penn was Intellectual History. People ask me if I use it and the answer is: yes, every single day. Intellectual History, or the History of Ideas, is all about how different people have thought about the world's biggest questions across time and culture. Intellectual History taught me how to take a step *way* back in examining problems.

It taught me how to put myself in others' shoes.

As this book gradually transitions from my experiences to what I've learned, I figured I might as well share a little bit about the courses I took.

The first of these courses (not chronologically, just from a storytelling perspective) was a course on the Scottish Enlightenment. It was taught by a visiting professor from the Netherlands. Of course, being Dutch, he explained that the Scottish Enlightenment was simply an outcropping of the Dutch Enlightenment. The coursework dovetailed with my own mother's work. The Scottish were masters of the feedback loop and the organic system. Adam Smith's Invisible Hand and moral philosophy came from Scotland. My mother was fond of pointing out that the French invented steam engines before the Scots did. Only the French steam engines kept blowing up. The French thought they could actively control the pressure and temperature. The Scots realized it was impossible and put in a pressure regulator that let off "excess steam." In other words, rather than trying to control, the Scots sought to balance. I almost wrote a thesis on this concept: in Continental Europe, G-d was the clock maker. In Scotland and England, the clock represented a hellish imposition.

One of the most important areas of Scottish impact involved education. Instead of trying to teach people how to fill a particular role (as is common in most societies), Scottish education focused on teaching people how to learn. It was that concept that defined American liberal arts education, at least historically. Put another way, most educational systems tried to teach people how to be gears and cogs in society's great machine. American and Scottish education, true Liberal Arts education, taught them how to be the oil. My parents could build houses because they had that traditional American Liberal Arts education.

This course allowed me to see that our understandings of how human society functions have actually changed over time. People might claim that there is nothing new under the sun, or that concepts of human interaction have hardly changed since Aristotle, but it just ain't so. The course also (initially) reinforced my strongly libertarian leanings. I actually earned a scholarship (and healthy stipend) to a libertarian educational course at George Mason. Attending the course, and seeing how far they had to stretch certain ideas, resulted in me becoming *less* of a libertarian.

The most practical thing I learned from that course involved the homework. Every week every member of the class was assigned a book and a question. The books were huge. There was no way we could get through them. The professor told us, on that very first day, that if we tried to read the entire book, we were fools. Our job was to answer the question. We were supposed to dig into the book only *just* enough to complete that task. Come the next week, he'd quiz us about the book and the question, and we'd have to perform.

This approach to research, which is really quite normal, has helped me tremendously. I've learned how to quickly research what I need to know in order to write fiction convincingly set almost anywhere in the world,-. I don't need to know *everything*. I don't need to immerse myself in a culture. I just need to know what I need to know and rely on a *feeling* of truth for the rest. Somehow, almost always, it works.

The second class was Japanese History from ancient times until the Meiji Restoration. The history was interesting, and I still share aspects of it with my kids. But what was life-changing was my introduction to the Japanese concept of beauty. Coming from Judaism, which always looks up, beauty is a happy ending. There's a reason Hollywood tends to have them. But the classical Japanese concept was different. Beauty was the cherry blossom. It would reach its pinnacle, just for a moment, and then it would fall. Beauty was collapse on the pinnacle of greatness. Beauty was refusing to yield what made you great, even as it destroyed you. I'd never considered such a completely different concept before. At first, I was put off by those ideas. I tried to resist them. By the end of the course, though, I embraced them. I could even see beauty in the hopeless kamikaze pilots who almost killed my grandfather.

I can't even remember what the third impactful course was about. All I remember is that it was a required writing course. We had to take a minimum number of courses with special instructors to help with our writing. I knew I could write, but a requirement was a requirement. I had a problem I didn't recognize, though. Honors Math had left me writing rigorous and dry arguments. At one point during that course, I realized I could do better. I wrote *two* papers. One dry, and the second built (almost) around a story. Both got an A, but I knew one was far more engaging. That's when I started using stories to tell deeper truths.

I took, and dropped out of, Evolutionary Biology. The course was taught by a woman who insisted on demonstrating to the class – again and again – how stupid religion was. She couldn't stay on topic. It was my first exposure to truly *political* science. Those who disagreed with her were wrong-headed idiots. I had no problem with evolution. I still don't. I had a problem with her assumption that she understood my religion and could – with arguments I saw as infantile and uninformed – somehow debunk it. It was a certain kind of hubris and I hated it. I ended up taking Physics for Architects instead. I had one of the top grades in the class – which is why I'll always hire an engineer before I build or alter anything in my home.

Perhaps the most boring class was a high-level course called the Origins of Constitutionalism. I *think* I read the Nyal Saga there, which was cool. I also learned about proto-Parliamentary Norman governments in what is now France and Sicily. Most of the class was spent reading hundreds of years of texts debating the meaning of the phrase: *Plenitudo Potestas*. What does it mean? Well, that's the question. It means something like plenty of power, or total power. It can imply absolute power or power that is somehow limited. The term was used to describe the power of a King. Its definition was critical to the emerging idea that a King could be subject to law. It was mind-numbing and I didn't learn from it what I should have. I didn't learn that fundamental ideas are changed in exactly this sort of way. Gradually and through a shift in consensus. Being raised to value standing alone, I didn't really get how important slowly bending those around you can actually be.

A course on Roman Law was interesting because it showed how much fundamental overlap there was between Jewish Religious Law and Roman Civil Law. It has always made suspect an unhealthy degree of cross-pollination. It also ruined the study of the Talmud for me. I just kept seeing Roman ideas, which aren't the ideas I want to subscribe to.

The most prestigious course in the Intellectual History department explored 17th and 18th century thought. Basically, the Enlightenment. I saw another example of change, far faster change, in that class. Although the professor, a great advocate of the Enlightenment, wouldn't have appreciated it, the class also taught me that I didn't have to look at the world through the post-Enlightenment prism of "rational" thought. I could see and appreciate how other structures of knowledge could be assembled and validated.

That professor was a very prominent (and not terribly subtle) atheist. Attacking G-d was a critical part of what he did. But he did it far more intelligently than the biologist had. My religious perspective was challenged (although ultimately strengthened) by the experience[1]. Among the various texts we read Pascal's Pensées. Pascal was famous for his precautionary principle in relation to G-d. But I remembered another part of

---

[1] The professor loved the footnotes in Diderot's Encyclopédie. I remember reading one of them while visiting a family in Maryland. That single note was the single greatest challenge to my religious perspective. Ultimately, it was something my mother wrote in *Reflections* that resolved the challenges it raised.

his writings. I actually misremembered it. In Chapter IV, *Of the Means of Belief*, Pascal argued that G-d could be proven by alternate means.

> *The heart has its own order; the intellect has its own, which is by principle and demonstration... We do not prove that we ought to be loved by enumerating in order the causes of love; that would be ridiculous.*

The way I always remembered it was: "Do you love your father? Prove it." I could almost swear I had it right, because I was surprised at the reference to one's father instead of mother. Ah, well.

Pascal's writing (even his antisemitism) spoke to the beginnings of a post-Enlightenment (almost Romantic) worldview. It spoke to the currents of thought that gave birth to Chassidic Judaism (Pascal died 40 years before the Baal Shem Tov was born). That those currents were taking root in the mind of a prominent mathematician at the beginning of the Enlightenment was fascinating. It also made me further reconsider just what a Proof is; and what it had to be.

The most impactful course of all was *War and Society*. The Professor was the single most popular professor at the University. She won multiple teaching awards, she was a finalist for the Pulitzer Prize and the National Book Award, and she had a class with 300 students (and a significant waiting list). She went on to become President of Harvard, a position she held for 11 years.

She also had a seminar with only a half-dozen students.

I was one of them. I had no idea how lucky I was to be admitted to that elite group.

I'll confess, I tended to nod off in this class. Being stuck in a dark room for three hours will do that to me. Heck, I can nap anywhere and at any time. But I still learned. The focus of the course was on how people's thoughts and perspectives changed in times of war. On the one hand, we read countless letters from soldiers in different wars. But we focused, most of all, on the experience of mourning in the South. We studied how Southerners mourned so many, including many who may not have been dead. Most of all, we studied how the idea and interaction with the very concept of life and death was fundamentally altered by the mass experience of it — and the almost total absence of funerals.

Even today, I can't put a finger on what I learned from that course.

I guess that's the highest praise of all.

I did well at Penn. I graduated with a Magna Cum Laude level GPA. It wasn't that hard. I was an Intellectual History major, after all. Despite the reputation of "Ivy League grading," not everybody flourished. Most of the kids at Penn had been at the top of their classes, wherever they'd come from. They weren't used to being middlin'. The adjustment was seriously hard for many of them. It broke some of them. For my part, I'd never been anywhere near the top of my class — not since the third grade. There was no shock at the level of work; I worked harder in high school. As my identity was never challenged by the level of competition or the amount of work, my confidence only grew with time.

At one point, I was even invited to the Honors program. I didn't end up joining it. I couldn't sort out the necessary paperwork without setting off alarms about having not graduated High School. I ended up settling for a good GPA and graduation.

You have to pick your battles.

Whether it was technique, luck or blessing, the paperwork ended up coming out in my favor. There was a limit on transferred credits for incoming Freshmen. I definitely exceeded it. I transferred some credits on arrival. But I had many left. Thankfully, my file was transferred to another administrator in my third year there. *That* group didn't know about the transfer limit. That's how I became a Senior only a few months before graduation.

It saved me tens of thousands of dollars in tuition and other fees.

I was pretty good at slipping through the bureaucratic cracks.

I learned at Penn, but I knew that the education I was receiving was almost certainly sub-par in comparison to Chicago or Columbia. The problems were structural. Penn had no basic shared course all the students went through. Even within specific individual liberal arts areas, no such background existed. As a result, an advanced history course couldn't simply assume that every student had a working understanding of broad historical trends – or even methods of study. Every course had to start from scratch.

Because of that, we learned far less than we could have.

The most important part of my time at Penn had nothing to do with the education. It had to do with funding that education. My family helped out with Harvard and Columbia. But they couldn't help with Penn. This created some real problems. These problems were compounded by policies the school had. For example, during your freshman year, you had to be enrolled in a meal plan. The only Kosher meal plan was *obnoxiously* expensive. I remember paying something like $18 for dinner and $12 for lunch. It might not seem like much but, added up over a school year, it came to thousands of dollars I didn't have. Once I got off the meal plan, I could stretch a single bag of ground beef over an entire semester. I was *good* at being cheap while still eating well enough. Unlike the rest of the tab, the meal tab couldn't be added to the school's overall bill. I coughed up the money, but I think it was the last support I ever got from home. By the end of my first year, I was over $20,000 in debt. I knew I needed to save everything I possibly could if I wanted to continue my education.

That's how I ended up homeless in New York.

Near the end of my first year, I lived in what everybody knew was the gay dorm (I kept odd hours and it was the only place I could get my own room). I remember being in the computer room and overhearing a discussion among the other students about internships. I had *no idea* what an internship was. I joined the conversation and realized two things. First, I couldn't afford an internship. Second, even if I could have afforded an internship, the window for getting one had already closed.

It was all for the best, though.

When summer came, I headed up to New York. It was probably my sister's idea. While there, I became a temp. Specifically, an Administrative Assistant (what non-Administrative Assistants call a 'Secretary'). It was easy to get work. My credentials were perfect. I was an Ivy League student, I could type 85 words a minute and I once I figured out all the temp agencies gave pretty much the same tests, I learned how to ace them. In the space of a few days, I went to 5 or 6 temp agencies (choosing the least promising ones first), got to 100% on the tests they gave and then, a day or two later, work started coming in.

I was really focused on optimization in those days. I was proud at how quickly I carried out particular tasks. 10 minutes to shower. 10 minutes for lunch (my only meal of the day and something I splurged on), 1-minute/cross-town block on foot (for real). Hustle, hustle, hustle. The work wasn't challenging, so I did what I'd done with those old Quarterly Report mailings – I took pride in metrics. Not just the optimization of my day, but the optimization of my tasks as well. I made a challenge out of *everything* and took pride in besting my own performance.

The place I worked most of all was Pfizer. At one point I was supporting an executive in the overseas drug trials group. I remember we were dealing with heart patients. I only worked out later that we were investigating what later became Viagra. That first year wasn't terribly busy as the guy I was supporting was always on the road. I didn't have anything to optimize, so I played a lot of Solitaire (tracking my scores across thousands of games to see just how bad the odds were). I also got a second job. I worked with my mother to create the first *Inventing America* textbook for Lewis and Clark College.

Pfizer taught me a bit more about class. The secretaries, in those days, moved with the executives they supported. But there was a hard line. No matter how much they knew about how the company worked and who made it function, the secretaries themselves could never be in management. They were conscripts, not officers. I got along wonderfully with them, but the class lines bugged the heck out of me. At the time, I saw the interns working in the file room. They were doing the most boring work possible. They weren't getting paid. They were the bottom tier. Except, they weren't. Pfizer wouldn't have considered extending *me* a real job offer. The interns expected one. I know the internships didn't exist to keep the poor kids out, but they sure had that effect. At least in the most prestigious corporations.

I worked other places as well. I spent a day at a mob fire suppression company. I heard them talking about signing paperwork on behalf of a guy who'd died a few weeks earlier.

They had an Excel problem, and they were very, very threatening when I said I couldn't fix it the way they wanted (it didn't logically work). Nonetheless, I did fix it – another way. I got back to the temp agency to find my handler was delighted. Every other person she'd sent to the place had quit halfway through the day, literally crying. It wasn't an easy job, it didn't feel like a *safe* job, but I'd been around some tough people before. Nonetheless, I declined their invitation to return. I didn't need to be party to what was clearly a less-than-legal operation.

I also spent a month or so at Bayerische Landesbank. The entire department I worked in (IT) was black. I, the temp, was the only exception. I think the bank was meeting their affirmative action quota by putting all the black people in one department. I was there to update their emergency protocols document. It was basically editing and reformatting a document which somebody had entered as you would a typed document. For example, actual page numbers were typed at the bottom of each page. If you added a few words, the formatting of the entire document was destroyed. I was stunned by how detailed those plans were. There were lists of who to call and exactly what each party was to say. There were directions to the backup facilities, and backup directions to the backup facility.

I guess, given 9/11, it all had its place and purpose.

The entire time I was at Bayerische Landesbank, I was the subject of *continuous* Jewish jokes. I suppose that's what led to me getting conned. I was so eager to show the strength of

Jewish culture that I let myself get taken by an Israeli con-artist while walking to lunch. I think he actually felt bad, once he realized I was broke. I suspect this because he actually reduced the amount of money he was asking for. Nonetheless, he got $300 from me – that meant a lot to me in those days. I even brought him to my office as I got my wallet from my desk (and to show off that we Jews looked out for each other).

The con man was good, but not perfect. Like most marks, I ended up blinding myself. I learned a lot from the experience. I couldn't have parted with more than $300 in those days. But those $300 bought me a very valuable bit of education.

It also burned like hell.

In general, I basically got along with the people in that office. They didn't mean anything bad by their jokes. Well, they might have, but I could take it. Plus, they had to deal with how badly I smelled.

As I saw it, it was a fair trade.

Why did I smell so bad?

The issue was simple: in order to save money, I was illegally squatting on the seventh floor of Columbia's Earl Hall. I wasn't a student. I had a key to the office on top of the elevators. I kept my clothes and cot in a file cabinet, I got up early every morning and came in late every night. Occasionally, I had to break into the building itself. But it wasn't hard. The outer locks were very easy to pick. On a few occasions I had to get into *another* building and then use the old tunnels to get to Earl Hall. They closed those off – or at least put code-controlled doors in – the next year. One time, late at night, I heard noises in the basement below the building. An *actual* student was living there. I had the better deal, though. I had windows and a beautiful view over Barnard and even glimpses of the river.

I'd wake up in the morning to the one cassette I had (Dire Straits Brother in Arms). I'd pack my stuff away before any of the staff showed up. And then I'd go to work.

My problem wasn't with the accommodations. It was a very, very comfortable kind of homelessness. My problem was with what the accommodations *didn't* have.

Namely: showers.

I used to go across town to shower at my sister's. But her husband (very ex-husband, now) didn't like me. So, he stopped me from coming. The security guard at Barnard knew me. Her mother was a cleaner and she'd let me into the visiting *men's* locker rooms. They were never used (Barnard being a woman's college). The problem was, they were only available after 9 and I had to be at work by then. So, I used to go to work for an entire week without showering. In New York. In a suit. In the summer. Not only that, but I walked *everywhere* once I was in midtown. I had no kitchen, so my one luxury (and only daily meal) was fast food. Generally, the kosher stuff was a mile or two from work. I walked a lot. I was *not* pleasant to be around. But I *was* good at my job and so they kept me.

I could deal with some Jew jokes if they could deal with the stereotypical stench of this particular Jew[1]. Plus, they taught me my favorite Jew joke.

Q: "Why is money green?"

A: "Because the Jews pick it before it's ripe."

I thought it was particularly funny because I learned it while working at a German bank.

Despite the lack of a shower, I never went more than a week without showering. On Friday afternoons I went around the Upper West Side. I found young Jewish men. I explained that I was homeless and needed a shower for Shabbat. Not one of the people I asked turned me down. Some even just told me where to get the keys for their apartments because they wouldn't be around. People criticized that community as less than charitable, but I never could. To me, their generosity was amazing.

In fact, I want to apologize to those whose showers I used. You see, I didn't realize I was supposed to bring my own towel. If you are reading this and you offered me a shower and I used your towel – I'm really, really sorry.

I won't do it again.

Probably.

---

[1] In Mein Kampf, Hitler writes: "The odor of those people in caftans often used to make me feel ill. Beyond that there were the unkempt clothes and the ignoble exterior."

A few weeks before school was scheduled to start again, I got an email from the finance department at Penn. They informed me that, because of my outstanding debts, I was not welcome to return. I wrote them a passionate email about how I was homeless, just so I could save money to pay them. We came to an understanding. I could continue to attend so long as I paid $1000 a month. There would be no aid and no discounts. Everything I didn't pay would still be due once I graduated.

I worked every break. My most profitable period was as a paralegal over Christmas and New Year's. The year after, the rate was raised to $1,800 a month. I got a job during school. I was working for a Philly-based commercial real estate firm (reworking their webpage and creating a database of listings).

After I graduated, the school wouldn't admit I'd attended. One of the first companies I worked for was a since-disgraced recruiting firm. I failed their background check (which is pretty ironic[1]). I showed my yearbook, with my name in it. But that wasn't enough. I called the school again and said that if they wanted me to actually be able to pay them back, I needed them to admit I'd gone there. They agreed, for a few prearranged hours, to admit I'd graduated. It was enough for me to get the job.

Years later, I was out of work again. This time, I couldn't come up with my $1,800 a month. I asked for reduced

---

[1]They are now back in business after their founder's stint in prison. He'd been convicted of reckless homicide while sharing drugs with minors at his home.

168

payments for 6 months. They agreed. Then they sent me a contract to sign. There would be no payments for 6 months, then I'd owe them the full remaining amount (close to $60,000) in one lump sum. If I failed to pay, they could take any assets I had as well as directly garnishing my future earnings. On the advice of my wise younger brother, I refused to sign. I intended to honor my original agreement, though. Six months without payment and then a return to the prior deal.

Six months in, as I was preparing to start paying again, I got a call from a debt collection agency. The school had *automatically* sold my debt as I was six months in arears. Their software told them they were unlikely to collect much of anything. The debt collection agency had bought it for pennies on the dollar. My younger brother negotiated on my behalf, and we settled the whole thing for a healthy discount[1]. Even better, the school wasn't in the business of regularly loaning money and so, while they had referred the case to a debt collector, they'd never reported me to any credit agencies.

Once again, the paperwork had come out in my favor.

During those years at Penn, I worked for many different companies, and I was exposed to many different corporate cultures. My academic work was teaching me how to *study* culture, but my work was teaching me how to *feel* it[2].

---

[1] I borrowed the money I needed from my in-laws.

[2] Interestingly, almost everywhere I worked things looked really good on first examination. Once you dug in, though, you discovered that people weren't nearly as competent as they let on. In all the companies I've worked for – and I've worked for many – only two

During my time at Penn, I was also beginning to develop my theological perspective. It combined that cross-cultural touch with the lessons of that Shabbat at Columbia.

My first year there, when I was 17, I wrote the following:

The Artist

It floats in the air, a strange luminance radiating from its uncertain shape. Like a cloud, it floats, shapeless, bodiless, shifting with the slightest movement of the world around it. Its borders are unclear. Its mist stretches out in every direction, never seeming to finally dissipate. At its center one can detect nothing. It is both there and not there. It defies definition. It is a raw substance, awaiting the magical hand of a craftsman to shape it, bend it, and fold it into a new form.

It must be sculpted.

From an unseen recess in the room a figure appears. Mighty and strong the figure bears no tools but his hands, delicate in shape and perfect in movement. The figure moves forward, appraising the shapeless mass before him. Like a child testing his food, the figure leans forward and, quickly brushing, shapes a small part of the mist. The figure stands back once again, looking, judging, wondering what to do next. Once again, his hands gently skim a part of the cloud. That part too gains form where there was none. Again, the figure, the artist, stands back, looking, afraid that a wrong move will be irreparable, that a wrong move would destroy the work. With a

---

have been as good *after* you scratched the surface. The first was Pfizer. Their corporate ship was administered beautifully. Quite possibly their overhead was extreme – but things worked. The second... well, we'll get to that later.

singular gentleness, the figure moves forward and lovingly caresses another part of the cloud. A valley forms. A flick of the wrist, creating a light wind, tunnels itself into the cloud. Like waves, the undefinable elements of the cloud take beautiful form. A ripple here, a dimple there, a crater in yet another place. But the ripple, when viewed again, seems to have attained more than one form. The dimple, so easily described, attains a life of its own, beauty emanating from its shape. The edges of the crater are unclear, everything flows perfectly.

The sculptor, moving this way and that, striking out here, blowing lightly there, shaping in yet another place continues his work. One part merges with another, they form a single whole, so perfectly joined that they seem to have never existed apart. Quickly, the artist works, his masterpiece taking on form after form. The sculpture, no matter how examined, still defies even the most basic definition, dodges the most basic attempts at understanding. Even the smallest element rests easily beyond the grasp of the imagination. The form, so beautiful, so unique, so complex, so seemingly simple, slips through the mind. The sculpture takes on all forms, and yet becomes none.

The sculpture, flows as it always will, as if by its own initiative. Still, the sculptor works, his hands never failing him, forming something, which alone among all things, defies the power of the written word.

The sculptor stands back. Once again, he appraises, viewing his own work. The sculptor stands back, his hands, unique among all hands, capable of working the material He has formed.

The material is unique as well. It alone is worked by these unique hands.

It was evening. It was morning.

The seventh day.

171

The sculpture, the soul, leaves, still malleable, to be finally shaped by itself.

Please G-d this work shall not offend you, king of kings, mighty and merciful, our lord and creator.

Over the coming few years, I would build on this idea. The underlying concept was that G-d was a collector of art. Our souls were that art. Whether we were near starvation in Indonesia or suffered from development issues in New York or had all the material and mental blessings a person could wish for, we had the same challenge. We had to try to form something beautiful of our souls. Challenges were only there because they could bring out that beauty. And death came, sometimes early, because the pinnacle of possibility had already been reached.

There were two holes in that perspective, holes that would gnaw at me for decades.

First and foremost: why help others if their struggles were some kind of blessing for the development of their souls? Charity wouldn't be doing them any fundamental good.

The second hole is best explained with a story.

I met a woman whose father was part of Mao's Long March. He'd later fled China. I asked her if her father had any regrets, given as he'd contributed to the deaths of tens of millions of people.

"No," she said, "At the time, he felt that he was doing what was right."

That jibed with the cardplayers' maxim: what matters is how you play the odds, not whether you win. But it didn't work for me. He *was* culpable in the deaths of tens of millions of people. "I meant well" was no kind of excuse. Dedication in the face of resistance wasn't enough to yield a beautiful soul. Somehow, it couldn't be.

In fact, my concept of a self-beautifying soul was lacking that one key feature: a definition of beauty.

So many of the people I knew at Penn had *plans*. I used to call it the world's most prestigious vocational school. People were confused by my choice of degree. After all, I didn't want to be either a lawyer or a professor. Many were also confused by the reality that I didn't have plans. On one level, I'd seen so many plans fail. I never trusted plans. On another level, I didn't know *how* things worked, I didn't know the people who made them work and I didn't have or even comprehend what kind of connections to build. I had friends who had internships with the Supreme Court. They either had *connections* or knew what connections to create. I had other friends who were just so brilliant that plans presented themselves whenever they needed them. I wasn't in either category. I'd learned how to make an impression, but I was still far from learning how to *work* with others. I valued, strongly, standing alone and making my own path.

All the normal plans just wouldn't work.

A good friend of mine told me that she was jealous of me because, no matter what situation I was in, she knew I could land on my feet.

I might land on my feet. But there are very real limits to what you can do when all you're doing with those feet is standing alone.

The entire time I was at Penn, I spent a little of my time involved with the family business. I didn't really have much to offer. My father wanted me involved. My mother wanted me as far from the business as possible. I vacillated between the two positions.

The summer I was homeless, three members of my father's family died in a year. Two cousins and an aunt. Substance abuse was a major factor of all three cases. When my aunt died, I was at work. I went for a 30-minute walk just to process what had happened. In a way, it felt like things were collapsing. My father's family's troubles were eating away at it. At the same time, my mother's family had real troubles of their own. I came back to my desk (this was the not-so-busy summer) and wrote something for myself. Just to understand.

The way I saw it, only the combination of the two families – Jewish and not – had proved stable. But I didn't know that it would be stable in the future. Among other things, the business worried me. I wrote a letter to a friend describing it as a train, racing towards a mountain, trying to build up enough speed so that it could fly. I couldn't tell if it would take flight or smash into the mountain – with all the speed it had gathered making the aftermath all that much worse. I guess that's the way to describe any venture. You have to risk things, and build up a head of steam, in order to take flight. But it still scared the heck out of me.

My friend gave me good advice: do your best to help the train fly; but try not to be (to mix metaphors) the captain.

I took that advice.

My sister was divorced while I was in college. Her husband was abusive. This was why I had no shower access. The ex-husband was afraid of me and wouldn't let me visit. He never gave me an excuse, in the moment, to attack him. But had my sister asked, I would have happily done so. Once he locked me out and my sister did ask me to come in. I broke open the door. That didn't help with his fear.

But my sister stayed with him. She stuck it out. She was modeling herself on our grandmother. She stayed until our grandmother told her that she regretted not having left my grandfather. That was the end of the road for my sister's marriage.

At least it was the end of the marriage as a *functioning* marriage. But the religious marriage lived on, like some zombie relationship. My sister was an agunah – a religiously chained woman – for years. Early in the divorce process, some Rabbinic authorities in New York offered to help negotiate things. In order to level the playing field, they asked my sister to submit all the evidence she had of abuse. Bruises, hospital reports etc... She was required to submit *all the copies* of the evidence. She trusted them. Then, the Rabbanute (the Rabbinic authorities) *lost the file*. Just like that she had no evidence to push her case.

I can't even imagine how angry I would have been. But I know how angry *she* was. She'd been betrayed on so many levels. She hated the Rabbanute, and she hated marriage. Her bitterness was palpable. At one of my *sheva brachot* (a celebratory meal in the days following my own marriage), she sat across from us explaining how evil the institution of marriage was. She kept insisting that my wife needed a prenup to protect her from me. I knew enough not to take it personally. I also knew enough not to tell her we had no such prenup.

Just as with the grandfather-in-law's non-kosher meat and my mother's faux Communists, this lack of upstanding behavior eliminated any sort of special respect I might have had for Rabbis. For me, Rabbis are now simply people with a specialization in religious law. Some are quite a bit more, but I never start with that assumption.

Amazingly, despite her hatred of Orthodox Judaism, my sister still guided others down the Orthodox path. I met a man who went on a date with her – in her angriest phase. As a result of that date, he decided to become a Torah-observant Jew. I still can't explain it. My sister can't either.

When my sister did eventually get "married," to a man she'd known since college, she didn't *really* get married. He became a concubine. As far as I know, that was the first Jewish relationship in a few thousand years to be based on the concept of *pilegesh* (concubinage). The arrangement was elegant. She and her "husband" would be together for a year. They had a one-year contract with everything, from who did the dishes on up, laid out and negotiated. If the contract wasn't renewed, the relationship would be automatically terminated. It wasn't a pro-forma deal. She and her "husband" spent three months renegotiating every year. They had an annual signing ceremony.

She demonstrated, as well as anybody, a willingness to solve problems in her own way. In the meantime, she too has learned to work with others.

One final note of caution from this period in my life. When I was in New York for Shabbat, I would go to Mount Sinai Hospital in New York to visit the sick. There was a religious protocol to interacting with the patients. The man who went with me followed every single rule he could find. He was that kind of guy. I didn't even know the rules existed until he told me. One of the rules he told me about was to talk about the patient, not yourself. I violated it, every time. I used to entertain the patients with my stories. I didn't agree with the protocol. I thought the patients needed to escape the hospital, and I could help them do that.

Then I met one patient, shared some stories, and saw him crumble. He had terminal cancer. All he heard when I spoke was that he'd never really lived his life.

It's not always a good idea to be a cowboy.

If any of my friends happen to be reading this, I want to apologize to them if I haven't included them here. They are good and interesting people. It's just that this isn't a *real* autobiography and I'm already pushing the tangents to an extreme.

Waltham

After college I moved into a house with my little brother and a few friends. We had a little web development business. It made a little money, but not enough to support us.

I almost died two times in those first two years after college. One of those occasions was while driving north from New York. It was about 2AM and I noticed an unusual blackness in front of me. I slowed down in a hurry, confusing the other passengers. But it was a good thing I did slow down. A semi-truck had jackknifed across the highway. The bottom of it had no lights. All we could see was darkness. Thank G-d, that was enough.

The other story was far more unusual. My brother and I, as well as an employee and a friend, were driving to Philadelphia for Simchat Torah (a Jewish holiday). Just a mile or two from home, on a feeder road for the freeway, I noticed a pipe sticking out of the road. I debated what to do. I could stop suddenly, but it seemed unnecessary. I could swerve, but the car was pretty well loaded and not exactly great at cornering. So, I decided to drive *over* the pipe, but somewhat more slowly. I slowed down, cruised over the pipe, and heard a 'clink!'

I looked in my rearview mirror just in time to see the beginnings of a flame.

I stopped the car and shouted, "Get out of the car!"

Nobody moved.

I shouted, "Get the F-CK OUT OF THE CAR."

And everybody did. We ran to the embankment as the line of lit fuel ran – Die Hard style – straight for the car. The thing went up in a massive ball of flame. It didn't explode, because the gas tank was full. It was just a fireball. A very big fireball. My little brother was traumatized by the experience. One passenger had exited the other side of the car and we weren't sure she'd gotten out. He'd freaked out and ran back towards the burning car to try to open the door, but it was just far too hot. I never tried. I thought the woman had gotten out and I knew, that, if she hadn't, there was no point in trying to save her.

My brother may not have been as cold and calculating as I was, but he reacted with honor and courage.

Numerous fire trucks and police cars came. Even an ambulance. After a careful examination, the Fire Inspector came up to us and asked who was driving. I said I was. He asked, "Were you aware your gas tank was leaking."

I wanted to say, "No sh-t, Sherlock." But I didn't. Instead, I walked him back to the pipe, showed him the pipe and the beginning of the slightly darkened pavement. And then I asked, "Do you think the pipe might have something to do with it?"

The police report came in exactly as I described it. Almost word for word. Everybody agreed on what happened.

The car, with me looking inside of it

That didn't help us much. We had to pay to have the car towed and junked. All of our clothes (we didn't have much) were in the car. Well, except for what we were wearing. We had almost no money. What we did have we spent buying some jeans and cheap T-shirts at Costco. We decided to sue the city. A friend of a friend was a lawyer. He was willing to work on commission. There were only two caveats. We had to come up with the filing fee and the maximum amount the city could be sued for was $5,000. In theory, we could have sued the construction company, but they too were protected.

We didn't have $300 for a filing fee. So, despite having a completely solid case against the city, we never saw a dime. We actually lost money on the tow job. I'm glad they didn't make us pay to fix the d-mned road.

I know the purpose of the filing fee was to prevent spurious lawsuits. I get it. But a fairer system would have allowed us to sue. Perhaps it could have put us on the hook for the city's costs if we lost. Or perhaps there could have been some sort of one-time asset or income exemption on the filing fee. You know, like a video review in sports. If you win the case and you can use your exemption again. If not, it is burned forever.

In the aftermath of the fire, my younger brother went for mental health counseling at his school. After hearing some of his story, the counselor told him she was happy to treat him. Just not for trauma. No, his real problem was that he was a pathological liar.

While living in Waltham, I did a few things I regret. One of them was helping a cousin and my girlfriend overcome educational barriers. That all sounds nice, and I meant it that way, but I exceeded my original intent in both cases.

My cousin was pursuing a Master's in Education. He had to write a thesis. It was suggested that I could help him. The original arrangement was simple. I'd help him and he'd pay me for my time. The problem was, as I worked with him it became more and more clear that he was beyond help. And so, like the proverbial frog, I ended up taking on more and more of *his* task. I ended up writing a Master's Thesis in Education. Thankfully, he dropped out of the program for other reasons and so I didn't help him *actually* get a degree. Whew.

The paper itself was interesting, on a personal level. It was about ADHD treatment and effects. Basically, I went back to first papers about using stimulants to treat kids (back in the 1930s) and progressed forward in a sort of meta-analysis. What I came up with was that stimulants (e.g., Ritalin) *greatly* improved concentration and behavior. What they *didn't* improve (at least not much) was grades. This lines up with my own experience. All the time my mind was wandering as a hyper and distracted kid, I was actually taking things in. I was learning, just not the kind of learning that shows up on a grade. If you'd focused me down through stimulants, I would have lost all that ancillary data collection.

Years later I met a man who ran a quantitative method of testing for ADHD (the TOVA test). He reported that 95% of diagnosed kids weren't actually 'ADHD'. More critically, he described a performance curve. With a little stimulation, ADHD kids would perform *better*. But then as you increased it, their mental performance would significantly drop off. He recommended that most kids just needed a Coke or a coffee in the morning. *Not* Ritalin.

It was a bit troubling that I could write an acceptable thesis for a Master's in Education. Then again, I'd consulted (this time for somebody who *didn't* have me write anything) on a paper for a doctorate from MIT. She'd been working on her thesis for years, but she'd completely lost sight of the actual *thesis*. You know, the singular point she was trying to make with all her research. I suggested a thesis and then a few days' worth of rework to restructure the paper around clearly supporting it. You know, to actually *say something* in the paper. She demurred. She didn't want to put in the effort, and she suspected that even lacking a real thesis, it was good enough. She was right. She's now a professor and a respected expert in her field.

Maybe the field of education isn't so bad.

The second case was my girlfriend at the time. I dressed up her credentials and described her doing more with our company than she had. She used that to get into a graduate program, a program she probably wasn't qualified for.

Last I heard, she dropped out.

It was kind of a theme. In the three cases I helped more than I should have, the students couldn't manage the programs. I tried to just do a little, to *nudge* them along. But the nudge just grew and grew. *When* you help, it is important to lift people up, not shove them aside. If you can't lift them all the way, then you gotta' be satisfied with a partial boost. This is why my own kids get no help on school projects or presentations. I'll show them how to do something, but I'll never do it for them.

I was wrong before, but I try to learn.

After the little business slowly died (in part, because I didn't put in the intellectual effort to learn the web exploitation of databases), I got the job at the recruiters. Then, I moved to a startup. I started as a technical writer but was then promoted to be a Product Manager. Not for a real product, but for our demonstration product.

I learned a lot there – mostly how not to design a quality system. The quality manager was a hardware expert in a company that depended a whole lot on software. They raised tens of millions and lost it. They were bankrupted by a paperwork-induced inability to innovate.

I still have a few thousand shares in that defunct venture.

A few of my co-workers were legal gun owners (unusual in Massachusetts). There was a shooting range across the street. Massachusetts law forbade leaving guns in cars, so I used to store my pistol and rifle under my desk. That was definitely a little weird. I can't imagine it in the United States today

One of the other folks who worked there (and went shooting with me) was a proud Pole. His father had apparently been the head of some branch of military intelligence. He didn't realize there was a whole genre of jokes that could be centered on that juxtaposition. Nonetheless, the Pole, whose name I've since forgotten, lived in New Hampshire. One day, he explained that he never ate poultry that he hadn't hunted and shot. As Torah-observant Jews, we don't hunt. We can only kill to eat, and you can't eat that which isn't killed properly. Shooting doesn't count. The only animals that you can kill properly (from a practical perspective) are domesticated. To me, his approach to fowl seemed downright barbarian. You had to hunt and kill all your poultry? I asked him why that was important to him? He said that hunting and shooting the animals reminded him that they had been alive. He wasn't buying some impersonal, shrink-wrapped bit of meat on a supermarket shelf. He could appreciate the *living animal* while I, who bought a chicken in shrink wrap, could not.

He could appreciate the animal's sacrifice.

Today, I'll admit, I can't see meat any other way.

I'm not a vegetarian, but I make a point of acknowledging the life of the animals I eat.

At one point, my cubemate was an Indian (an actual Indian) who'd grown up in a West African dictatorship. I was fascinated about what he thought about his homeland. He would not say *anything* about it, though. Only after months did he finally admit that the place might be somewhat corrupt. But he reiterated, he could not talk about it. After all, his family was still there. His fear of that West African government extended across the Atlantic and into Boston's Route 128. It stunned me. I'd known Russians with that kind of fear. Today, you might find Chinese or Iranians like that. There are practical reasons for those fears. The Chinese, Iranian and Soviet states have/had tremendous reach.

But West Africans?

The internalization of fear, even of regimes with rudimentary methods of suppression, was stunning. Today you can find Arabs with that same fear. I've met with people who were unwilling to talk about anything substantive, until they saw my face. They wanted to be sure, or as sure as they could be, that I wasn't working for the regimes they so hated and feared.

One day, while still in Waltham, I'd gone to a laundromat to wash my clothes. I was there when a man stepped into the laundromat. He'd come from a nearby bar. He was drunk and angry. As per Massachusetts law, despite having a carry permit, I'd didn't have my gun. The guy wasn't big, but his friends could see what was going on. I could have kicked the crap out of him and still not made it past the front door.

I was trapped.

So, I did the only thing I could do. I talked.

I asked him *why* he hated Jews. After all, despite being one of the people who controlled the world I was here washing my clothes in a laundromat. I couldn't even afford a laundry machine.

It turns out he was a philosophical Jew hater. He subscribed to 'Eastern' philosophy. He envisioned a truly harmonious global society. He was attracted to the Platonic vision of perfect coordination. The only obstacle to his vision was the Jews. We wouldn't integrate. We wouldn't get along. We insisted on being different. It wasn't an unusual position. Haman, from the Purim story, had a very similar perspective.

> *There is a certain people scattered abroad and dispersed among the peoples in all the provinces of thy kingdom; and their laws are diverse from those of every people; neither keep they the king's laws; therefore it profiteth not the king to suffer them.*

The Spanish had a beautiful vision of the perfect state in service of G-d. Jews didn't fit. The Soviets (often led by Jews)

186

had a beautiful vision of the perfect state in perfect equality. The Jews, at least practicing Jews, didn't fit. The Nazis had a beautiful vision of a perfect racial society too. And, of course, the Jews didn't fit.

In all these cases, Jews violated the goal of harmony.

That argument wouldn't help me get out of the laundromat, though.

I had to convince the guy that that the violation of harmony was actually a *good* thing. I had to argue the dynamism enabled by a people who enabled change and growth and the organic development of ideas was a good thing. We had quite a long conversation. At the end of it, we shook hands and he said, "You're all right, for a Jew."

He left.

I grabbed my laundry, and I got the heck out of there.

These sorts of incidents were rare in those days.

I fear they're all too common today[1].

In the late 90s, two major world events changed my life.

---

[1] Years later I had a kind of similar discussion while working at Mercedes Benz in Australia. One of my German colleagues explained to me that Jews ruled the world. I was kind of shocked that this well-educated German thought that. He pointed out that we ran the banks, the governments etc... He didn't mean anything *bad* by it. I explained that Jews are indeed prominent, but we don't *agree* with each other. That kind of eliminates our ability to actually run anything as a group. At the end of our conversation, he confided that he was only repeating what a Jew had told him over drinks. Poorly thought-out pride, including Jewish pride, can be a dangerous thing.

First, I remember being crushed by the Asian Financial Crisis of 1997. I actually cried at the effects of that collapse. So many people's hopes were crushed when the Southeast Asian Tiger economies were laid low. Millions were pushed under the poverty line, governments were brought down, and violent Islamic movements were strengthened. It is believed over 10,000 people in Hong Kong, Japan and South Korea committed suicide as a result of the crisis. All of it was caused by problems with the structuring of debt within financial systems. That crisis kicked off my desire to understand how markets could be better structured. I wanted to understand how markets could be protected from the kind of financial contagion that undermined so many ambitions.

I didn't have any answers then. As with all the good questions, the answers would take me decades to begin to understand.

The other major event was 1998's Hurricane Mitch. Hurricane Mitch killed over 11,000 people. Honduras was hit particularly badly[1]. I'd grown up with a great deal of skepticism towards major international aid organizations. The Red Cross hid Nazis while the UN made them Secretary Generals. Live Aid raised money for food, which the Derg almost certainly stole in their Marxist-Leninist program of economic cleansing. Watching what was happening in Honduras, and the delays that plagued normal international aid, I wanted to help donors support more effective and direct support. I wanted to find and

---

[1] While oddly uncovering a treasure trove of jade in Central America.

vet charities already on the ground in potential zones of catastrophe. These charities wouldn't need to start from scratch, and they would already know how to work around often counterproductive governments. I called the venture *Who Can Help?* It didn't get very far. Some of the most effective local ventures were Evangelical outreach organizations. People objected to giving to these organizations. To this day, I don't really understand. As a Jew, I won't fund people trying to convert Jews. But I have no problem with religious organizations using their local connections and dedication to help out in a crisis like Hurricane Mitch.

Who Can Help? didn't survive. I still regret that.

In those days, I was still very much a weirdo. I'd cast myself as a socially awkward genius. I was good at my job, but I thought perceptions of my performance were enhanced by the slight mystery of how I ticked. I was *actually* a socially awkward weirdo. The "genius" bit was what I'd tried to add to the product that was Joseph Cox.

I had a girlfriend, despite being a weirdo. The relationship was serious. She wasn't a native English speaker. A few months after we broke up, we were at an event at Harvard. Somebody asked her how she possibly followed what I was saying. After all, I talk fast.

"I never did," she said, "I just nodded and agreed with whatever he was saying."

Whatever doubts I'd had before, that confirmed that ours wouldn't have been a very good long-term relationship.

Cambridge

I moved to Cambridge (MA) after my brother graduated from Brandeis and headed back to Oregon. I rejoined the Harvard community, after years had passed. My goals were pretty straight-forward. I wanted to find a wife and get married.

I didn't want to get married to just anybody, though. The way I figured it, if somebody couldn't handle a bit of my background up front, they wouldn't be able to handle the rest of it later. My prime method of filtering potential women was the rifle I proudly displayed in my living room (trust me, that isn't normal in Cambridge). Of course, the rifle might have been unnecessary discouragement. I was hardly a player.

I had fun, though. I was surrounded by some of the brightest people in the world. One of my friends was a professional chef. Others were professors. Still others were graduate students of all stripes. I drove a car I called the Pimpmobile. It was a 19-foot long 1979 Lincoln Continental with two-tone brown paint, fuzzy seats and a digitally tuned eight-track player. It had 365 horsepower but was so heavy it felt more like 75. I used to put opera on the eight-track. I don't even know which opera; it was just one of the few eight tracks I had. We'd cruise Cambridge in that car. It was a fun car. It also led to a particularly unusual experience. I was trying to sell the car and had a "For Sale" sticker on the back window. I was driving home, down the 128, when a man in another (newer) brown Lincoln Town Car pulled up next to me. He flagged me down. Figuring he might want to buy my car, I pulled off at the next exit. I'd learned from the laundromat, though. I unlocked and loaded my gun.

He drove up next to me and then, much to my surprise, he propositioned me. He wanted me to come home and "play" with him. I refused, as politely as I could. He was very persistent. Close to aggressive. Nonetheless, I wasn't looking to be any middle-aged man's boy toy. I suspect it wasn't the first time I'd been scouted as a candidate for that particular position.

At least I didn't need the gun, right?

Another time, the car died. I didn't have a cell phone. So, we were parked on the side of the freeway, for *three hours*, waiting for a cop to show up and help us out. After three hours, I climbed down the embankment to take a leak. *That's* when the cop showed up.

He wanted to ticket us for public indecency.

My relationship with cops was still less than perfect.

In fact, I got pulled over three times in less than one month. Once, a *fleet* of police cars pulled me over. It turns out somebody in a late 70s Cadillac had been driving near Hanscomb Air Force base. When the cops tried to approach, he sped away. Late 70s Cadillacs might have had that kind of umph, but I didn't. After an extensive check, they finally let me go. My Massachusetts carry permit was my out. They *knew* I'd been through a ringer of a background check. They were a little annoyed though. I'd taken the time to get a Massachusetts gun permit, but I still didn't have a local driver's license.

They didn't get my priorities. But I did get a local license soon afterwards.

I almost hurt myself badly while I was living in Cambridge. I got sick, coughing up blood sick. I was coughing up blood for days, but I wanted to tough it out. Finally, I gave in and headed for the hospital. I hate hospitals, and so I became very funny (it isn't my usual form). The doctor doubted I could possibly have pneumonia. But I did, and a pretty serious case too. I wasn't hospitalized. I got medication. It didn't kick in right away though. I was really having a tough time and considering calling an ambulance (even though it was Shabbat) when things finally took a turn for the better. It was one of three times my life has definitely been saved by modern medicine. Think about that for yourself: how many times would you have died if you'd been living in 1900?

From that point on I had a new rule: if I couldn't sleep, I'd get medical help.

At least until I knew what was ailing me.

It was while I was in Cambridge that I took my next major stab at changing the world. It was called GiveDaily. When I was a kid, in London, the Sassover Rebbe challenged my father to give $18 a day, to a different charitable cause each day. It could be an individual or an organization, but it had to be different *each day*. The experience was awesome for us kids. We got to do all sorts of research and we got to help out quite a few people just a little bit.

GiveDaily tried to scale up that experience. People would give a donation via our webpage and every day we'd give a slice of that donation to a different charity. We'd then email the donors to tell them what they'd supported. We created different funds, around people's different priorities (I learned that from the *Who Can Help?* experience). The goal of GiveDaily was this: to encourage charitable giving and teach people about worthy charities.

I formed a 501(c)3 (and learned I didn't need an overpriced lawyer to do these sorts of things) and I raised money. Not much, about $50,000 over three years. But we gave money to hundreds of charities. I learned a lot about coding (everything was managed via a webpage), printing checks and the kinds of worthy work people all around the world were doing. We received all sorts of wonderful letters we shared with our donors. I still have relationships with some of those donors, and even with some of the people who ran those charities.

The organization never really grew. I just wasn't attracting enough donors to make all the work worth it. I created new funds and fund managers. I went to a weekly format, so those managers didn't feel so stressed about choosing charities. I even tried launching a school program where we'd mail out lesson plans and charitable boxes. The fact was: none of it was enough. GiveDaily never really took flight.

Early on in the process I'd sought the advice of a Rabbi who was very good at raising money. He told me one thing: raise money from people who have it. He didn't get what I was really trying to do. The IRS didn't either. They rejected my original filing because 'encouraging charity' was not a cause they'd ever heard of.

Neither of them understood that I wasn't trying to raise money for a cause – I was trying to raise money just so people could experience the joy of giving.

In the end, the mission was beyond me.

While I was in Cambridge I learned, through a very non-rational experience, that people could exude emotions. People could sense and feel when somebody was engaged and involved and interested. At least it worked for me. The reactions of people around me were completely different (and more involved) when I intentionally exuded what I called Emot-Ions. It *almost* felt like a physical experience.

My best friend in those days was a brilliant scientist and heavy metal lover. He taught me how to banter. One weekend we went to New York. We'd dared each other to line up as many dates as possible. I managed to schedule 7 dates over a single Shabbat. He had about 5.

We ended up cancelling them all.

The fact was, I wasn't interested. I didn't want to play 'the game'. I wanted to find a wife. I'd visited the hotbed of Jewish single life on many occasions. That final time, I hadn't been afraid to approach anyone. I'd opened and developed every conversation I'd wanted to start. There was no fear, no hesitation. There was no failure. Despite all that, I hadn't found anybody who had any chance of being a match.

That weekend, I knew my hunting for an East Coast bride had come to a close. I don't remember how I met her, but I ended up dating a girl from Oregon. Not rural Oregon, but Portland. Our relationship didn't last long, but I headed back West anyways.

It was time to try something new.

Back in Oregon

Not long after getting back to Oregon, I found myself single and living in my brother's basement (thanks, bro!). Luckily, I had a very engaging job. I'd started as a technical writer, but before long I'd finished my "full-time job" and I'd been tasked with something more involved. My job became researching global transaction tax and coming up with systematic ways to determine which jurisdictions were due which tax. I became an expert in VAT, GST and Sales Tax.

I never filed a return, but I knew how tax systems worked everywhere from Europe to Brazil. After about a year and a half of study and development I had my 'Aha!' moment. In a single page-and-a-half-long memo I described a clean and systematic coding system that could manage tax determination everywhere from Idaho to India. A patent was filed, but I wasn't informed, and I wasn't on it (another learning opportunity). The system ended up being adopted by numerous Fortune 50 companies.

The most informative part of that job involved Indian taxation. Tax law all around the world shared a common structure: "Here is the general rule, here are the exceptions..."

Indian tax law was different. There was *no* general rule. There is now, due to one of Narendra Modi's biggest reforms. But there *had been* no general rule.

Every other country had a rule, but not India. Indian thought was just fundamentally different. Where the rest of the world sought generalizations at the cost of mastery of the details, India seemed to embrace all the details at the cost of generalization. The contrast was yet another reminder of how differently the world could be approached and understood.

Despite the rewarding work, I had a problem. I was in Oregon, with a tiny Torah-observant community. I was 25 and eager to get married. I'd given up on the Northeast and I wasn't looking to restart my life by moving to Israel. I knew that if I wanted to take the next step, I'd have to go online.

It was 2000 when I started actively looking online. My approach was informed by a twisted sense of economics. I figured the best 'product' had already been picked up in the larger markets (like New York). I'd experienced that. So, my best chance of finding a high-quality partner lay in finding people effectively stranded in small Jewish markets like my own. I found people in places like Nebraska and Honduras. Initially, I took my time carefully crafting messages around the other party's interests. Nothing came of my attempts to reach out. One interesting profile was posted as a joke. Others just never responded or just told me to go away. By the time I encountered Rebecca (who had no picture) from Melbourne, Australia I'd given up on crafting careful messages. I just texted her, via the website, "Check out my profile, you might be interested."

Rebecca, for her part, had also had her time wasted. She'd met somebody online who'd lied about many things – from age to previous marital status. She wasn't actively looking to get married, certainly not to somebody online. She was just looking to network in anticipation of a move to London. She saw my message and replied, simply, "Can't you do better than that?"

I was smitten.

I *could* do better. My brother lived in a daylight basement with a fantastic view. I started describing every day's sunset to her so she could wake up to the description.

Online dating, in those days, involved no video. Even voice was hard to set up. So, we just emailed, for the first few weeks. Then we got to talking. She sent me a gorgeous photo. I showed my friends at work. One of them, a very nice young woman, asked, "Joseph, does she know anything about you?" It was a pretty good indication that I was hardly a socially adjusted individual.

Eventually, we set up a first real date. She'd fly to Vancouver, Canada. I'd drive up and get her. It was a thousand dollars cheaper than me heading to Australia. Her father had his Rabbi call a Rabbi in Portland to confirm I wasn't dangerous. Nonetheless (and unbeknownst to me), Rebecca had a backup ticket to Chicago; in case things went sideways.

I picked her up. In person, we didn't hit it off. We'd been speaking for months, for hours a day. But never by video. It wasn't an option then. In person, neither of us was what the other expected. Neither was quite the person we thought we knew. Rebecca hated the way I laughed (like a poorly educated hillbilly) and she was driven nuts by the way I talked about the traffic when I drive. That's not a good thing when the drive from the airport is over 5 hours long.

As she told me later, "I was just asking myself – what did I get myself into?"

Despite these initial hiccups we committed to giving the five days we had together a serious shot.

When my mother heard Rebecca was coming, she made me promise *not* to do two things. The first was to go shooting. The second was to meet my father. Both of these were filters for me. If Rebecca, a proper woman from gun-free Melbourne couldn't handle them then our relationship wouldn't survive. I brought her shooting first. Then, we visited my parents. My parents *loved* her. I knew it because as we were leaving my father called out, insisting I open her door. That was the first time they'd ever asked me to be nice to a woman I was involved with.

My mother added just before I got in the car, "Make sure you don't do the other thing." Of course, we already had done "the other thing."

Rebecca just smiled.

That Sabbath we had lunch with a Rabbi and his wife (as well as a crowd of other people) in downtown Portland. I learned later that the consensus at the meal was that we had no future. It was a reasonable reaction to us. But we did, in fact, have a future.

On the five-mile-walk back to my brother's, Rebecca told me what she didn't like. My laugh wasn't brought up. My talking while driving wasn't brought up. My barking in public was, though. Rebecca's advice was basically a continuation of my first girlfriend's advice: "concentrate on sticking out in useful ways." I committed to doing exactly that. She accepted it. By this point, I was already adjusting to her as well. There are benefits to learning how to control yourself and your emotions. It is more than control though – which is what our modern ears believe is all you can do. I have learned how to actually change myself. We'll get to that later.

It was on that walk, through the beautiful forest that lines Terwilliger Boulevard, that we committed to giving our relationship a serious run. Rebecca's favorite car, at the time, was the PT Cruiser. I promised her one if we got married.

I never delivered.

I flew to Australia next. We spent a few weeks in Bundaberg, Queensland. We were staying in a motel owned by a retired English couple. One day, we borrowed their car and drove out to a beautiful park near the town. The park had a lake completely covered by lily pads. That and geese who (given that it was the off-season) were desperate for treats. We had to abandon our picnic and climb a table just to get away from the extremely aggressive waterfowl. That wasn't what was important. What was important was the ring from the Coke bottle. I placed it on her finger and less than six months after meeting online we were engaged.

My trip came to an end in Melbourne. Rebecca's parents were not the least bit surprised by the engagement. But Rebecca had kept my existence a secret from her friends. Most of them hadn't even known that she'd gone to the states. They met me, for the very first time, at her engagement party. This is a community where everybody knew everybody else – and had for years. They were not impressed. A group of them got together to stage an intervention. The husbands brought me out to play pool. I had no idea what was going on. I only knew I was completely failing to build any sort of connection with these men. I didn't know I was being separated from Rebecca so their wives could convince Rebecca to do the right thing and leave me.

Lucky for me, the intervention failed.

Rebecca has never been very good at taking direction.

A few months later, I returned to Australia.

It was September 11th, 2001.

I was in the air when the twin towers were hit.

On December 27th, 2001, we were married.[1]

---

[1] My father flew to the wedding on Emirates. He sat next to a Pashtun warlord who explained that the Pashtun were historically Jews. They had a great time together, the Chassidic Jew and the Pashtun warlord. They apparently scared the heck out of the other first-class passengers. On the way back, my father was in the first-class lounge and seated next to the Syrian Minister of Defense. Not

LANE CHANGE

I started writing the next part of this book the same way I wrote the prior part. Something roughly chronological with a few themes and lessons thrown in. The problem was: it *really* wasn't engaging. We were broke then, we did X, Y and then Z, we moved here, we moved there, I worked for this company and then that company – whatever, right? I put together around 20 pages and realized that if I was falling asleep *writing* then my readers would have no chance. Yes, exciting things happened. We spent 5 and a half years trying to have children. We moved homes 15 times and changed continents 4 times. We had triplets. We visited Ethiopia with an infant (and five other kids). I wrote 10 books (this is #11). I worked on mortgage servicing after the 2008 collapse, then with Nike shortly afterwards and then on designing a new aircraft system. All of this was fun and (I think) interesting.

---

wanting to show fear, he proceeded to put on his Tallis and Tefillin. As he reported it, the Bangladeshi and Filipino "help" had no idea what he was doing, but they were loving it. Whatever it was, it was making the Arabs in the lounge incredibly angry. Thankfully, our relations with the UAE have improved greatly since then.

But it wasn't exciting enough to justify the rest of this book. I mean, how involving can "we packed our boxes this way and filled out the paperwork that way" be?

Right?

But despite the *events* being more mundane, the *learning* hasn't been. I've learned a lot since I was 25. I've learned a lot since I was 35. I've fundamentally changed the political, economic and moral positions I held less than 10 years ago. Things have happened, it's just that they're best looked at through relationships, not through a timeline.

So instead of the events being used as a way of dropping in on ideas, the growth of relationships and – dare I say it - wisdom[1] is going to be used as a way of dropping in on events.

You wouldn't expect anything less from a wannabee intellectual historian, would you?

I'll see if I can pull it off.

One last thing... before I dig into a bunch of life lessons. I'm not going to lecture you about marriage or raising children or Torah or dealing with adversity or any of that. My own experience is just that, *my own experience*. I am not you; your family members are not my family members. What you need

---

[1] Wisdom isn't intelligence. It takes time to learn how to drive a car. You know you're good at it when you just understand what to prioritize and focus on; and when you intrinsically understand how to maneuver. Wisdom is the same thing, just for life. Put a more brutal way – wisdom is when you know what to do despite not being anywhere near as smart or swift as you were when you were twenty. Eventually, though, that lack of smarts catches up with you. Then you lose your license.

spiritually is not what I need spiritually. Not only that, but I don't want you to *become* me. That's why all the growth I'm going to talk about isn't a guidebook to anything. It is just a sharing of slices of our own story, some of which might be useful to you.

Even worse than lecturing would be stating the completely obvious again and again. Unfortunately, there's a fine line between the obvious and the insightful. I'll only share what *I* think is insightful. I apologize in advance if it makes me look a bit simple-minded.

G-D

By the time I was married, my general religious perspective was stable. It had been stable for almost a decade. I believed we were here to make our souls beautiful through the choices that we made. Generally, those choices involved how we *tried* to help others. Specifically, as Jews, they involved how we walked in the path designated for us by G-d[1].

Within my own personal life, and specifically my marriage, the goal was to create a *bye'it ne'eman b'yisrael* – a "pleasant house in Israel." I wanted ours to be a house of warmth and

---

[1] Which is why we discourage conversion. In very broad terms, it is easier to get to Heaven if you aren't a Jew.

love enriched by our long tradition and the many practices that defined who we were as a people. I guess, through our own efforts, we'd try to serve as a bit of model to help others beautify their own souls.

I dwelt on the Torah that reinforced my beliefs. I read the standard pamphlets (some beautiful, some technical) that explored the Torah readings. I shared the explanations I already had and accepted there weren't explanations where those same sources claimed explanations were impossible. My only real critical thought focused on the outsized impact of Platonic thought on Torah thought. I happily walked in a path I did not understand, that act of faith being part of my challenge as a Jew.

I'd had problems with this model, particularly the non-Jewish parts. What about the Maoist who was *really* trying to help but contributed to the deaths of tens of millions? And what about the charity that might lift a person out from a struggle they were meant to face (and thus mar their souls)?

I had answers of course, but they were sort of rough workarounds. We help people out so they can face 'higher' challenges, whatever those might be. And perhaps what we *do* matters more than what we *intend*, although as mere mortals we really can't understand the impact of our actions. I wasn't satisfied with those answers, but they weren't enough to force a reconsideration of my general model, much less my Jewish one.

Then it all began to change. The change actually had very deep roots. It started with how I was brought up, intellectually.

In our family, my mother was the intellectual powerhouse. She was a brilliant woman and thinker. Her magnum opus, *Reflections of the Logic of the* Good, argued that there *was* good and bad, but there were nearly infinite ways of measuring it. A particular Inuit might not be very good at map reading, but my mother knew from personal experience that that same particular Inuit could navigate a canoe over what she thought was a featureless landscape in darkness and end up getting exactly where he intended exactly *when* he intended.

As bearers of the Western intellectual tradition and post-Enlightenment values, we tend to dismiss other ways of thinking and engaging with the world. Nonetheless, they have a value all their own. This *doesn't* mean all values and approaches are equivalent. Within that Inuit context itself, you could discriminate between "Good" navigation and "Bad" navigation. There is a separate axis of judgement – but an axis of judgement, nonetheless.

Before you can criticize something from another tradition, or even really engage with it, you have to be able to appreciate the axis (or even multiple axes) of "good" on which it lays. It is all too common a trap to analyze it within your own understanding of reason. Things that hold together, suddenly hold no water whatsoever and you lose the opportunity to learn from what can be a radically different perspective.

This approach has been reinforced throughout my life. Not only through my mom's writing and thinking but through my interactions with people who held diametrically opposed worldviews. Worldviews that could not be squared through argument because the fundamental axioms were distinct. Growing up, we were around far-right militia types, leftist Jews, sophisticated city folk, backwoods hillbillies, reason-centric Torah scholars and mystical Chassidim. As I got older, I was exposed to more and more alternate ways of approaching the world – including through those randomly struck up conversations.

My undergraduate education in Intellectual History attempted to teach me to place *myself* within disparate historical epochs of thought. It sought to teach me to look at the world through long-dead eyes.

I've not only interacted with others, but I've also inhabited a variety of my own realities. I've been an Ivy League student. I've been homeless. I've worked packing boxes and I've had the opportunity to propose the reorganization of an entire Fortune 50 company to its CFO. I've been unemployed for years of my professional prime. I've worked – and not just on an entry-level – in high-tech, mortgage servicing, taxation, aerospace, print services and more. I've lived in the country, and I've lived in the City. I've been rich and poor and a whole variety of things in between. I've been childless and blessed with many children.

All of this exposure left me with a single question:

What's *really* important?

The more perspectives you learn to value, the harder it is to answer. The real vexation is that the more perspectives you learn to value, the more important an answer becomes.

As the old saying goes: "If your mind is too open, your brain will fall out." We don't want our brains to fall out.

Years ago, during one of my multi-year bouts of unemployment, I started a project called "Bible4Community." The idea was to recreate, online, my experience of studying the Five Books of Moses as a child. The site would break down every word in the Five Books of Moses, showing parts of speech, tenses, roots of words and even how to pronounce the text itself. I built the site, including an engine for entering the data reasonably quickly (by sharing common parts across the text automatically). A friend of mine, Rabbi Nahorai Kotkin, populated it with data[1]. He got half-way through the book of Exodus (with later words that shared structures with earlier words already being filled in). So, he got about two-thirds of the way through the Five Books of Moses. In the process, he produced a dictionary, the *Hebrew Root Dictionary*, which was based on his work. It is excellent and I highly recommend it.

The site never went anywhere. It had two regular users: myself and my older brother. I'm not very good at consumer marketing (i.e., *terrible*), but beyond that my vision wasn't one many others seemed to share. I wanted to enable non-Biblical Hebrew speakers to interact with the text *directly*. In the

---

[1] The site itself is no longer up. I have it backed up but lack the bandwidth to put it back online.

original Hebrew[1]. I wanted them to be able to analyze and build up their own understanding of what was going on.

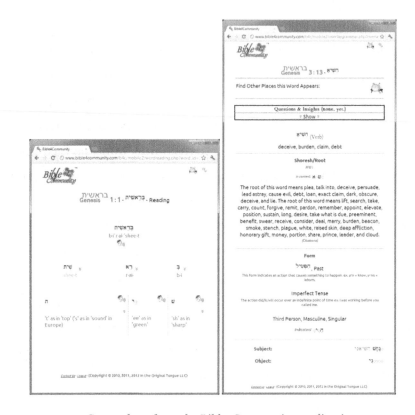

Screenshots from the Bible4Community application

Most religious traditions *don't* embrace this approach. It can certainly be dangerous. Even in those traditions that do embrace it, most religious *people* don't embrace this approach. Normal people wanted a more packaged understanding while

---

[1] The actual name of the company was In the Original Tongue. We called it IOTA, a play on the lost Greek letter Iota and the Hebrew letter Yud.

scholars wanted more technical detail than the site was designed to provide.

But Bible4Community wasn't a total failure. Kotkin's dictionary has sold well; and *I* acquired the tools to study the Torah as I never had before.

Although I didn't quite know it at the time, those were the tools I'd need to eventually appreciate the axis of "good" on which the Five Books of Moses themselves lay. That understanding would, in turn, transform my religious and political philosophy.

A few more years had passed, and we'd joined a Sephardic community in Portland. It was an odd little congregation that rarely exceeded 20 attendees. Unlike many Mizrachi (Eastern) communities, it wasn't Arabic-speaking. Instead, Ladino and Spanish were the primary ancestral languages[1]. Although I do now know some liturgical Ladino tunes, I wasn't of this tradition. My brother and I supported the synagogue (he, far more than I) because it was important to us to have a variety of Torah-observant options and approaches available within the broader community.

Within the community, Torah knowledge was somewhat limited. I had more of the basic tools than most. I could sing (although not in the Sephardic style), I could read Hebrew and I knew some Torah. I led prayers on occasion, I blew the Shofar on Rosh Hashana. I was made Gabbai of the synagogue.

---

[1] Sephardic actually means 'Spanish.' But Sephardic tradition closely mirrors other Mizrachi traditions and so the term is used as a catch-all for Eastern Judaism.

The job was simple: I called people up to the Torah for honors (although it would have been easier if I was any good at remembering names). Every Shabbat there are seven Torah readings plus a little add on at the end (other Holy Days have other numbers of readings). So, every Shabbat, I called seven people up for Torah-reading honors. They didn't read the Torah themselves; they said the blessings on behalf of somebody else who did the reading[1].

A year or two into this role, I asked the Rabbi if I might give a very very short sermon before each reading. The reasoning was simple: most people in the community didn't have much exposure and the readings could get seriously boring or off-putting for them. They were often seriously boring or off-putting for me. I wanted to add a little color and spark to the proceedings while smoothing things out. In addition, it would be a continuation of an ancient tradition of providing basic interpretations before each reading.

The Rabbi approved and I started the next week.

The Rabbi and I had diametrically different approaches to Torah. He was a Mizrachi Rabbi from Spanish-Morocco who could speak at great length and came from a tradition that quite simply didn't use reason in the way post-Enlightenment Europeans did. I was coming from a far more European approach and my Torah snippets were never longer than 60 seconds in length. I was very much trained in post-Enlightenment thought.

---

[1] Not *me*. Although I have *layned* (or read) almost the entire Torah I am legendarily bad at it.

At first, I had a pretty good idea of what I was going to say. I knew what my preconceptions and beliefs were. But as I was standing there, defending and explaining Torah, I realized both the axioms and the axis of good that *I* used simply didn't match up with the text. Thankfully, I was able to recognize this and accept it[1]. It isn't always so easy.

The fact was, I'd seen people cast the Torah in both a right-wing and a left-wing light. I'd seen it used to justify individualism, communitarianism, environmentalism and pretty much every other -ism you could find. The text seems to work for all of that, so long as you *ignore* the bits that don't. It is so tempting for Jews and non-Jews alike to say, "those bits are antiquated, these bits aren't" and then recast G-d's word in their own light. They are making G-d in their own image. While I don't try to interpret Jewish Law from the Torah, I do try to find moral guidance within it. Deciding that half or more of the text can be ignored because it doesn't fit with what I believe wouldn't work.

To give an example... I once heard a speech about how the Torah is fundamentally supportive of environmentalism. The evidence was that the Torah forbid the cutting of trees to build siege engines. The Torah clearly loved trees. Here is the quote:

> *When thou shalt besiege a city a long time, in making war against it to take it, thou shalt*

---

[1] Years earlier, I'd had a long argument about encryption technology with a relative of my wife's. At the end he emailed her and said, "Joseph is more interested in winning than in being right." That criticism struck home and changed what I try to achieve with my argument and analysis.

not destroy the trees thereof by wielding an axe against them; for thou mayest eat of them, but thou shalt not cut them down; for is the tree of the field man, that it should be besieged of thee? (Deut 20:19)

The speaker's argument seems to make sense... as long as you ignore the very next verse:

Only the trees of which thou knowest that they are not trees for food, them thou mayest destroy and cut down, that thou mayest build bulwarks against the city that maketh war with thee, until it fall.

Which is the reality? Is it environmentalist? Is it warmongering? What is the underlying reasoning behind these verses?

For my own part, I was a religious liberal (we'll get to that later). Yet, the Torah on many occasions is *definitely* not liberal. Not by *any* definition of that oft-reinterpreted word.

I faced a challenge. But I also had the answer to that challenge. It came from my mother: Before you can really engage with something from another tradition, you have to be able to appreciate the axis of good on which it lays.

Because I was commenting on *every single reading* in the Torah, I had to strip down my preconceptions and beliefs. Instead of seeing Torah on a modern axis of Right vs. Left, or on an older Jewish perspective of Legal vs. Mystical or on a philosophical axis of Platonic vs. Aristotelian, I had to find the Torah's own axis. Part of that involved really understanding the purpose of each bit of the boring bits (e.g., Mishkan) and understanding how to reconcile the hard bits (e.g., Sotah).

I delivered my short little speeches every Sabbath, 7 times a Sabbath. I broke down the Torah. After a few years, I ended up with an unpublished book of about 590 little Torah *pensées*[1]. Then I began to reassemble the pieces, bit by bit. Only instead of building them around my previous philosophy and politics, I was trying to build them around *their own logic*. I wanted to assemble the *simplest* understanding I could to knit them together. In particular, I wanted to understand the many *Chukim*. In many traditions, *Chukim* (translated as statutes) are considered to be beyond reason, but I believed that *Chukim* are simply symbolic commandments, and they are eminently comprehendible once you understand the symbols and their underlying purpose.

All that said, the process of building back up what I had broken down was *not* simple. It took years. On more than one occasion I found myself asking G-d Himself (or Herself) for answers to riddles I could not unravel. Remarkably, whether though relaxing my own thoughts or being helped along by a Greater Power, I got my answers within minutes of asking[2].

---

[1] I thought about publishing it but then I showed it to a few people. One, a very learned scholar, said it was a treasure of Torah. The other, not so learned, couldn't understand a darned thing I was saying.

[2] I believe anybody can ask questions of G-d, and receive answers. For me, that experience is the closest I've ever come to seeing the

Eventually, I assembled one lens into Torah. Because it was compelling to me, it impacted my understanding of a person's basic relationship with G-d and the world.

In the beginning of the Torah, G-d creates many things. He then defines them as Good. Four things are *not* Good. Man, Heaven, Shabbat and Night. These four things are *not* associated with creation. From this, I understand that Good is associated with Creation.

When man was in the garden, man was *not* creative. Given everything he needed, man just hung out, probably smoking weed[1]. The problem was that man had been created in the image of G-d. He was to be judged not as a creation, but as a Creator. More fundamentally, I believe man, as an independent and *different* being was created in order to relate to G-d (just think how lonely the world is if you define *everything*). But a man who did not create had no basis of

---

hand of G-d... almost. One year, a very modest man whose identity I won't share was visiting our house. It was the holiday of Sukkot (the Feast of Tabernacles), so we were eating outside. A rainstorm was coming and, having lived in Oregon for decades, I knew we'd have to go inside. The visitor, who was both a tremendous scholar and a very simple man, raised his arms to heaven and said "Hashem, these people are so nice and are having such a nice meal, so take away the rain." Just like that, the clouds just *reversed direction*. Such a silly little thing, but I'd never encountered anything like that before, or since. My brother, who lived a few miles away, spoke to me later that day. He couldn't help but comment how weird it was that the storm just vanished.

[1] You know the phrase... "Portland, where young people go to retire."

relation with a G-d who had done nothing *but* either create or rest from his creation to establish the holiness of Shabbat.

Because man was failing in his task, G-d sought an *ezer kinegdo* among the animals. An "opposite helper" who would push man to create. There was none. So, G-d created woman, figuring that would give the man a kick in the pants. No dice. G-d then *engineered* the eating of the forbidden fruit. G-d realized that man had to had least be aware of evil in order to be driven to do good. But even that didn't work. Man (and Woman) simply dressed themselves to protect against the evil they now understood. They were still *not* creators.

But even more critically, they denied responsibility for what had occurred. They were neither creators nor *responsible* agents of their own destiny.

They had nothing in common with G-d and so they could not relate to G-d. They served no purpose in this state. This was why they were expelled. They had to create, and to take responsibility, in order to survive the Evil of the world outside the Garden.

It was better for Man and Womankind to know Good *and* Evil than it was to know neither. To borrow coarsely from another tradition: it is better to have a Yin and a Yang than just a gray circle.

But Good and Responsibility, aren't the only aspects that matter. The Torah is not unipolar. The other critical pole is Holiness. A Rabbi I respect greatly had challenged me to define holiness and after a couple years this is what I came to: Holiness is connection to the timeless.

Charity can be Holy because it enables people to look past the pressing challenges of the here and now. It gives them a chance to relate to the unchanging. Offerings can be Holy because they connect to G-d. Shabbat is Holy because we step outside of time.

There is a sort of dualism here: Creation is change while Holiness is unchanging. One does not directly touch the other, but they still influence and impact one another. In the Five Books of Moses, we use Goodness to establish Holiness. We have to invest our tangible and time-bound reality in order to touch the timeless. We abstain from work and live off our weekly production on Shabbat and the past year following the Sabbatical Year. We invest our produce in offerings. We give our money as charity.

In order to experience many forms of Holiness, we also have to be distant from Evil. We have to be *tahor*, or pure. Exposure to evil – to loss of potential creativity – is *tumah*. We avoid mingling *tumah* and *tahor* whenever we can.

These principles explain the vast majority of *Chukim* (and of the laws that apply to Jews alone). Humanity is inherently exposed to loss – we live in a world of increasing entropy. The only thing we can do beyond minimizing loss is connect to the lossless divine through symbolism.

A lot of the Torah is about exactly that.

This framework enables us to define, in understandable ways, the *Mishkan* (Tabernacle), the offerings, the *Parah Adumah* (Red Heifer), *Azazel* (the scapegoat), the *Arba'at Haminim* (Four Species) and so much more.

The key for me was that *this* lens on Torah (and I totally accept there are many faces of Torah) sought to engage with the text on its own terms. On its own axis of good. So much of what we study today is an attempt to see Torah as if through layers of colored film. We've got the ancient Greek and Roman layer of philosophy and law, then the Medieval European layer of Christian and Muslim theology, then the Enlightenment layer of "rational" argument, and the post-Enlightenment (almost Romantic) layer, and then the modern layers. When we look and try to understand the purpose of the original document, we look *through* all of these layers – as if they are all somehow part of that original layer. Given the number of obvious things missed that you can discover if you try to read the text in its own context, I believe the symbolic reality of the Five Books of Moses was as distant from Greek and Roman thought as it is from modern thought. Trying to understand it looking *through* those later frameworks is very difficult indeed[1].

I wanted to strip away those layers and try to understand the core values of the Torah through its own lens (at least as best as I can) and then apply one layer of perspective – a modern layer that can make sense of it all to us today.

---

[1] This is not an argument against the Oral Torah. I follow standard Jewish Law (Halacha), derived from all these layers. In addition, I keep finding that our *oral practice* matches up beautifully with this underlying symbolism. I just think the intervening era's preconceptions have concealed what would have once been obvious *symbolic explanations* for our practices.

The next step was to identify the cycle of Goodness and Holiness (with growing responsibility) as a recipe for human fulfillment through continuous growth. It doesn't have to be individual; it can be societal (e.g., support for priests), but it raises people up nonetheless. This cycle, the cycle of human fulfillment, became something that deeply impacted my religious, spiritual, political and economic thought.

At its core, the cycle of Goodness and Holiness leading to ever increasing Responsibility isn't a unique one. It doesn't even apply to Abrahamic religions alone. Touching the timeless is a near universal longing[1]. Dedicating one's produce to achieving that is, again, a near universal thing. Even responsibility, although unevenly allocated, is a common theme across many societies.

Nonetheless, it answered those two questions that confounded my earlier and simpler model.

What about the Maoist? His philosophy was based not on maximizing human fulfillment but on trying to achieve fairness. These aren't at all the same things.

That ties into the charitable question. If the charity you give results in a person no longer being driven to create and then connect with the timeless, then your charity has become

---

[1] Non-religious care for the planet is a version of this. So is feeding Buddhist monks.

counterproductive. You can actually rob a person of their material and spiritual potential.

So, we must try to structure and give charity in a way that enables and encourages people to experience the cycle of fulfillment. Not just "a hand up instead of a hand out" (or teaching a man to fish), but helping a person appreciate creation while helping them understand that the way in which they use their productivity can have a fundamental impact on our world.

Struggling with the Divine Perspective

For me everything above eventually falls within a religious framework. We walk in the path of G-d in order to relate to G-d. But despite that, as I share in the following write-up, there must always be a distance between humankind and our Creator.

In the Five Books of Moses, G-d's role is cast in a way that is almost impossible to understand. There is a fundamental divide between the divine and the human perspectives and the Torah doesn't do anything to hide it. What is for me the most personal expression of this is actually quite subtly alluded to in the text.

Avram (Abraham) was one of Terach's three sons (I think they were triplets, given that they are described as being born the same year). One was named after the past (Av means father). One was named after the present: Nachor means "sneeze." The third was Haran, named after education or the future.

The kids were named after the past, present and future.

Then Haran died in front of his father and, a few verses later, Terach (their father) left his homeland of Ur Kasdim (Chaldea). The name of this place literally means "Destroyers of Light."

Years later, after Avram has just fought the war with the four kings, G-d promises Avram he will have many descendants. Avram believes G-d and is credited with righteousness. Then G-d says something striking. He says: "I brought you out of Ur Kasdim to this land to inherit it."

Avraham doesn't simply believe *this*. Instead, he says: "How can I know?"

There are many possible reasons for this response. One, that touches modern issues very closely, is that Avram didn't want to dispossess the people already in the land. We know from the war that Avram had a treaty with those people. Another possible reason is that Avram thought he brought himself from Ur Kasdim; or at least that his father brought them out. He doesn't credit G-d with bringing them out. A third answer, the answer I want to focus on, is for me the most difficult one.

In 1975, my oldest brother died in an accident in the Idaho wilderness. He had just turned seven. That same day, my parents left their home of 8 years. A home they had built nail by nail and board by board. They had built the hydroelectric system. They had hacked a life out of an incredibly inhospitable place. And, in a moment, they abandoned it when my brother died there.

When I read this verse, this is what I recalled. My parents left when their eldest son died. Perhaps Terach left Ur Kasdim for the same reason. Perhaps G-d (who is, after all, in control of everything) had taken Haran and driven Terach and his family from Ur Kasdim. From the place where light is destroyed.

Imagine being in Avram's shoes. Imagine that G-d, with whom you have a direct relationship, had just implied that He had taken your beloved brother *in order to make your family move*.

220

Your trust would, at the very least, waver.

G-d's response is to double down. He promises Avram's descendants will be driven into slavery and then subjected to genocidal attacks. Afterwards, they will be redeemed and brought out to their land. In the future, there will be no question that G-d brought the people out of a place of darkness. But G-d will do it *through* darkness. He won't just magically transport the people to freedom.

Instead, millions will die.

When the time comes for the first iteration of that reality (there is no country specified and I think it is speaking about Germany as much as it is about Egypt), Moshe resists G-d's vision. He constantly and consistently resists. He can't accept this vision.

The Torah doesn't hide this. It also doesn't diminish Moshe for his perspective. While Aaron does whatever G-d wants, Aaron isn't chosen by G-d.

Moshe is.

Moshe, the one who can't just agree with G-d, is G-d's chosen one.

In fact, this conflict of outlooks permeates the entire Five Books of Moses. In Parshat Vayikra (the beginning of Leviticus), the sacrifices are described from the perspective of the layman. In the entire reading, only one sacrifice is called Holy. The sacrifice of flour that is *eaten* by the priests. Everything else involves destruction. Animals slaughtered and burned in their entirety, even flour burned up into nothing. From the Everyman's perspective, this isn't Holy. And for those who like to point to animal sacrifice in other nations, it often wasn't holy for them either. They ate (as far as I know) the meat that they sacrificed. It was like a barbeque. But we burned it up into nothing. But in the next reading, which comes from the priest's perspective, almost all of it is Holy or Holy of Holies. These animals are somehow converted from physical reality to spiritual reality. Something greater is made. There is no loss and no destruction – just the instantiation of holiness. The Everyman, in this reading, can't see this. He doesn't really need to. There is more than one perspective.

There is this divine perspective. This divine reality. This reality in which people, *even people*, can be sacrificed for spiritual ends. Haran dies in Ur Kasdim. The result is the first family that moves between cultures and a couple – Avram and Sarai – who have the most influential marriage in the history of humankind. Haran would have died at some point – thousands of years in our past – and *we* can see the spiritual payoff. But we can also understand how Avram would have struggled with it. How he could never truly accept it.

We can even accept and celebrate the Exodus from Egypt. Yes, huge numbers of Jewish children were killed. Huge numbers of Egyptians died. Nonetheless, we see and celebrate the result. The positive, and spiritual survives, while the pain of those who are lost disappears.

In a way it reflects the divine maxim that kindness is preserved for thousands of generations while hate vanishes in three or four.

The Akeidah (Sacrifice of Isaac) brings it all into even sharper perspective. Hashem commands Avraham to sacrifice his son. Avraham cannot understand. And yet he performs the commandment. He accepts the divine perspective even though he cannot perceive it.

This is the Fear of G-d.

One of the members of my community was reflecting on the talk and, again and again, described the divine reality as a fundamentally irrational reality. But I don't agree with that assessment. It isn't irrational, it is just hard to internalize.

222

My understanding of this perspective is this: G-d created Mankind *so* He could have a relationship with us. But we needed to be fundamentally different for there to *be* a relationship. Otherwise, we'd just be windup robots. There needed to be some core distance between us. Death provides that distance. Death and sin. As is stated before we leave the Garden of Eden – if we were to eat from the Tree of Life we would become like G-d and that would defeat the purpose of our creation.

We need sin, we need death, we need fear – so that we can be different than G-d. We must be different than G-d. But then, in order to serve our purpose, we have to try to bridge that difference. *Not* by truly internalizing the divine perspective. If that were the case, Aaron would have been chosen and not Moshe. No, we bridge the difference by deferring to G-d *even* as we fail to understand the perspective we can never share with Her.

We build a relationship with G-d. A relationship in which we walk in the path of G-d as Creators who ultimately connect with the timeless. But a relationship in which we are *not* like G-d and do not see the world as He does. Only our priests, the Kohanim, take on that perspective. Like the first of their number, Aaron, they adopt that divine perspective. But that is not the place for the rest of us. We Fear G-d. We *accept* that there is a greater vision. We can even describe it. But we cannot internalize it.

As my mother used to say: "I can understand the music, I can analyze the music, but I cannot feel the music."

There are so many of this 'convert-the-physical-to-spiritual' commandments that we no longer observe. We rarely destroy the physical to create the spiritual. We don't offer sacrifices. We don't practice most of the art of ritual purity. We don't follow a wide variety of the symbolic restrictions on other activities. We don't subsume the natural to the divine.

But there are some of these commandments we still embrace. For example, we *can* choose to live without interest-bearing debt; we can ignore the opportunity to share real-world risks and instead simply pretend that they do not exist. With this commandment (and others like the Sabbatical year) we *can't* understand it. It makes no sense. And yet... if we have the Fear of G-d, we will embrace it.

We will understand that our perspective is not His, but we will follow His commandments nonetheless.

The centerpiece of the Yom Kippur service, in ancient times, beautifully illustrates the opportunity of the divine relationship. It also demonstrates, in a way, just a slice of that divine perspective.

The centerpiece is the ritual of Azazel, called the 'scapegoat' in many English translations. Famously, there are two goats. One goat is sacrificed, the second is loaded with the sins of the people and shoved off a cliff in the wilderness.

Growing up, we had goats. Goats are mischievous and rambunctious. In the Five Books of Moses' description, one goat is sacrificed to Yud-Key-Vav-Kay – the name of G-d that embraces the past, present and future. The second is driven away – and dedicated to Az-Azel. The name Az-Azel literally means 'goat of disappearance.'

For me the lesson is clear. We *all* die. But we can become part of forEver (Yud-Key-Vav-Kay) or – like our sins – we can be a part of ForNever.

We can be a part of eternity; or it can be as if we never existed.

Being a part of forever requires building a relationship with G-d. Not through belief (because we can never truly internalize the divine perspective), but through action.

Even – especially – through reluctant action.

MARRIAGE

Not long ago, it was common to compare Western and Indian marriages. Not Indian Love marriages, but Indian arranged marriages. The argument went that divorce rates and self-reported rates of happiness seemed to be higher among Indians who had arranged marriages than Indians or Westerners who had "Love" marriages. The way a classic Indian (or Muslim or Jewish) arranged marriage works is that the families identify suitable matches and then the couple meets a few times to ensure they aren't repulsed by each other and then they get engaged.

The bar is really low in terms of their personal "spark." Which is why no Westerner (with the exception of some religious folk) would submit to an arranged marriage. Obviously, being arranged, it can't be a true expression of that highest of emotions and aspirations: Love. So, self-reported happiness and marital longevity aside, it just can't be worth it.

Personally, I think the Indian model is impractical for reasons other than a lack of "Love." An arranged marriage is defined by the priorities of the families involved. The families are getting married, often even more than the individuals are. That just doesn't work in a society in which finding your own way is valued far more highly than adhering to the path of those around you.

But really, we all know it just comes down to Love. The West enshrines Love. Come to think of it, maybe that's the problem. Defining Love is a bit challenging, after all. We've got the old "somebody who understands and cherishes you just the way you are" or the "somebody who makes you truly happy' or the 'somebody you always want around" or "somebody who makes you go all aflutter." And, of course, you also have misdiagnosed Lust.

You get the gist. It's really hard to put your finger on Love. The real problem is that when you pick one of these definitions they end up, well, pretty wiggly. I mean, they *feel* like forever at the time, but once you get a few years in (or a few hours) things kind of just wear off.

"I cherished him/her just the way he/she was - until he/she bought a Corvette/$600 heels." That turns into separate bank accounts, which are apparently a must nowadays in order to protect Love because, you know, you can commit to spending your *lives* together, but you can't commit to sharing your *money*.

I mean, you've got to draw the line somewhere, right?

Or "he doesn't do the dishes" or "she never finishes anything." It was cute while you were dating, but it just gets grating – right? You're different people after all. Even if you were perfectly matched, you *change*. You may once have fit together like a hand in a glove, but maybe the hand put on a little weight and maybe the glove got put in the dryer. Perfection rarely lasts.

So, all these definitions of Love rarely last. Which leads to bleak disappointment and a commitment to nothing and a decision (if you have kids) that they'd be better off seeing you miserable and alone than miserable and together.

Soon enough, people abandon marriage as a broken institution. After all, it is the ultimate sign of Love and (pretty words aside) Love never lasts. So, people end up replacing marriage with either meaningless sex or "non-committed" relationships which become less and less interesting in their own time. I mean, getting off is nice, but it doesn't scratch the deeper itch you *really* need to scratch.

Then again, marriage isn't scratching it either.

Cue mass mental illness, vast amounts of loneliness (I saw a survey saying 62% of Americans felt alone *before corona*) and a really, really sad state of affairs.

And I'm just talking about what I've seen in the movies.

The awful thing it, I don't think any of this is inevitable. I really can't speak to your relationships, of course. I recognize everybody is different. But I can talk about my own relationship and maybe there will be something useful in there.

So here goes.

First off, Rebecca and I don't have an arranged marriage and we don't have a "Love" marriage.

We have a "self-arranged" marriage.

We met online, before video chat. We emailed for a week or two. We talked online – voice only. We established our *goals*. I could say *values*, but really *values* don't really speak to action and that'll end up being important. All we knew of each other was our words and the sounds of our voices.

We knew we were compatible in thought and conversation. I knew she was loving and caring and thoughtful and strong. But, critically, for those first three months, looks and mannerisms were off the table.

Then we met.

It was rough at first. Nonetheless, Bec knew we were going to get married within a day of meeting me in person[1]. It took me about 3 days to realize the same thing. We ended up getting formally engaged after spending a grand total of 3 weeks together.

Was this due to a sensation of instant and overwhelming love? No, it was not[2]. People who saw us together knew we weren't a fit. We had little personal chemistry – at least in person. We were great on the phone.

Nonetheless, we both knew our 'arranged marriage' qualities lined up. We knew we were compatible in many ways so we both believed we could work through all the other stuff. And there was lots of other stuff. In the "Practical" department we had to deal with living 8,000 miles apart, jobs, friends and

---

[1] Apparently, it had something to do with Filbert.

[2] I don't want to overstate things. We didn't *not* love each other at the beginning. We'd expressed love to each other. We certainly cared about each other. But the white hot passionate "I can't be without you" love wasn't there.

all that stuff. In the "Love" department, we had to deal with issues around attraction and mannerisms[1].

The marriage was built on the "arranged marriage" qualities – most critically shared *goals*. Only it was self-arranged, so the degree of *real* compatibility was deeper than any third parties could really understand. Nonetheless, just as with an arranged marriage, not every 'Love marriage' star had to align at the outset.

So, what were those goals? They weren't specific things like 'write five books' or 'have five children.' They were broad goals. In our case, I think our mutual goal was to live a G-dly life – whatever that meant. We tried learning Torah together, early on. We each bought and read "Derech Hashem (the Way of G-d)" by Rabbi Moshe Chaim Luzzatto. It didn't do anything for us, though. We got a few chapters in, but that was it. Part of living a G-dly life, of being committed to that, was figuring out what that meant.

That last point can't be stressed nearly enough. The fact is, as 25-year-olds, we had no ideas what the possibilities were 10, 20 or 50 years hence. I thought I had a pretty stable understanding of the world and my place in it, but as I already covered, I was wrong. We couldn't commit to specifics. They wouldn't last. The one thing we knew was that our potential would be uplifted by marriage. We could be more together than we could be alone.

----

[1] Oh, and my clothes. I wore sh-tkickers, for example. Even at my wedding. Bec managed to tolerate them.

That was the building block of everything else.

Of course, in order to achieve this, we had to shift the modern purpose of marriage. It wasn't to express Love. It wasn't to acquire happiness. It wasn't to avoid loneliness. All of these things could be achieved, by and by. But they were side effects. The primary point of marriage was instead to achieve a mutual goal.

With this in mind, what happens to the questions people ask about marriage in the modern age? You know:

"Does this make me happy?"

"What does my partner/fiancé/spouse do for me?"

"Do I love him/her?"

"Can I be my truest self with this person?"

"Would I be better off with someone else?"

All of those questions fall by the wayside. They aren't the point. Instead, a new question replaces them: "What can I do to make this marriage achieve its goals?"

To paraphrase JFK, "Ask not what the marriage can do for you, but what you can do for the marriage."

There's a Jewish tradition that on the wedding day a Bride and Groom are considered a King and Queen. The question is then asked (as it always is in Judaism), how long are they King and Queen for? The classic answer is: for as long as they treat each other that way. But what does it mean to treat somebody like a King or a Queen?

I actually learned the answer to this on my wedding day.

I wanted my jacket. I realized it would be better to ask somebody else to get it for me than to get it myself. As I was King, it was *an honor for them to serve me.* In an even purer sense, it was an honor for them to honor me.

This is what separates Queen Elizabeth from Moammar Ghaddafi. Ghaddafi had power, but it is honor (at least for many) to honor Elizabeth. It is an honor for many Japanese to honor their Emperor, even though historically the Emperor has almost never had any power.

It seems so simple, but that is such a foundational concept. For a marriage to really succeed, in my data set of one, it has to be *an honor* for the couple to serve each other. Not a quid pro quo, mind you, but an independent honor for each party to the marriage. That sense of honor can and should be cultivated, which we'll get to. But a pretty good starting place is the knowledge that the couple's goals are shared. When you honor your spouse, you are taking a step towards your mutual life goals.

This is how you address the problem of shifting understanding. What is a G-dly life? Understandings change. But if you know your spouse is committed to that goal then you can find honor in serving your spouse even as your spouse's understanding of that goal develops.

In fact, Rebecca and I have very similar understandings, but our emphasis is very different. My emphasis tends to be more outward – in writing and speaking and analyzing the world at large. Hers is more inward, focusing on the family itself. Of course, in mutual honor and respect, we intermingle constantly. I serve her focus and she serves mine and our mutual understanding grows as a result.

I know it hardly sounds romantic, but we'll get to that part soon enough. For now, let's stick with a basic concept: A marriage needs to be built around mutual goals and a mutual commitment to helping each other achieve those goals.

There is one caveat. Not every goal will work for this. The mutual goal has to be something bigger than yourselves. I talked about an itch that needed scratching. That itch is called *Purpose*. A purpose doesn't have to be religious, but I'll borrow from a famous Biblical story to show just how important it can be.

We all know the story of Joseph, right? Punk kid who thinks he's "all that" is ganged up on by his pissed off brothers who sell him into slavery. He goes down to Egypt, where he ends up being the big man in town and shows his brothers what's what. Great fun... somebody ought to make a musical.

Being named Joseph, and being a punk kid who thought he was "all that," I always identified with the Biblical Joseph. I still do, although for very different reasons and with some great reservations. When I began to really dig into his story, I saw a bit more to it than I had before. I've written more about this elsewhere, so I'm only going to touch on the relevant points here. Those points being focused on how Joseph interacted with those around him.

With his first set of dreams, Joseph just let them hang out there. They spoke for themselves, or so it seems. The brothers' corn would bow to his corn and the entire family's stars would bow to his star. Nothing says "I'm the man" quite like that.

But if Joseph had had a thought about what was bigger than himself, then another interpretation might have sprung to mind. His brothers would be dependent on him for food, and he'd provide it. And their fates (i.e., stars) – and the fates of all the family – would be dependent on him. And, again, he'd ensure their fates would be good. Instead of them serving him, *he'd be serving them*. The real hint of this is that his mother's astronomical sign (the moon) would bow to him as well. She was already dead. *She* wasn't going to bow to him. But her legacy would be dependent on him.

But he didn't say any of this, and so they stuck him in a pit and sold him.

With the next set of dreams, having experienced slavery and prison, Joseph has learned a bit. The two prisoners come to him with their dreams. One is a baker (Egypt was the land of bread in the ancient Mediterranean). In the baker's dream, there are three baskets of bread, and a bird comes and picks at them. The other was a vintner (Canaan was the land of wine). In the vintner's dream, three vines grow and produce fruit which are then served to Pharaoh.

Joseph interprets the bakers dream as suggesting he'll lose his head in three days while the vintner will press wine into his King's cup.

Through this we can see that Joseph is learning.

Why?

Because the dreams could be about nations, not *just* people. In three generations (three Pharaohs or Levi, Yocheved and Moses) the baker's already baked goods will be picked at from heaven (the birds) while the vines which have grown and sprouted (the children of Israel, who claim Canaan) will be dedicated to the service of the King.

Joseph doesn't say this though. He's learned not to piss people off. But he hasn't learned to *harness* them.

The vintner gets out of prison and promptly forgets about him.

The third set of dreams is where he gets it. He hears Pharoah's dream about the corn and the cows. He immediately conflates them – although they clearly mean two separate things (corn is about food, cows are about national potential). Then he does something remarkable. He talks about the problem, then he proposes a solution. But he wraps that solution in a key phrase:

> *let Pharaoh look out a man discreet and wise,*
> *and set him over the land of Egypt... so that*
> *the land perish not through the famine.*

He's not speaking to Pharoah's *needs*. He's given Pharoah the opportunity to serve something bigger than himself. The land. He's given Pharoah *purpose*.

Pharoah can't help but buy what Joseph is selling[1].

That sense of purpose then defines Joseph's behavior for the rest of his life. He does what he does to his brothers so they can see past themselves and serve others. He raises sons who are the first two brothers in Torah not to fight. I believe they don't fight with one another because have their eyes on a purpose greater than their own honor. And his wife, Asnat, is the only one of the wives of Yaacov's sons listed in the people who came down to Egypt. There are 69 names from Yaacov's descendants that are listed. But the Torah said there are 70 people. I believe she is the 70th – the mother of the first brothers who didn't fight. By the way, Asnat raised those boys. The Torah makes clear her husband was always travelling for work. She too was a paragon of Purpose.

Purpose is what motivates people more than anything else. I believe this is one reason why global warming is such a popular topic in the West. In a society that is less religious, people can still serve the land – just like Pharoah.

They can serve the planet.

This idea of Purpose is why the goal of a marriage must be something beyond the couple themselves. It can't be Happiness, that is self-focused. It can't be Love. It can't be Peace (even within the house). It can't be Honor.

---

[1] For years this was my primary interpretation of what was going on with the dreams. I've now added additional layers to it, but this isn't a book about Biblical exegesis.

It has to be something bigger.

For Rebecca and me, it was G-dliness.

We wanted to build a G-dly home.

The happiness, love, peace and honor would all come in time. They'd already begun to grow – we were certainly not unhappy, unloving or at war with one another. But they would truly flourish later. There is nothing in the world I prefer than being with my wife. I love her immensely. I love her more today than I did yesterday or five years ago or ten years ago. Our relationship has continually grown stronger and stronger. We fought once, in our first year of marriage, and that was it. We haven't had days or weeks or months – or even hours – where the relationship was in a lull[1]. Our marriage has been a constant and ever-growing reality and a source of every increasing joy. I hear people talk about how marriage is a "struggle", or you have "ups and downs", or you need to "make difficult compromises." I experience *none* of that. I know it's there for others, but I can't really understand it.

So how, aside from deep mutual respect and shared purpose, did we get here? Specifically, how did we build our love?

---

[1] Well, there is one exception. A few weeks ago, there was about an hour of lull. It was about a difference of opinion on maintaining decorum over the blessings at the Sabbath table (I was very unhappy with particular kids and expressed that quite clearly – Rebecca was not happy with the expression). We continued to have some differences (my hillbilly past deals with some things differently). Generally, we short-circuit disputes very, very early on so we can focus on the big picture.

In our day and age, people like to believe that feelings and emotions are immutable. Some things are immutable, sure. But not many. Most people, in most areas of their lives, occupy a point on a spectrum. It could be a spectrum of love for coffee. Or a spectrum of social skills. Or even a spectrum of sexual preferences. Put men in prison and a significant number will adopt homosexual behaviors. Take them out and they become straight again. Some men can't be anything but straight and some can't be anything but gay. But a lot of people reside somewhere in the middle. On the spectrum.

When I met Bec I had a strong preference for short and slender women. That's not Bec. She is *very* far from O'Beast (my cousin's word for really, really, obese), she just isn't slender. And she certainly isn't short. She wasn't my "type".

She was, as you can see in this photo, *beautiful*.

Just not my type.

Bec in 2007

I decided, in light of everything else, to make her my type.

I know that sounds horribly non-romantic, but it really isn't. You see, Rebecca was *and is* this magnificent person. My feelings about her height or her figure just had to be brought into line. And the two of us, together, could create something great – even Holy.

Again, the little stuff had to be brought into compliance.

Chassidic (and other) thought is fond of talking about the animal soul and the spiritual soul. The animal soul has certain desires. The question is what the spiritual soul does about it. Does the spiritual soul seek to minimize them or control them? Some would suggest that is impossible. I prefer the answer that says that the spiritual soul can and should seek to harness and redirect them. After all, we live on a spectrum. Most of us, in most things, are adjustable[1].

The thing was, I didn't know if I could actually adjust in this way. I was worried I wouldn't be able to. The process of self-adjustment actually ended up being straight-forward *and* rapid. Once I committed to it[2], it took days, not weeks, months or years.

---

[1] This is why seeking 'yourself' is often so unrewarding. You expect to find A Truth when in fact there is very little to be discovered. Very few things are immutable, and chances are you already know what they are. Instead of finding some core, rewarding, truth you're more likely to find emptiness, which sucks. If you want to grasp something great, look *outside* yourself and adjust your reality to fit.

[2] Thus, cutting back the concept of "what if?" Once you commit, "What if?" is a terribly counterproductive idea. You might explore it seeking some Truth, but there is no Truth there. There is just variance, variance *created* simply by questioning it.

The basic principle is this: in any person (or thing) you can find that which you like and that which you don't like. If you think about what you don't like, even or especially when trying to suppress it, you won't be able to think about anything else. But you *can* focus on what you *do* like. And you can think about that. And then you can build on it. Actually, you can build on it continually – throughout the course of a marriage. You can also *recast* that which you aren't so keen on into a light that is far more positive. These things can become a source of attraction. You can act on them and build that love.

It is *not* false. It is *not* shallow. It would be if you were lying to yourself. But in *most* areas, *most* people are adjustable. Your inner reality *can* be shaped. And then it becomes your truth.

The key is to *choose* which path you take in order to support higher goals. You harness your animal soul to your spiritual one. The "Love Marriage" is developed within the values and goals of the "Self-Arranged Marriage."

Although this approach isn't popular in our age of self-discovery and self-actualization it is a very very old concept. Aristotle wrote about it in the Nicomachean Ethics:

> *men become builders by building and lyre players by playing the lyre; so too we become just by doing just acts, temperate by doing temperate acts and brave by doing brave acts.*

I would add, "(wo)men become lovers by thinking thoughts (and doing acts) of love."

It took a few weeks to overcome areas of resistance. But that wasn't the end of the story. The process of continual growth, of continually *strengthening* the attraction and the connection, is still ongoing. And, although Rebecca might not explain it the same way, it applies to both of us. She really had to overcome my social issues; she couldn't fix all of them.

Of course, the cultivation of that attraction remains a servant to the greater purpose. To the holy life. To trying to do the best with whatever you're given. Bec and I have been through a fair amount. Nonetheless, every challenge has been placed within the context of that larger purpose. And each of us knew we were stronger together, so we leaned on each other for that strength. Because of that, those challenges didn't weaken our relationship. Quite the opposite occurred. Through every challenge, our marriage has grown stronger.

The Nicomachean Ethics quote is about more than physical attraction, of course. It can also speak to the concept of mutual royalty – of seeing one another as King and Queen. To extend it still further, I'd write:

> *we become servants to each other and our marriage by doing acts of service.*

We develop that mutual royalty by acting on it.

I started all this by critiquing love. But now I claim I am in love. So how do I define Love?

I define it in a Biblical sense. The Bible continually connects the concept of love with the concept of 'cleaving to' another – whether it be a spouse or G-d or even food. Love is a desire to cleave to another, to stick with them. To be with them constantly. Funnily enough, it leads to (almost) all the other definitions listed earlier:

- Somebody who understands and cherishes you just the way you are? The "way you are" had to grow and morph, but it is still true.
- Somebody who makes you truly happy.
- Somebody you always want around.
- Somebody who makes you go all aflutter.
- And, of course, misdiagnosed Lust.

All that is true. But so is one more definition:

- Somebody who makes you more than you could ever be without them.

This, thank G-d, is what we experience. Our "self-arranged" marriage has become a "Love marriage."

The best Love marriage I know of.

I want to qualify a few things, though.

First, Rebecca and I do not enjoy total alignment. We wouldn't make each other better if we did. In child-rearing (I'll get there), I'm more hillbilly. Not that our children can tell the difference[1]. One of our children, a master manipulator, came

---

[1] Well, if they're reading this, they can now. Kids: even though you know we don't *think* in lockstep, we'll still *act* in lockstep.

to me once and said, "I hate that you and mommy are the same person." The kid couldn't play us off each other. With very, very few exceptions, we move in lockstep as far as others are concerned.

But there's a more fundamental way in which we're different. Rebecca is the one with the better sense of the truly big picture. In all our lives, we have opportunities to touch the timeless. But we sacrifice the tangible to it. Sacrifice, in this sense, isn't a loss. It is instead an offering of the tangible in order to create the intangible. A simple example: going on vacation. I *hate* it. I'm sacrificing valuable time for something nebulous. In reality, the conversion is well worth it. But, especially considering family history, it is hard for me. Other things fall into the same bucket: spending money on a house. For me, even buying houses is hard if renting makes more financial sense. Or music lessons for a kid who almost certainly won't be a musician. Or nice shoes for a Bar Mitzvah.

I *know* all these things are worthwhile. I really do. I know they create an intangible beauty that is all the greater for being intangible. I *write* about this stuff.

But it's still hard to really grasp it.

That all said, she's my Queen. I *know* when I honor her, I raise us both up. And I honor her by recognizing and facilitating her ability to create the intangible by dedicating that which is tangible.

In the end, we both grow.

So, is any of this useful to anybody else?

Is it useful for our kids who might be reading this?

I don't know. But I wrote it, I'm sharing it, because I hope it might be. I know *Bec* is unusual. My brother likes to call her the world's only non-neurotic Jewish woman. I know everything I talked about above wouldn't have mattered a wit with some of the other women I dated. Bec is unusual, but so are *we*. With the exception of my mother's story of her own grandmother's married life[1], I haven't heard of anything quite like our marriage. So, I'm very reluctant to give advice. But if I have something to offer, it is this:

1. Try to cultivate the royal spirit. Whether you're in an arranged marriage, a love marriage or something in between, commit to mutual service. It's hard, especially since you have to give and not know if you're going to receive. But let it run for a little while and see if it can't grow.

2. Cultivate the positive in order to set aside the negative[2]. Harness the animal soul in service to the spiritual soul.

3. Find a greater purpose and cling to it. If you are not-yet-married, focus less on the spark and the undeniable attraction and instead focus on the goals – because with that, the spark, the love and the attraction can all grow. If you are already married, try

---

[1] With the woman who died when her husband called to her from Heaven.

[2] And do the inverse, where necessary, outside the marriage.

to find and develop a common purpose. I have no idea how you'd do this, but it can't hurt to try, right?

And that's pretty much it.

I'll end with a fun little story. Soon after our marriage, we lived in London. We lived near these two major roads in Edgeware. Right where they met there was this little gap in the buildings. That gap was Heronsgate, a little one-lane road leading away from the noise and hustle of the main roads. You'd walk down it and in less than a hundred meters, the noise and the busyness of the city would seem to vanish. You'd be surrounded by trees and quiet flats with beautiful gardens. You'd be in another world. I wrote my first two books while living there. For *me*, it was almost magical. Rebecca's experience was something a little different. That first year, Rebecca had been working *extremely* hard. She had two jobs and a monster commute to South London. Initially, I worked from home doing consulting for the global transaction tax company. While the consulting paid well, I didn't work that many hours. And so, quite simply, I wasn't working nearly as hard as she was. Beyond her work, Rebecca was also doing all the cooking.

I'd made a Shabbat meal a few weeks prior to our marriage. But I was living in a very low-end apartment and the oven was terrible and so was the food. Rebecca thought I couldn't cook (although I did blame the oven, she didn't believe me and just ascribed it to total lack of skill). Anyway, that whole first year, she'd been doing *all* the cooking (the Vietnamese fish balls were to die for). As well as earning most of the money etc... etc...[1]

Near the end of that first year, we went to dinner at my brother's family's apartment. In the middle of the meal, my sister-in-law asked "Joseph, do you still make that wonderful manicotti?"

It's funny now, but at the time Rebecca turned to me and said, "YOU MAKE MANICOTTI??"

I'd told her I knew how to cook, but she hadn't believed me. Really! I swear! Unfortunately, she'd been doing all the cooking because she thought *I couldn't*. I certainly wasn't trying to give off that impression, but I did.

Today? I rarely cook. She enjoys cooking and she's much better at it than I am. But I can, and do, pinch hit when called upon. She just knows she can call upon me now.

I never have made manicotti, though.

Childlessness

First up: the facts. Rebecca and I were married in December 2001. We had our first child in June of 2007. Considering that raising children was a critical part of our mutual Purpose, this wasn't easy. It was the biggest challenge we've faced. It is also a struggle we talked about freely. We wanted people to know the challenges we were facing as we faced them. We didn't want

---

[1] Our fight had been about me not doing the dishes despite how much work she was doing. She was totally in the right which was why the fight lasted about a minute and a half.

people going through similar issues to somehow feel ashamed or alone.

The basic story was pretty simple. We expected problems. We had problems. We talked to providers, picking the one that seemed to know what he was doing[1]. We went through what was then a normal course of treatment. Clomifene (no effect). Metformin (bad effect). Then the hard-core stuff: gonadotrophins. They'd just come out with a pre-mixed, dosage controlled, system (a cool pen with a dosage-selecting twist cap) – but it cost more. So, instead, each month, we picked up these sets of glass vials from the back of a Thriftway. They cost thousands of dollars. The vials came in pairs. One vial had powder, the other bacteriostatic water. We'd crack the glass off the powder (I *hate* snapping the glass tops off of vials), mix it with the water, draw it with a massive needle and then inject into poor Bec intramuscularly[2]. I can't remember the frequency, but I think it might have been as much as twice daily. The whole time, Bec was undergoing tests. Blood tests almost daily, and ultrasounds to see how our progress was going. And then, at the end of each cycle (which we couldn't do

---

[1] We visited one doctor who explained why multiple rounds of treatment had a lower and lower chance of working. His argument was that somehow the IUI potency dropped. He didn't get the math of it – that if the IUI was able to work at all, the likelihood of you being in the 'it will work' group dropped each time it didn't because the possible successes dropped out of the population. It seemed he was either simplifying the math to a stupid level, or (even worse) that he didn't understand it. As an important aside, after 6 rounds of treatment, you'd have about a 5% chance of success.

[2] One time, I was mixing drugs and injecting her in the parking lot of a closed Fred Meyers in a Seattle suburb. Nothing says illegal activity quite like that. Thankfully, we garnered no police attention.

every month due to timing) we'd do the IUI. You can look it up to get details. One time we had to do it on Shabbat. The clinic was a good 10 miles away. After some halachic (Jewish legal) review, we prepaid for a cab to the clinic. It was worth it if we could get pregnant. But it didn't work.

Each time we tried, we failed to get pregnant.

The protocol in the United States was to do three rounds of IUI and then step up to IVF. With the fourth round, you only have about a 10% chance of success. The problem was, I couldn't understand why IVF would work any better. So, while that was the protocol, I basically felt that if IUI wasn't going to work, nothing else would either. But protocols are protocols, so we were ready to step up to IVF.

IVF came with its own challenges, though. First was cost. All in, IUI was maybe $5,000 a cycle. Considering our medications, IVF was closer to $15,000 to $20,000. It was a whole 'nother level. But we were willing to do it. Which brought us to the other challenge: Jewish religious law.

Portland didn't have the Jewish infrastructure to do IVF in a Halachic way. We knew what we wanted and so our choice was clear. I had a contract with Intel, but it was wrapping up. I applied for Permanent Residency in Australia and not that long after we moved Down Under.

We expected to start up with IVF using a Jewish organization that focused on just that. We expected a very similar set up as we'd had in Portland. But pretty much *everything* was different in Australia.

In Portland, we'd see the doctor every few days. In Australia, we saw the doctor twice over the course of months. The process we were going through was routine, and so there was really no need to see the doctor.

In Portland, you went through three rounds of IUI and then IVF. In Australia, they went through three rounds of IUI and then conducted an exploratory surgery to make sure everything was flowing properly. If you passed that test, then they did another three rounds of IUI. After all, there was no special reason why IVF would work in that situation. In the US, the surgery could run $15,000+. It didn't add up, considering the cost benefit analysis. But in Australia, the surgery was $1,800 – Australian. Thus, it made sense to do it.

What was the difference? Australia had a somewhat *market-based* economy for healthcare. Providers could charge whatever they wanted, but the government and insurance companies would only pay a fixed amount for particular services. You'd get a bill in your doctor's office and then run your insurance card and the insurance would pay their pre-agreed fees. Anything extra came out of your pocket. The result of this was *price competition*. You'd shop around, and we did, for cheaper services. For our surgery, we had to select the anesthesiologist, the clinic and the surgeon. We paid each separately. But each of them was competing for our business.[1] We didn't see the doctor much because we didn't need to, and

---

[1] My father, a total foreigner, spent 2 days in isolation in an E.R. Total bill, as a foreigner with no insurance or government subsidy? $1,200 USD.

it would have cost a lot to make her available. The system had faults, but my current ideas on healthcare build on it. It was quite a bit better than what we'd seen in the U.K. or the United States.

After about six months, we'd gone through two more rounds of IUI in Australia. We were down to our last round, with a 5% chance of success.

The entire time we'd been going through this, we'd been pretty level-headed. We'd kept our hopes down, as much as we could, with each round. We'd picked ourselves up quickly after each failure. We kept asking and figuring out what the next step would be.

All the stuff you're supposed to do.

On the religious front, we prayed. I bring a 'How to Win Friends and Influence People' approach to prayer. If you want G-d to bless you, you've got to have a plan for how you'll use those blessings to bless Him/Her. A bit of a quid pro quo. I think of G-d a bit like I think of a *good* parent. If your kid whines to you, you don't want to give them *anything*. You shouldn't give them *anything*. But if they come to you with a good *reason* for why they should have something (e.g., they've earned it, you promised it, or they'll use it well[1]) then you're likely to help them out. I prayed like that. I didn't really have an argument for why I deserved anything, and G-d didn't make *me* any promises. So, my prayers tended to fall into the

---

[1] This triumvirate of reasons dominates the Rosh Hashana prayers and Torah reading. We have Pakad (for earned blessings), Zocher (for promised blessings) and Teshuva (for blessings we'll use well).

category of "Here's what I want and here's how I'll use it."
Basically, I would try to raise my child in a way that was a
credit to G-d.

Jewish prayer has a place for those sorts of prayers. The
very end of our standing, silent prayer (the part we add things
to), reads:

> Act for the sake of Your right hand. Act for the
> sake of Your holiness. Act for the sake of Your
> Torah.

I'd had plenty of those prayers.

But we'd never gotten pregnant.

In the planning ahead category, we'd gone to educational
events about adoption. In Australia at least, it is *so so so* much
harder to adopt a child out than it is to simply abort one. The
paperwork and confirmations and later access rights places
such a terrible burden on adoption that almost nobody gets
adopted in Australia. Australia had 343 domestic adoptions in
the fiscal year 2019. That was a very high year. This is in a
country of 25 million with about 80,000 abortions a year.
Australia isn't alone in making it hard. But they are pretty far
up there. Just consider that in Australia there are over 230
abortions for every adoption while in the United States the rate
is 6 to 1. In Australia, at least, there are no protections for
unborn, and far *too many* for the already born.

The result is the loss of a lot of children who would find
loving and eager homes.

We were in our last round. The next step was going to be
IVF. Then we'd probably go back to the US and try to adopt

there, quite possibly internationally. It would be years until our family would be blessed with children.

During that sixth and final round, I remember driving up the Dandenong Highway (just before it goes under the train bridge into Caulfield). I remember it was dark. And for the first time, I let myself get angry. I was angry that we couldn't have children. I don't remember what I said, but the gist seemed to be that we were ready for children, dammit. We deserved a child, we'd raise it well, and it was time for G-d to finally step up.

The burst of anger only lasted a minute. I didn't regret it though. And, maybe, it was what worked. Maybe G-d just wanted a bit more passion. Whatever it was, we discovered we were pregnant just before Rosh Hashana. I remember reading the story of Sarah, who was visited by angels because she was *pakad* – she was deserving. Sarah who had a child at 90. And I remember crying with gratitude. A few weeks later, I was called up to the Torah reading of *n'arim* (where all the children are brought up to their once-annual Torah blessing). The community didn't know we were pregnant. The honor of being called up to *n'arim* was given to us as a bit of ritual good luck. I remember crying then as well.

And then, before too long, our eldest daughter was born.

Nava was delivered by a doctor trained at Saddam Hussain University in Baghdad. He was a substitute for my wife's regular doctor (who was on vacation). As an obviously religious Jew, I checked out the delivery doctor *politically*. I wanted to make sure he wouldn't harbor any ill-will towards us.

He checked out and then some.

Delivery was a bit exciting. We started off with a group of top-notch nurses. And then this emergency came up on a highway somewhere and that emergency came up in another part of the hospital and soon we were left with the C-team. They were led by a nurse who had her keys and ID dangling loosely off a long chain around her neck (less than appealing during examinations). This nurse told Bec she was almost there (and even summoned the doctor), when she had five hours to go. The nurse had no idea how to properly measure dilation. And then, at one point, she happily mentioned how cool it was that our daughter would be born on 7/7/7. It was cool, and I can remember her birthday, but it isn't what you want to tell a woman in labor.

Oh, and one more thing: Bec refused painkillers because she wanted to experience *everything*.

After Nava was born, we held her naming in our synagogue.

A young Yeshiva student came up to me and said, "Do you know why G-d makes it so hard for some women to have children?"

I knew the standard answer and I *hated* it. The standard answer was that G-d wanted the heartfelt prayers of righteous women. To me, that answer simply made G-d out to be cruel and evil-minded. I told the student I didn't want to hear what he was about to say.

"No, no," he said, "This isn't *that* answer."

"Then why?" I asked, gruffly.

"Because" said the student, "Some souls require more convincing before they're willing to come down from heaven."

It was a beautiful explanation. It moves from somehow blaming the mothers (or G-d) to praising the children. And it holds just as well. All the famous women in Torah who prayed and prayed for their children were granted *remarkable* children.

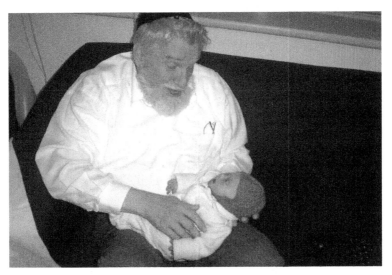

Nava, reacting to meeting my father

Blood on the Carpet

As the following digression reveals, our experience in the final stage of childbirth taught me that allowing for a less than perfect solution can often yield a better reality.

After Nava was born, we were moved to another part of the hospital. We had 'Private' care and thus a little more up-class than the 'Public' system (we had a double-room instead of a ward). I remember being stunned by what I saw. The United States was going through a *still* ongoing hospital-borne infection crisis, but this hospital had carpeted floors (I even found blood on them) and real curtains. It seemed like a cesspool for infection. I looked up death rates from hospital-borne infections and found that almost nobody in Australia was dying in that way. I couldn't understand it. I attributed it to a lack of data collection. But the *overall* hospital death rates didn't support that.

I dug deeper and I *think* I now understand what was going on.

At the time, in Norway, there was a totally different model for dealing with hospital-borne infections. Instead of trying to keep the entire hospital a bacteria-free zone, the hospital only treated the patient and the bed. Why? Because when a bacterium evolves to be drug resistant, it necessarily gives up on other evolutionary advantages. It becomes very good at dominating an anti-bacterial environment, but terrible in the wider community. This is why hospital-borne viruses haven't exploded in the wider world. In a hospital that only treats the patient and the bed, resistant bacteria can't survive except on the patients and the beds. Other bacteria overwhelm them. But because they have such limited anti-bacterial environments (both in space and time), they lack the opportunity to evolve drug resistance.

If a resistant bacteria strain happens to evolve on one bed (from a very limited population), it gets eliminated by more competitive bacteria when the bed is taken out of service.

In a fully treated hospital, on the other hand, that bacteria can survive on any surface that isn't totally sterile. It has no competition. It can then spread throughout the facility and even – through the transfer of patients, doctors and equipment – to other facilities.

The second order effects of trying to eliminate bacteria from a healthcare environment (like trying to eliminate forest fires) can be devastating. They can also be irreversible. Once those new bacteria have evolved, it isn't necessarily so simple to walk back to a system that discourages their evolution.

Six months after Nava was born, we returned to the US. We decided to have another go at kids. We knew IUI worked so we went back to the same clinic, which followed the Australian doctor's protocol (we were actually so eager for more kids that we'd begun the fostering process in Washington State).

At the time, we had close friends who had twins. Their twins never slept at the same time. They ran their parents ragged. Nonetheless, we were in catch up mode. One day, while playing with their kids and listening to their father[1] complain, I made the comment "It'd be nice to have twins."

He replied, "May you be cursed with triplets!"

Six weeks later, we were in the clinic – checking things out. The blood work suggested Rebecca was pregnant. Rebecca thought it might be twins. The doctor po-pooed the notion. The blood work suggested nothing of the sort.

---

[1] He is a great character. I'll rename him Moishe for anonymity. Once when he was a kid his mother sent him out to the street to watch the men from the council repair the road. He came back in a half-hour later. She asked him what he thought of the men, and he said, "They're stupid."

"Why?" she asked.

"Because I keep telling them my name is Moishe and they keep calling me 'Bugger Off'."

Then, during the ultrasound, we saw his face drop. These clinics don't like having multiples – they win when they hit the sweet spot: single baby pregnancies.

"What is it?" asked Rebecca, "Is it twins?"

"No," he said. Then after a long pause. "It's triplets."

I almost did a fist pump. I was delighted. Rebecca was a little more uncertain, given the risks of such a pregnancy[1]. Nonetheless, the curse had come true.

Rebecca was pregnant with triplets.

Bit by bit we began to limit her activities. Our bedroom was on the second floor of a converted Officer's house in Fort Vancouver. We planned on moving her downstairs as the pregnancy progressed. Then, 25 weeks in, we went for a routine checkup. We had no idea, but Rebecca was having contractions. That was a *little* early.

Going home was no option. Our doctors (a crew of three fantastic perinatologists[2]) started calling hospitals. This one didn't have 3 NICU (Neonatal Intensive Care Unit) beds. That one didn't have a mother bed. Eventually, they found us a hospital that had what we needed. Bec was brought by ambulance to Emmanuel Hospital where she got a beautiful room overlooking the river. I spent Shabbat with her, under high observation. On Sunday, they managed to move her back

---

[1] Another doctor at the clinic actually suggested we abort one of the babies because otherwise our oldest child would spend her life caring for three three-year-olds.

[2] We actually recommended them to other people who'd had many many failed pregnancies and they managed to get them through to a successful delivery.

to St. Vincent's (where the perinatologists worked). We were quickly enrolled in a study comparing different forms of breathing assistance for severely premie (premature) babies.

Our kids being used to study oxygen delivery was kind of poetic, in a way. Rebecca's mother had been a charge nurse at the Cook County NICU in Chicago before she went to Australia (yes, she is that kind of battle axe). They didn't have enough money for oxygen in that hospital. That lack of oxygen, in that hospital, under her care, was the basis for a major shift in premie care. It turns out, contrary to all conventional wisdom at the time, that excessive oxygen blinds premies. It just goes to show: when it comes to medicine, always pay attention to the weird stuff.

Anyway, we were on high alert. I remember praying in my way that we'd make it to our first Rosh Chodesh (New Month). Rebecca's mother came to the United States to look after our oldest. I slept in the room with Rebecca, driving up to my parents and back to bring our daughter to see her. We had enormous community support – but nobody provided more support than my sister. The nurses and doctors were also fantastic. And, of course, Rebecca was amazing. She was such a delight in her hospital room that the nurses even bought her a present – a glass Magen David (Star of David) to hang on her window.

Most importantly of all, Rebecca's labor was kept under control.

Then, at week 30, we had a major crisis.

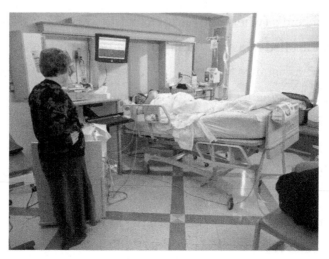

Sister visiting Rebecca, Week 5 (inverted)

Baby A's cord was protruding. If Rebecca's labor proceeded to the next stage, the baby would immediately lose oxygen and could suffer major lifelong complications – even death. We were moved to the room closest to the operating theater. Rebecca was inverted (her head was lowered below the rest of her body, to try to use gravity to pull the cord 'up'). And then our doctors asked us to make a choice. We either delivered all three babies then (very early) and improved Baby A's chances or we waited and risked Baby A's death.

We had 24 hours to decide (assuming events didn't force things sooner).

This was, of course, an impossible question.

We don't often ask Rabbis halachic (legal religious) questions. But we did then, urgently. There had to be a halachic preference between knowing three would face serious risks; and risking that one would face catastrophic risks[1].

The question was run to New York-based experts in religious-medical ethics.

The response was this: "Do what the doctors tell you to."

It wasn't much of an answer.

We prayed, of course. And I did research. What were the risks at 30 weeks? How much danger or disability would those other kids face? It was surprising to me that nurses (and even doctors) didn't know the statistics I was researching. The statistics weren't obvious or easy to find. They were also constantly improving. Despite all that, they could be roughly assembled[2]. They doctors were looking at each case, each person and relying on their own experience and feelings. It was a perfectly legitimate way to work but it couldn't address our question which was concerned with the relative risks of our decision.

Our research was done and our decision was made by the timeline. We decided to pull the kids out and then just do the very best that we could.

---

[1] The same moral quandary faces self-driving car logic today. If the system only has two choices – plowing into a car full of people who might be protected by their vehicle or running over a single little girl.... What does it do?

[2] I learned one fascinating thing in pulling together that data: Cubans in the United States have a far higher rate of complications than Cubans in Cuba. It was held up as a testament to the quality of Cuban medical care. It was pretty convincing, until I worked out that the Cuban government *requires* the abortion of any high-risk pregnancy. If there are no high-risk cases, your likelihood of post-birth complications goes way down.

G-d was giving us a task and we'd do what we could to fulfill it.

We'd been calm throughout, insisting on working our way through the problem. Insisting that that was what we'd do for the rest of these kids' lives. We'd been calm, but Bec had had a miserable time. Being inverted is no fun at all. The nurses kept saying "It's for the good of your babies." And Rebecca kept thinking, "At this point, I'm not sure I care." We thought about buying a projector so mothers in her position could watch movies on the ceiling.

We never did.

The next morning, the ultrasound equipment returned.

We told the doctors our choice.

They did one more scan before we were to proceed.

But, miracle of miracles, Baby A's cord was no longer protruding[1].

We no longer had to make a choice.

I remember thanking G-d for getting us to the new month, twice. When the third month came, near the end of Chanukah, I remember saying, "It's okay now, you've done enough."

The delivery was scheduled and a few days later, the kids were born. Rebecca ended up carrying those babies to 34 weeks and 5 days. The kids were 4, 4.5 and 5 pounds (1.8, 2 and 2.2 kg). The Apgar of one kid (Baby 2, now that he'd been

---

[1] We were going to be on high alert the rest of the pregnancy. Daily ultrasounds became the norm.

born) wasn't awesome. The nurses expected him to be in the NICU for weeks, at a minimum. But he recovered quickly. Three days later, all the babies came home with their mother. The two boys[1] had their *brit milah* (ritual circumcision) on the eighth day. Aside from being tiny, they had no health complications.

They were (and are, thank G-d) all healthy.

Ten weeks in the hospital, ten weeks of labor, one major scare, and in the end three perfectly healthy (although tiny) kids.

The nurses said it was a miracle.

We agreed.

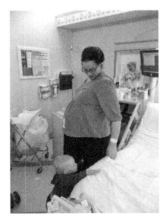

Rebecca and Nava right before delivery

---

[1] We hadn't wanted to know the kids' gender. Then we tried to pick first and middle names. It was too hard to pick *six* sets of names. We gave in and asked if they were all the same. The answer was no, so we only had to pick four names – those of two girls and two boys.

About 6 weeks later, we were having lunch at a friend's house. Those same friends who'd cursed us with triplets were there. Our then 18-month-old was sitting with us, and the triplets were lined up like sardines in a Port-A-Cot. They were napping peacefully and in unison.

Moishe, the man who'd cursed us, turned to me and said, "Joseph, when I cursed you with triplets, I didn't mean like this."

Triplets shluufing like sardines

Once the triplets could shower themselves, we decided to try again. We went back to the same clinic. There was a new protocol he wanted to try. It was a cancer drug (letrozole) that had some interesting effects on fertility. It was simple and easy to use. We'd decided we'd try only once. More kids weren't a total necessity, and we were already planning to move to Israel. There was only so much complication we could deal with.

We followed the protocol, for that one cycle. It worked.

We moved to Israel with Rebecca about 10 weeks pregnant. Yaniv was born here, exposing us to yet another health care system. Then, a few years later, we had our first 'volunteer' baby – Revital. It turns out it is quite common in our situation. There's a hormonal shift that occurs when the mother is in utero (e.g., Bec) and the effects wear off as women approach their early 40s.

Now, thank G-d, we have six kids.

We were childless, and now we are thoroughly blessed.

I know many are not as fortunate as us. Many never have children. Others have children severely damaged by premature birth or accidents during birth. Still others have major health complications when young.

I have my theories about G-d and the nature of blessing and curse. But I have no answer, no consolation, no understanding for why *we* have been blessed and *they* have not. All I can say is that I can appreciate their challenges. I can understand them. And, in my own human and limited way, I can hope that *we* can help. After all, so many people helped us along the way.

I know, at the very least, that Rebecca and I can lend a few sympathetic ears.

We can't promise things will turn out well. We can listen, though.

We can listen and we can share just a little of the pain and in time, G-d willing, the joy.

CHILDREN

A few people have suggested that Rebecca and I pen a book on child-rearing. We've demurred. Again, it is presumptuous. Are we good parents or are we just blessed with good kids? Are our kids good or do we just need to wait a little longer for them to morph into proper teenage and adult monsters?

How do you measure or judge "good" kids?

I'm not asking these questions facetiously.

My grandfather used to say, "check back when they're 30." He was right. You *never* know whether a kid has turned out well. It can even be hard to tell if they've turned out badly. Beyond that, it can be d-mned hard to tell whether the parents had any role in *either* outcome.

So, the following isn't a guide to good parenting. It is simply an exploration of what we've done, why we've done it and what we've observed as (we think) a result.

Happiness

Let me start with a single, perhaps controversial, statement: our goal as parents has never been to raise happy kids. It isn't that happiness isn't important. It is just that it isn't the *most* important thing.

Way back when I was at Harvard, I took a survey course on intellectual history. The professor asked a question: "If there was a drug that made people happy and had no side effects, other than stopping them from doing anything else, would you require all of society to take it?"

You could pose the question a little more gently: "Would you *let* people take it?"

The professor posed the question in class but didn't answer it.

Privately, though, he did.

"Yes," he said to a small group of us, "I would require people to take it."

He was obviously a utilitarian – somebody who values the most happiness for the most people as the highest goal. Aside from practical considerations (e.g., how would people eat?) happiness was *the goal*. This perspective has faced some challenges, even from proponents. There's the classic distribution of happiness question. Another big one is: how do you measure happiness? It is darned near impossible, especially if you find people claim to be happy and you just can't believe them because you disagree with their life choices (e.g., Haredi/Ultra-Orthodox Jews). The next natural step was to find something you *could* measure. Something *material*. That, of course, was money.

I believe this is how money became a *proxy* for happiness[1].

In Western societies, once you got well into the 20th century, lower classes had increasingly – quantitatively – better lifestyles. The poor got fat. But they weren't happy. Absolute wealth obviously wasn't a proxy for happiness. So, people turned to *relative* wealth. People looked at the super-wealthy and said: the uneven *distribution* is at fault. After all, once you get past a certain level of wealth, the happiness return/dollar lowers. People with that level of wealth are hoarding a whole lot of happiness others could exploit far more effectively than they can. And $10,000 in your pocket means a lot more than it does in the pocket of a billionaire. Obviously, it isn't fair to distribute happiness so unevenly, so justice demands balancing the scales.

I'm not arguing against or for redistributive economic policies (at least not here). I *am* arguing that they miss the point. Happiness is *not* money. And happiness is not The Point. A life lived under a drug that makes you happy but stops you from doing anything else is the life of a pickle: it has no purpose. Actually, the pickle has more of a purpose. At least it

---

[1] For a long time, I thought it was a good proxy for happiness and thus an argument for capitalism. It turns out the correlation is more complex than it might seem at first glance.

can be tasty. As far as I'm concerned, happiness is *not* the goal. It may well be a side-effect, but it shouldn't be the goal.

Even more critically, in practical terms, aiming for happiness *does not result in happiness*. There's a whole class of things like this. I'd add Love, Honor and Peace to the list. They're all best acquired indirectly. Playing tough makes people less likely to pick a fight with you, leading to peace. If you are always seeking peace, then others who aren't seeking peace will take advantage of you. Seeking Honor gets awful close to kissing others' rear-ends in order to gain their respect. It doesn't lead to honor. Instead, *ignoring* others and doing what *you* believe is right is more likely to yield their respect. Desperately broadcasting how much you need Love is likely to drive others away. Playing "hard-to-get," or at least acting as if some other goal is more important, is far more likely to attract a mate[1].

The same rules apply to Happiness. Leading a *fulfilling* life is more likely to lead to Happiness than seeking Happiness directly.

Happiness plays "hard to get."

You've got to let it come to you.

As we see it, raising children who have the tools to lead a *fulfilling* life is more likely to lead to their happiness. That happiness will be a side effect, sure – but it will be all the more

---

[1] Expressing a desperate need for an individual is far better than broadcasting *general* love neediness.

real because of it. There will be a basis for their joy, rather than joy wavering uncertainly over a pit of emptiness and despair.

Killing Yourself

Early in Nava's life, we went to the United States. She'd been sleeping through the night at about 4 months, but then she stopped sleeping through the night when we got back. We expressed a bit of confusion to a friend, and she recommended a very controversial book: *Contented Baby* by Gina Ford. Now, *Contented Baby* is a bit *crazy*. But it made sense. Gina Ford had worked for years with kids with terribly sleeping patterns and she'd corrected them. Our case was milder. Buried in the book, she had tables for feeding and sleeping by age. It turned out we were already keeping to the table the with exception of one 2:00PM bottle. We added it and Nava has slept through ever since (although she no longer needs a 2:00PM bottle).

We applied *Contented Baby* "light" to all our other kids and all of them were sleeping through by four months of age[1]. It's the only parenting book we ever really used (another reason to be reluctant to write one – why contribute to a genre you don't follow?).

The most important part of *Contented Baby* wasn't the timetable. It was the philosophy. Gina Ford had a simple foundational principle: happy parents make for happy kids.

---

[1] I can't tell you that the sleep management was due more to luck or to Gina Ford. I can tell you that without Gina Ford, it wouldn't have happened so smoothly.

Specifically, well-rested parents make for contented babies (thus the clever title).

She'd regularly encounter parents who didn't get this. They thought that their exhausted reality was an expression of their love and sacrifice on behalf of their children.

It is an expression of a form of love. And it is an expression of sacrifice. But it is *not* best for the parents *or the children*. It is a sacrifice that only serves to make reality worse.

Our children aren't there to grind us into the ground. Whether we had a single baby, four kids under 17 months or six kids, we've always wanted to meet their needs with the *least* amount of effort required. It isn't just about *us*. It is also about *them*. *They* need to learn how to sleep, then how to occupy themselves, then how to take care of themselves and then how to be fully responsible adults.

Excessive parental sacrifice can undermine all of this while making for a very grumpy house. Especially with triplets.

When they were young, if *we* were well-rested, they'd be more settled and confident. As they've gotten older, our increasingly hands-off approach has given them the opportunity to grow into the fullest versions of themselves.

Everybody wins. Knowing when to do less can actually be the truest actualization of parental love.

That's why every time I see a TV show with the parents waving their exhaustion around as a matter of pride (and with only one or two little babies in the house) I just want to scream: "YOU'RE DOING IT ALL WRONG!"

Incentives

Enough poetry. How do you get it done?

Or, rather, how do *we think* you get it done?

I know I might sound like some new-age Upper West Side Hippy installing speakers with Mozart in her womb when I say it, but it all starts very, very early.

Yes, I'm sure living in a calm and peaceful and well-fed pre-natal environment helps. It probably also helps if the mother eats peanuts (gotta avoid those later allergies). But I'm not really talking about *that* early. I'm talking about the very first days of life *outside* the womb.

NICUs today – or at least NICUs when my kids were in them – don't use breathing monitors. They use blood-oxygen monitors. With more modern electronics, blood-oxygen monitors are probably simpler than breathing monitors. They are also measuring, if you will, a more vital sign. Breathing monitors may correlate with danger, but blood oxygen's correlation is stronger. All that said, neither simplicity nor directness are the reasons we use blood-oxygen monitors in NICUs. Instead, it had to do with another of those NICU studies. They tested two groups of babies. Both had blood-oxygen *and* breathing monitors. One set had the conventional setup – alarms attached to breathing monitors. The other only had alarms based on blood-oxygen levels.

Now, it is very easy for a baby to stop breathing. It is quite a bit harder for them to bring down their blood oxygen level. When they ran the study, trying to verify that the blood-oxygen levels were kept within a safe level without the breathing monitors being alarmed, they found what I believe was a surprising result: the babies on breathing monitors *stopped breathing* far more frequently.

But why?

The answer has to do with manipulation. Whenever the babies stopped breathing, the nurses would come running to help them. They'd get a lot of attention. So, they *learned* to stop breathing. As pre-mature infants.

This, of course, endangered them.

With the blood-oxygen monitors, the nature of the cause and effect was far more tenuous. For starters, the babies had to take things a lot further and in ways even adults have a hard time comprehending. For the baby's own good, it was better to let them stop breathing once in a while than to *teach them* that they were rewarded for doing just that[1].

Aside from the health impacts, the breathing monitors were making the children *dependent* on the drug of attention. Part of independence, part of fulfillment, is learning how to stand happily alone.

When we lived in Oregon, I read an article condemning an Eastern Oregon family for child abuse. Among the various charges, the local paper's most magnificent claim was that the

---

[1] I'm generally quite skeptical of scientific studies claiming to provide universal rules. I am here as well. This tells me children can manipulate from a very young age. It does *not* tell me that this is *all* children do. Humans are deeply complex and *very few* rules successfully define us.

uncle was said to have said – on multiple occasions – that raising children was like raising cattle.

The thing is: there's a lot of truth to that statement.

It is not evidence of child abuse in and of itself.

Children learn from incentives. You've got to be very careful about which incentives you use or how far you take them – after all, you don't want to undermine their ability to be full-fledged people[1]. But they, like every sentient creature, respond to their environment. The environment you provide them with must guide them towards a fulfilling reality. That's why ours is a house that seeks, at every stage and in every way, to empower our children. Physically, socially, mentally, economically, and yes, spiritually. We don't use incentives to *control* children. And we don't *ignore* incentives in the belief that they need to express their true selves. Instead, as much as possible, we use incentives to *guide* them down the path of self-control and self-empowerment. They must ultimately learn to define themselves around one or more purposes (although they need to find those purposes) and then reinforce the aspects of themselves that reinforce their chosen purposes. This will raise them up, making them greater than themselves.

Put another way, learning self-control leads to learning self-empowerment which enables us to become the highest form of ourselves.

So, how?

––––––––––––

[1] We never used candy or food as an incentive. Enough people have problems with that already.

Here's a simple example. If our children screamed for their bottles, they'd get them. But *not quickly*. We'd switch from normal efficiency mode to SLOOOO-MO. We'd make a big deal out of it. Soon enough the kids would learn not to whinge (a wonderful Australian term) for their bottles. They'd have to ask (or be willing to wait while their parents prepared the bottles if they weren't yet able to ask). With triplets it was even easier. We just gave the kid who screamed the most the last bottle. We created a race towards more pleasant behavior.

As an aside, raising triplets can actually be very, very efficient. You only have to sleep train once, basically. And certain activities are much less time consuming on a baby-by-baby level. Take feeding solid foods. Instead of waiting for a child to finish their morsel before spooning in the next one, you just move onto the next baby. By the time you're ready to feed baby one again, they've already finished their first bite. Feeding three kids only takes marginally longer than feeding one.

Lunch time after a busy morning. Guess which one is the foodie now?

Kids could play the game too, of course. A favorite of every child is to make noise in synagogue. You're sure to get what you want then, right? Your parents will give you candy or whatever just so you won't make a scene. Our approach was simple. If a kid made a scene, we stuck them outside by themselves in the stroller for a minute or two (so long as the weather was fine).

Soon, our babies were quieter than most of the 5-year-olds.

The four-baby Stroller of Exile

From an early stage, we paid our kids for chores. Early in life, payment was in rides[1]. By default, they'd get rides, but if the toys weren't picked up, they'd lose them. If they went above and beyond, they'd get extra rides. Misbehavior could cost them. I'm good with rides, so it worked. When they got

---

[1] I would give any sort of ride they could imagine. Tree rides, scare rides, elephant rides, car rides (they'd steer me by the ears), rocket rides, couch rides and many, many more. One of the best was the "I don't know" ride, which I'd give when I'd ask them what ride they wanted and they'd say, "I don't know." The whole system was not only a lot of fun, but a real challenge for my imagination.

older, we transitioned to points, which were convertible to money.

That's still the system we have today. We have a job board where we rotate everyday and pre-Shabbat tasks. The everyday tasks earn points, and they can't watch anything until they finish the pre-Shabbat tasks.

And if *we* end up doing their chores?

Then they have to pay *us* from *their* points.

The incentive regime continued in other ways. We never ever gave in. Even with newborn infants. Screaming and whinging just hardened our positions. The cost of going "the easy way" is a whole lot of the hard way. If you don't start this young, you face an increasingly steep road in trying to implement it later[1]. If the kid *expects* to get what they want by screaming, it is pretty hard to change that belief. They can put up a hell of a fight if they haven't already learned that *not* putting up a fight is the best way to get what they want.[2]

It goes back to prayer. I want my kids to ask "their father and mother who art in the Kitchen" by making an argument – not by pulling a fit.

---

[1] We're going through this process now with one of the kids. I suspect the going is particularly hard because the child is effectively receiving the opposite message at kindergarten.

[2] It is a bit trickier with newborns. They communicate by crying and you need to ensure they are fed, kept clean and loved. You want to stay *ahead* of the need to whinge. Understanding *when* they are *just* whinging requires both knowing the kid very well and ensuring the kid has what he or she needs – and that includes cuddles.

Reality

At the same time that we treated our children like cattle, we also made a point of treating them like real people. They can't deal with the real world unless they have exposure to reality. Reality ends up being a heck of an incentive.

Again, this started at the very beginning. We spoke to all the kids in full sentences, in a normal voice, from the day they were born[1]. Respecting that they had real desires and that a lack of communication was deeply frustrating (and a legit cause of crying), we taught our kids very basic sign language. Words like "all done," "more," "please," "milk." "water" and "poop." We wanted them expressing themselves as soon as possible. Beyond that, we wanted them to be able to more effectively impact their reality. If screaming isn't effective at changing your reality, then *something else* needs to be.

The real people principle extended to our threats and promises. We only made *real* threats and *real* promises. We were very careful with each because walking things back (or enforcing the unreasonable) really hurts the child involved. We also never promised our kids it was all going to be okay or that we'd always be there for them. We can't deliver on those promises and so we can't make them. I like to think the

---

[1] When Nava was about 18 months old, she started getting some serious vertigo. We called the advice line for our health fund.

The nurse asked, "what are her symptoms?"

We said, "She's dizzy."

"How can you possibly know she's dizzy," said the nurse, "She's 18 months old?"

Rebecca just put the phone on speaker and said, "Nava, how do you feel."

"I feel DIZZY!" said Nava, and that settled that.

promises we do make have more power as a result. They are more comforting than that which cannot be trusted.

We were, and are, realistic with the kids. We explained, continually, what we were doing with them and why. We know, as with many of these things, that they didn't get it at first. They couldn't comprehend it. But eventually, it clicks together[1]. Things become a lot easier then. They can get (and stay) with the program because they understand it.

Perhaps the most important "real" principle was honesty. We were always honest, sometimes brutally, with the kids. There was only one exception to this: older kids' activities after younger kids' bedtime. We lied, on two occasions, about the big kids watching a movie after the little kids' bedtime. We didn't just conceal our intent, we lied about it under interrogation from those younger children. We only did it twice. The older kids were so upset by the deception that some of them refused to watch the movie. Oh, and when Yaniv wouldn't eat kreplach, we called them Monkey Brains. We've been calling them Monkey Brains ever since.

That's it in the deception department.

---

[1] Years later, when I was tangentially involved in setting up a school, I visited an American Classical Christian School. They had a three-stage learning process. Stage One was Grammar. In Grammar they memorized countless fact-filled songs – from songs about Pythagoras to songs about history. Young kids are great at memorizing songs. Stage Two was Reason. That was when they started using the facts that had had no meaning before. I think of our almost rote explanations of child-rearing as belonging to the same category.

Reality is more than parents just speaking honestly. During Ethiopia's brief spring with the rise of Prime Minister Abiy, we brought our entire family to the country. We saw other white people there; what we didn't see were other white children and babies. Local people were fascinated by the eighteen-month-old girl we had with us[1]. Why'd we do it? The trip wasn't for us. All I learned was that Ethiopians vastly prefer Toyotas to any other cars and that mannequins *in Ethiopia* are white – which says *something* about the nature of racism[2]. No, we went because we wanted our children to see *poverty* – to understand the extent of the challenges in the world. We also wanted them to see what was, at the time, a hopeful society – despite its poverty.

We were only there for two days, but it made a lasting and valuable impression. We've always exposed our children to

---

[1] One girl at a rural church site asked what our daughter's dummy (pacifier) was. Bec explained through an interpreter that it was so she wouldn't cry. The girl asked why our daughter didn't just use her thumb. The interpreter was also curious. Rebecca was going to answer, something to do with future orthodontics. Then she literally stopped herself and said, "It's a First World Problem." At that same church we were going to visit the grounds dressed as Jews. Just before we got out of the van, the guide explained that churches in Ethiopia were carved out of rock because a 9th century *Jewish* queen had burned all the wooden churches and monasteries. We tucked in our tzitzit and took off our yarmulkas. Shortly afterwards, we visited a local family and they made us coffee. We shared some of our food with them. The sharp English cheese was *not* appreciated. But again and again, when we offered our salami, they checked that it had no pig. They were Christians who would not eat pork.

[2] We were next in Australia, where a black Kenyan Jew said we really had to go to Nairobi. "Ethiopia is backward," she said, "Because it was never colonized. That's why Kenya is far more advanced." Right or wrong, that's not the perspective you hear about on American college campuses.

reality, as messy and as horrible as it may be. We've tried to educate throughout that process.

After all, if our children hope to change the world, they have to know about it.

Ethiopia with the family

Expectations

Now kids can be pushed and prodded and enticed with incentives. But there is something even more important: *expectations*.

We are, after all, social animals.

To give a basic example: my grandmother expected us *not to swear* in front of her. She expected better from us. Because of that, better is what she got. If you expect *less* from your kids, or if you assign them a basket of expected behaviors, your expectations will become reality.

The classic example is parents freaking out when kids hurt themselves a little. If the parent acts like it is all cool, the kid will think it is all cool and everybody will *actually* be better off[1]. This is why, when my kids used to scrape themselves and start screaming, I tended to administer immediate comic amputation or defibrillation by blown raspberries. It actually led to better outcomes.

In a much more serious and broad case, the recent news has seen a rush of teenagers suffering from tics. Tourette's-like tics. It is believed the rapid spread of tics is due to (I kid you not) Tic Toc. Teens see videos of other teens with real or simulated tics and their brains seem to reprogram around what is expected. They then develop uncontrollable tics of their own.

Every kid has strengths and weaknesses and challenges. But you have to manage the impacts of expectation when facing them. In *almost* all cases, we believe you really need to micro-focus on the particular and damaging issue at hand. If a kid is hyper, work on helping them settle themselves down (or get them into an environment where they *can* be hyper). Don't label them with ADHD and the whole suite of other behaviors that come with it. If you do, they'll start exhibiting those behaviors too[2]. You'll expect it, their teachers will expect it and so they will adopt it unconsciously. If your kid is poorly

---

[1] Rebecca taught me that even when things *are* serious, running around in a panic will only make things worse (e.g., increase the chance and severity of shock).

[2] Even worse, you might *unnecessarily* stick their young and growing minds on psychotherapeutic drugs which have *got* to mess with things. Sometimes it is necessary, but it'd sure be best to avoid it.

adjusted socially, don't put them "on the spectrum." Work on individual issues, whether it be eye contact, noticing and responding to cues, or whatever. Be aggressive about addressing *those issues*. After all, they can certainly spiral out of control. But be very reluctant to apply a broad-spectrum label[1].

Unusually, for my thoughts on these matters, a recently published study backs them up. A *JAMA Pediatrics* study tested normal interventions vs. an intervention that taught parents to interact with their babies even if there was no eye contact and to play with them in a way *sensitive to their particular issues*. As the study's authors said "Many therapies for autism have tried previously to replace development differences with more typical behaviors. In contrast, this works with each child's unique differences and creates a social environment around the child that helps them learn in a way that was best for them."

The study reduced eventual autism diagnosis by 70%.

We are social animals, and we love to adhere to expectations. By ignoring the "package deal" and focusing on individual challenges, we can get past the expectations the "package deal" created – to the benefit of our children.

That social component is a core reason why I believe little kids should *never* be exposed to little kids' TV programming. The shows are tuned to maximize attention and delight.

---

[1] This applies to syndromes, which are simply oft-correlated collections of symptoms. A disease is different.

However, they mess with kid's ability to understand real-world cues. The screen *seems* to be interacting with them. But it isn't *actually* doing so. Even if it is a computer game, it still isn't reacting as a *human* would. The more convincing the faux interaction, the more it messes with our social programming.

I remember watching part of a basketball game with two of the triplets. They were under the age of two. I pointed at one player (Travis Outlaw) and said, "That guy can really jump!"

One of my sons promptly turned to the TV and said "Jump! Jump!"

He *couldn't* know it wasn't real and that Travis Outlaw couldn't hear him, not until he was older and ready to compartmentalize the screen.

Our older kids watch shows and use computers pretty freely. For a while, we strictly limited it. We still do with the younger ones. With the older kids, we focus on talking about the risks while making sure the screens aren't impacting their ability to otherwise grow.

Expectations don't only have downsides. They also have upsides. We expect our children to do their best and to improve on their weaknesses – this helps them do exactly that.

It is impossible to measure, but our expectations seem to help.

Growth

When Rebecca was in the hospital with the triplets, we got our hands on a few books advising how high-order multiples should be raised. Every book said you had to make your friends and visitors do the dishes. They will all want to feed the babies – the books advised – but make them do the dishes! We didn't do that; it just didn't seem nice[1].

Plus, people really enjoyed feeding the babies.

Other than that one point of disagreement (which we set aside), the books differed widely.

One set of books said the first year was fine, but then it all spiraled out of control. The other set said the first year was a living hell, but then it got better. It was quickly clear what the difference between the books was. The control-freak mothers had a fine first year. Once the kids got older, they could no longer control them. And the mothers who had no sense of control couldn't handle year one; but were better adapted to later years.

Learning from these examples, we went for a mix. Total control early on and then, whenever possible, relinquishing that control. We had a baby chart indicating the order of feedings. We cycled the kids through sleep, food and attention on a synchronized schedule[2]. The kids were all sleeping through by four months. The synchronization continued in these basic areas, but we began to let loose more and more over time.

---

[1] Plus, our community provided us with the first six *weeks* of meals after we got out of the hospital. Six *weeks* of prepared meals. How can you ask somebody who's a part of that to wash your dishes?

[2] *No* face-to-face or voice contact during sleep time – including feedings or changings.

Early triplet navigation, we quickly shifted to simply calling out 'single-file duck style'

The principle explained to them – and acted on – was that as soon as they demonstrated good decision-making in an area, we would relinquish control over that area. At this point, with a 14-year-old and three 13-year-olds, we don't check homework or tests unless half-year report cards come back bad. But they don't come back bad. Our kids have earned our trust. One kid concealed his poor performance a few years back, and so we watched him carefully for a few months. He's back on track. One kid used to lie regularly. That has stopped, due to clear repercussions. We now believe that child as a matter of course. She's earned it.

Step-by-step, day-by-day, we encourage and reward their *self*-control. As part of this, we aren't safety nuts[1]. As 12-year-

---

[1] Although our second youngest has gotten himself into some serious trouble (eating a toilet bowl cleaner, walking into a busy

olds, two of the kids would take the bus to Tel Aviv alone and walk for kilometers while there – even at night. They tell us they are at friends' homes, rather than asking for permission. Our thumb is continually being pulled off the lever of their lives. It would be, no matter what; they are growing into *de facto* independence. But we believe our encouragement of it makes it all easier while still (we hope) leaving them willing to sacrifice some independence and turn to us when they need help.

Law

As part of that growth track, we created a system of family laws to adjudicate issues between the kids. They started with laws created by the parents. But by the time the kids were five, we were working *with* them to help fashion their laws. At the time, the laws were primarily about toy ownership and control. That mattered to them. As time has passed, we've encouraged more and more self-control as a "community of children."

As an example, when two kids have a dispute they can't resolve, they can call a *beit din* (a Hebrew word for House of Judgment, or Court). Three other kids sit on the Court and hear the claimants' cases. They set the rules of evidence and presentation. After hearing the two sides, the judges ask questions and then argue about what the outcome should be. Eventually they vote on a decision. When two judges agree on

---

street at 18 months and pulling a cupboard of glasses onto himself), he hasn't suffered any serious harm.

something, it is settled. Critically, later cases can refer to those judgments and their reasoning – making the judges reluctant to decide things on the basis of personal bias[1]. Laws have been established around couch usage, table setting, seat choice and, yes, toy control.

The *beit din* doesn't come up often and it has weaknesses. The biggest is that enforcement of decisions relies on each child keeping in mind that *others* will thus adhere to similar decisions in the future (something our grown up courts might learn from). One kid had a run of very unreasonable actions which led to an expectation on that child's part that they'd never win a case. It fell on me (the bailiff) to enforce the law, but I really had very few tools to accomplish that.

It's since resolved itself, but that was a tough period.

For me, the best part of the *beit din* is hearing the judge's reasoning. It is pretty cool to see the logic of a legal system emerge. Especially if it is about toys. It is even cooler when judges come at things from totally unexpected directions and end up setting precedent as a result. The kids work out sometimes beautifully elegant rules that have never occurred to us as parents.

Deeper Issues

Children, of course, are people. They aren't carbon copies of their parents' ideals. As parents of non-identical triplets, we know this better than most. They have been raised in very

---

[1] Laws are not allowed to differentiate based on individual people or personal characteristics.

similar fashions and yet they are very different people. They aren't blank slates. As I'm fond of telling them when they struggle in one area or another "every person has their own kind of intelligence and gifts." More critically, every person faces very real challenges. When those challenges hit your kids, you either have to help them through the challenges – or help them come to accept a harsh reality and work around it.

It sounds horrible, but for years, I shared a very peculiar kind of advice with my kids. I talked to them about their weaknesses and how they could be improved – almost like life was a test and they just had to focus more on the subject matter they were weak on. I didn't expect a socially awkward kid or the one with self-anger issues to be the most adjusted or stable children. I just wanted the edge taken off so that they could best leverage their real strengths. Those years of conversations worked. Each kid is different, but no kid has a glaring problem that is likely to undermine their own goals.

But even with this, some issues just get bigger and bigger and bigger. Two challenges have stood out above the rest.

The first was a very long-term lack of confidence on the part of one of my kids. That kid was considered almost doll-like by many when younger[1]. The *expectation* was that that kid was stupid (not our expectation, but the universe is bigger than the family). The kid got convinced, deep inside, that they weren't smart. It didn't help that the kid didn't consider many conventional things easy to think through. The child is very

---

[1] It's genetic. My mother was kidnapped by a mentally ill woman who thought my mother was her doll.

bright, but every strength comes with other weaknesses. So, the kid was a mediocre student who covered for the many things the child didn't understand (out of fear of seeming stupid when the kid asked for help). Even more challenging, the kid loved to create chaos in order to have some feeling of control.

We stayed the course. We kept insisting that we knew the child could do well, even as that wavered. We also made a strong effort to listen to the kid's questions, especially those the child thought were *stupid*. We worked to ensure the kid slept enough (a continuing problem, it turns out almonds help). We had the kid ask their own teacher for help, privately, so the child wouldn't feel stupid in front of the class.

Then, the child switched teachers. The new teacher had no idea the kid been a poor student. There was an opening to establish a new self-identity. In one year, one summer really, the child went from mediocre student to a very good student. The kid's confidence, behavior and *non-academic* intelligence (shown in art and interpersonal understanding) improved as well. When I met with the teacher and told her the child had been a poor student, the teacher was incredulous. The teacher had never seen any of that.

Our kid is most at fault for the improvement, but as parents I like to think we opened the door to a better reality.

Another kid, the one who almost broke the Beit Din, was harder. The child would pull terrible, destructive, disruptive fits. They weren't like my fits (which were cries for justice, at least as I recall). The child's goal seemed to be to make everybody as angry and unhinged as he was. Using a maxim from my own father that some kids really need physical interaction I'd give the child these long hugs, but they didn't really help. It's hard to say, but they may have simply pissed the kid off even more.

To help things out, we'd tried Friday night appreciations. You know, we'd go around the Shabbat table and have everybody appreciate somebody else. But it didn't help much. There was no real *underlying* appreciation.

Things were getting worse and worse, and it was impacting the entire family. At one point, I felt like everything was falling apart. I remember praying outside on the street just wondering what we could do. That child had just told one of my other kids that they wanted to hurt themselves.

That was a major major, major red flag, and I was really worried. Growing up I'd seen where it led. I wasn't just praying that night in my standard quid pro quo fashion. Instead, I was begging for insight.

The Shabbat before (I believe) I'd attended a lecture given by a local Rabbi. He wasn't talking about child-rearing or psychology or dispute resolution. I *think* he was talking about prayer times. During his lecture, he mentioned a Jewish community in medieval Europe that had a ridiculously stupid custom. Every Sabbath, after morning prayers, the people in the community would share the grievances they had with others. One Shabbat the dispute lasted so long that they missed the afternoon prayer.

As I stood on the sidewalk, praying, the thought entered my mind: "Grievances?"

It was dangerous. Stupid dangerous. It could blow up in our faces. But it was worth the cost. I came in after prayers, proposed it to Bec and then, that very night, we tried it. We went around the table and asked people to share their grievances. There were rules (of course). The grievance had to be about some*thing*, not just some*one*. People had to listen to the grievance against them before they responded. Voices couldn't be raised. And the discussion had to focus on finding resolutions or agreeing there were no resolutions to be had.

The grievances were all over the map. Boys going into the girls' room. Kids not giving each other enough time to use the plug to charge their phones. Me angrily wading into disputes without understanding them. I don't remember the rest. But, either through commitment or simple purchases (e.g., plug splitters so kids could charge simultaneously) we either *resolved* the issues or showed good faith to improve the problems.

The very air in the house seemed to clear. We've only done grievances once or twice since. The kids tend to bring them up more proactively during the week. And people who committed to improvement (including me with my wading in) are continually improving their behavior.

What about the child who was threatening self-harm?

The child is fine now. The child sometimes gets down on themselves for doing things they think are stupid, but the child's disappointment is very limited in both extremity and in time.

This must have happened early during the coronavirus. Through the course of the lockdowns, the kids and family just grew stronger and stronger.

The lockdowns were, in our little microcosm of a world, a beautiful time of familial peace and growth.

It sounds totally counterproductive, but grievances were the best thing to happen to our family.

I guess we're medieval idiots.

Goals

In many cases people like to cast things as direct tradeoffs. Freedom vs. Discipline. Independence vs. Control. Communism vs. Capitalism.

A child who's a rebel and a total pain in the behind might be just the kind of child who challenges the improper order of things when they grow up. On the other hand, a well-behaved child might lack the gumption to address injustice or much of anything else. Forgetting kindness and justice and all that, the rebel kid is more likely to do what's needed to take care of him or herself while the well-behaved kid is more likely to be walked over.

So, which do you emphasize?

Facing this incredibly simplified cross-section of behaviors, our answer would be to pick another ideal. You want to raise *considerate* and *caring* kids. Guided by consideration and caring, the kids can be rebels when it's called for (giving dad a grievance for wading into fights like an idiot) or disciplined when it's called for (helping dad take care of the little kids when mom is out of town). We've always tried, with our kids and with life, to find a way between the common tradeoffs to something greater.

To me, the greatest path between the tradeoffs is the path of Goodness and Holiness. Enabling your children to live a life of fulfillment, (rather than happiness-seeking), ought to be the goal of any parent.

Conclusion

Many parents are eager for vacations away from their children. Not us. We've done it a few times since they were born, but it is never all that rewarding. Sure, the dishes, clothes, etc... can be a lot of work, but the kids aren't. They are increasingly pleasant and interesting to be around.

I'm far from a perfect parent, of course. I do raise my voice – but I am improving. And the kids sometimes battle – but they tend to resolve those battles quickly and without a whole lot of bad blood.

We all have the tools to improve, and we all know we are, in fact, improving.

The biggest gap in my own parenting is that, despite working from home, I don't spend enough time with my kids. I have a lot to offer most of them – from teaching them to write to teaching them code to simple discussions about life. I tried scheduling a half hour a week for each kid, but I didn't sustain it. My best conversations with them tend to be either while I'm driving them around or while we're having our daily family dinners. I have a hard time stepping away from my work, from the productive side. I have a hard time sacrificing the tangible to create the intangible. I never regret when I do it, though. The result can be magical.

Are we good parents? I have no idea. Parenting isn't an experiment you can run. Every kid is different, and parenting *should* be flexible. "Success" can have many different definitions. You can't rerun your children's lives. That said, our kids push themselves and think seriously about the world. That's pretty much all we can ask for. I like to think we played a role in this, but maybe we didn't. I have no idea. That doesn't stop me from giving a bit of summary advice, though. So here it is:

- Focus on outcomes, not self-sacrifice
- Be honest and real with your kids
- Aim for fulfillment, not happiness
- Continually improve and encourage independence
- Use expectations to bring out the best
- Help them internalize the rule of law and responsibility
- Think creatively when faced with the hard stuff
- Keep off the screens in the early years
- Avoid assigning syndromes
- And always seek to improve

There are lots of little practical things – like not making eye contact with babies at night or asking your children to tell you the best part of their day before they go to sleep – but the overall guiding ideas are these. Oh, and *always* make sure your kids know that you love them. But that's so obvious, it didn't get its own section.

Is it scientific? No. But the 'scientific' way of raising children is also deeply flawed. It not only tends to reflect the biases of the scientists (science has shown that scientists of the softer sort tend to "prove" what they already believe), it also tries to boil unimaginable complexity down to simple questions or statistics. In other words, it misses the enormous beauty of the unmeasurable. Science can't see or feel love. It can't sense the myriad challenges of a real life. It can't tell which child will be empowered by challenge and which overwhelmed. All it can see is vast patterns – like my premie statistics trying to replace the doctor's sense of the individual case. Most critically, scientists often miss the *second order* effects. Making a kid happy in the short term can undermine happiness in the long term. Going easy on a kid so they learn more readily can leave them unprepared for stressful real-world environments. We try to find these effects, but even when we do so, the scientific approach is coarse by its very nature. Dangerous playgrounds for young children lead to fewer injuries later in life. But *some* children never recover from the trauma of injuring themselves.

We are complex. It is precisely because of complexity that common sense and paying careful attention to *your own* children can be more effective than the best scientific and academic reasoning – no matter the metrics. You have to think about the kid, think about how they respond, and constantly adapt. There is no magic shortcut.

When we were looking at fostering and perhaps adopting children, there was a universal, scientific, rule. The household could have *no* negative feedback. No criticism. No punishments. If we hadn't been so desperate to have more children, it would have been a dealbreaker.

Sometimes the negative is needed. Sometimes, even with traumatized children, it can be necessary for their growth.

Every child, every person, is an individual. There is no recipe for success. We forget that only at our own very great peril.

A Note on Education

I grew up (and remained for many years) a strong proponent of home school. The educational outcomes I experienced were superb. In addition, home schoolers had more opportunity to preserve their Truth and Virtue by simple dint of not facing social pressure. Rebecca, and practicality, gradually weaned me from my attachment to this model.

In Portland, Rebecca got involved in founding a Jewish Day School. We were reasonably bit players (me especially), but I'd had a long-term fascination with education. In my various explorations, I came across the American Classical Christian Schools (ACCS). They were funded by a less than exemplar individual, but the educational structure made an enormous amount of sense to me. I exchanged a presentation and discussion of Judaism with their Senior Class for an exploration of their administrative and financial model. Their system was structured to enable absolutely minimal administration (a principal, a secretary and a janitor for 187 students), a very high student to teacher ratio *and* some of the best educational outcomes in the State (they are the fifth-ranked private school by SAT scores).

With the exception of modest capital expenses, the school was entirely funded by tuition. Even today, tuition at the Beaverton, Oregon school starts at $5,700 in kindergarten and rises to $10,800 by the end of High School. Portland Public Schools spend over $16,000 per student while the prestigious Catlin Gabel charges over $37,000.

Exposure to *this* school helped drive my preferred educational funding model.

Public schools in many countries are very weak. Outcomes would be improved with competition. But I am *not* a fan of traditional school vouchers. Like flat fees for healthcare or subsidies for college, they inevitably drive-up costs. Sure, better outcomes are rewarded by such choice – but efficiencies are not created. Vouchers only create a cost floor, a floor that is gradually raised so lower income students are not priced out of educational opportunities.

My approach to education funding would mirror my approach to medical funding. A median rate would be paid to any provider and parents can get 5% back – so long as their children *pass* standardized achievement tests. If they save money by going to home school, they can get hundreds of dollars back (in addition to covering their expenses).

When both outcomes and costs are incentivized, opportunities are extended for all students – no matter the wealth, color or social standing of their parents.

There would be one ripple on this model. In order to qualify for funding, I'd require primary and secondary educational institutions of whatever ilk to participate in exchange programs. So if you send your kid to a Torah-observant school, they'd have to spend a week a year someplace else – whether secular, Muslim, Christian or other.

There's a real benefit to knitting together a broader society even as you *encourage* the diversity of distinct sub-cultures.

As a final aside, if there hadn't been a Torah-observant Jewish Day School in Portland, then Rebecca and I probably would have sent our children to the evangelical Christian ACCS school I toured.

COMMUNITY

What is the purpose of a relationship with a community? For many Torah-observant Jews, community is a central bulwark and definer of their religious practice. But that wasn't the case for me or my siblings. My family became religious *without* a community. For my parents, community was never all that important. A synagogue was where you prayed. Your friendships, your family and your faith would survive just fine outside of it.

For the most part, we didn't even pray in a synagogue. Our relationship with the synagogue was pretty tangential. Community, as defined by a synagogue, wasn't *that* important.

And yet, we had community. We had Camp Cox. We had people from many different walks of life who were a part of our lives. We were a part of theirs as well. There was some overlap with the Jewish community, but not *only* the Jewish community.

In our marriage, Rebecca and I have had many people from many backgrounds in our home for the Sabbath. From Indian Jains to Nigerian Christians and from Pakistani Muslims to Israeli Jews (we've even had a few people who professed no religion!). Our "communal life" didn't so much center on synagogues as encompass them (Rebecca and I attended separate congregations). Even when we had our own congregation (see below), we didn't define our social circle around it. Instead, just as with my parents, our community was centered on our home.

That home-centered-community reached its pinnacle in the year before we made Aliyah (moved to Israel). In that year, we had 90 people stay in our house for Shabbat (over the course of the year, not all in one week). We were a go-to place for meals and lodging. We had an Orthodox long-distance trucker[1], Intel employees, tourists and many, many others. All had stories. Many opened their homes to us later on *our* journey. In a way, they were community. The height of how we might have defined it at the time.

Our sense of community (aside from our family within our home) was essentially transitory. We weren't committed to anything. We were willing to contribute – even to work hard in order to contribute. But our souls were not in those places. We wanted to do the right thing, but we didn't *really* care.

----

[1] He'd been an urban combatant in the IDF. It had scarred him terribly. He left to explore and decompress and wound up suffering a coma due to a fall in Peru. When he woke up four months later, a Chabad Rabbi was sitting by his bedside. With that, his religious journey began.

We knew, in a few years, we'd simply move on.

Our family and our home, though? That was another matter. Those were going nowhere.

Our souls were with them.

That reality remained even after we moved to Israel. Rebecca and I continued our somewhat separate and separatist ways. She prayed at two different synagogues, alternating weeks. I added in a third, a *bnei Yisrael* Indian congregation. I had nothing in common with them or their traditions, but I deeply appreciated the opportunity to widen my own appreciation for the scope of religious Judaism by associating with them as I had with various other communities[1]. It also reminded me of communities outside Israel in that it was trying to preserve a vanishing tradition. While our house was much smaller (we had 5 kids sleeping in one room), but we still hadn't really shifted our sense of *home* outside its doors.

Community, outside the home, wasn't central to our lives.

It still had no permanence.

When we first moved to our current neighborhood, it was much the same. We bounced from place to place. We were looking for a place to fit. We thought we had a possible match, but it shifted religiously, and we moved on.

We'd meet people at shul. We'd talk. But we were never grounded in any institution.

---

[1] To this day, in my Shabbat davening, I maintain snippets from Chabad, bnei Yisrael, Rhodes Sephardi, and Spanish-Portuguese davening.

And then came *Lechu N'ranena.*

Over the course of this book, I've spoken a lot about purpose. I've talked about how important the vast and broad goals of G-dliness and then the fostering of Goodness and Holiness are to us. I've also mentioned, briefly, how every day was Rosh Hashana for me. Every day, I was reassessing and reanalyzing whether what I was doing was fulfilling my purpose. Whether I was using the tools I had been given well.

I'd spoken at the Sephardi synagogue in Portland. I'd even delivered the occasional dvar Torah at the bnei Yisrael congregation. I'd written for the Jewish Press and Arutz 7 Online. But these were always steppingstones; they never really made me feel like I had found my path.

Not long after *Lechu* started, I spoke in synagogue about Kashrut and the death of Nadav and Avihu. We were meeting in a little *gan* (Kindergarten) then. I spoke almost every Shabbat for a year after that. My vision and perspective unfolded and gathered steam. Occasionally, I flirted with the drug of pride; I'd never had this sort of opportunity before. I also debated how much I should actively promote *myself*. After all, ideas need a front man/woman. They need a brand. But, aside from wearing a somewhat distinctive white hat, I stayed away from this. My name isn't even on most of my work. I still don't know if that is really for the best. I keep with it, though. My goal was never to impress with my logic or erudition. On a basic level, I approached speaking as I approached prayer. I was there to serve others. If I did that well, then more and greater opportunities would present themselves. If I did that well, then I could take pride in what I had accomplished.

I started a little custom in those first couple years with *Lechu*. Before I speak in front of the synagogue, I silently utter a phrase from our daily prayers:

אֲדֹנָי שְׂפָתַי תִּפְתָּח וּפִי יַגִּיד תְּהִלָּתֶךָ
O Lord, open my lips, so that my mouth may
praise You.

The goal was to keep everything on the right channel.

I was speaking for a purpose.

After a while, I happened to notice that, for the first time since I'd been six years old, I was no longer asking myself whether I was fulfilling my purpose. I was using my experiences, my past, my education, and my study to build up those around me. I was using all the tools I had, and I was using them well.

I was where I belonged[1].

After that first year, I backed away from speaking. It is important to have a variety of voices and one perspective can get boring. Also, everybody should have the opportunity I had.

---

[1] At one point, I entertained notions of trying to build on that speaking – of trying to use the community to share the ideas more broadly. That didn't happen. I realize now that it *shouldn't* have happened. A community needs a diversity of attitudes, approaches, and opinions. A community organized around one set of ideas (even mine) is far less dynamic and everybody within it would suffer as a result.

I still speak and give classes, but only once every few weeks. Instead, I shifted to writing. One year, I wrote a short story every Shabbat. The stories were related to the Torah Readings and the Holidays. People both inside and outside of the community have told me those stories were life-altering[1].

Then, this past year, in preparation for an actual Rosh Hashana, I found myself asking the same question. "Am I fulfilling my purpose?" I wrote a Yom Kippur greeting that was not entirely positive on that question.

I once again felt I wasn't achieving what I ought to be achieving. In its way, the greeting was quite self-centered. Then, while praying on Yom Kippur, I realized what I needed to do next.

I didn't need to ask others to raise *me* up, I needed to raise *them* up.

I didn't need to expand outward and try to work on a grand scale. I needed to focus on the community itself and work on the personal scale. I decided then to profile members of my community – interviewing them and writing about how *they* walk in the path of G-d. I believe I am empowering those I interview, spreading what they've learned. And I believe I am empowering my readers, by sharing the examples of others within the community. I'm building community, using all tools that I have.

---

[1] I published them in a five-volume anthology of Torah Shorts.

I'm not the Rabbi of the community. I never will be a Rabbi[1] and I've grown increasingly uncomfortable with the idea of followers[2].

Nonetheless, *I am fulfilling my purpose.*

People ask me sometimes why I take so much time for these side initiatives.

The answer is simple.

My goal since I was a very young man has long been to live a G-dly life.

For me, these aren't side initiatives. They (along with my family and children) are my path to Holiness.

Today, *I* am grounded in an institution, but *our* home is once again growing in importance. We just bought our first house in Israel. We've remodeled it and organized it so that we can support the sort of home community we had in Oregon (with a serious kitchen, indoor seating for 30 and outdoor seating for another 100). Rebecca and I are both hoping that our home will build up a community of its own. Even as our connection to *Lechu* continues, we hope to use our house to build deeper connections to all those around us.

In the past, our soul has always been in our *home*. But it has never been in a place. Every place, ever *makom*, has simply been one we were passing through.

---

[1] That Talmud study still evades me.

[2] I was never comfortable with the idea of followers to begin with. I've had some wannabe followers before. I instinctively try to drive them away. So far, I'm batting 100%.

This place, this community, this house, are different.
Our *souls* are here and *here* they are flourishing.

Vermont Street

The below shares a bit of our experience with another community.

At one point, my wife and I, together with my brother's family,
wanted to have a mainline Orthodox synagogue in our
neighborhood. There was already a community there, but they were
walking five miles to the old synagogue in downtown. Given
Portland weather, that could be a challenging experience. So, we
started a little community, called Vermont Street.

We rented a little house. I was the speaker and often led prayers.
My brother organized and cooked (as did Rebecca). We had dinners
and lunches for the whole community. There were others deeply
involved as well. We started off with Friday nights alone. We
weren't planning on extending to Shabbat day for a while – we
didn't have a Torah reader. Then, a few weeks in, the Rabbi at a
synagogue we were attending during the day gave a speech about
the evils of people who had no business starting a synagogue
starting a synagogue. We sat through it, out of diminishing respect.
The next week we attended the special Torah reading of Shabbat
Zachor. In it we are commanded to destroy our greatest enemy,
Amalek. Amalek gets defined in all sorts of ways – depending on
the speaker's pre-existing biases. Lo and behold, the Rabbi starts
speaking about how *we* were Amalek – because we were starting our
own synagogue. *Then* we walked out. The Rabbi's wife came at us
like a tornado, shouting that we were disrespecting her husband by
walking out on his speech. I guess it hadn't occurred to her that we
were worthy of some modicum of respect, too. At that point,
though, the split was final. We began to have weekly Shabbat day
services.

They weren't good. Our *minyanim* (prayer groups of 10 men) were sporadic. I did Torah reading, which was a nightmare. But the atmosphere was warm and loving. And we accomplished our goal. Just over a year later, once we hired a Rabbi to up the stakes, the mainline synagogue moved from downtown. By that point Rebecca and I had already left town and Vermont Street shut down, its mission accomplished.

The biggest challenge of having a community in Portland involved the issue of conversion. There is tremendous emphasis in the Orthodox community of what is or is not a valid conversion. The road to conversion is made very, very difficult to follow. One of the reasons for this is because we are obligated to discourage conversions to Judaism. Another oft-cited reason is that converts have to accept the Torah and they can't do that unless they already understand it. For my part, I doubt the vast majority of people (myself included) really understand the commandments and how there are reflected in Halacha.

In Portland, every local family has a convert. Many, though, are not accepted; the wrong Rabbi or Rabbinical Court carried out the process or the individuals who converted failed to adhere to an Orthodox lifestyle. Some of these people prayed at Vermont Street. If we accepted them, we would be considered illegitimate. If we rejected them, then, well, they would be rejected. I consulted with our family Rabbi, who had studied the topic for over a decade. He said, simply: if three Shabbat observant men are witnesses to the conversion process, then the convert is Jewish. Not Rabbis, not a highly respected court. Simply three Shabbat observant men. He was in favor of accepting almost everybody. A helpful scholar who disagreed decided to educate us about the complexity of real-world halacha. My older brother (who did not live in Portland), and I did a multi-month course on conversion. We ended up right where we started; there was no solid justification for the exclusions that were being practiced. At the worst, if there were questions about whether the Rabbis involved were actually Shabbat observant, then three men from our community could have reconverted questionable cases. I think, at one point, we made that suggestion to a controversial family. They were so insulted by the concept of being required to reconvert – even in a quicky manner – that it never went anywhere.

Vermont Street never got to full acceptance of questionable conversions. We kept ourselves in line with the broader community. We had enough controversy without certificating conversions.

I came across the story of the rabbis of Salonika (while writing a profile of a Holocaust survivor from the city). This city strongly supported the claims of conversos – those who had converted to Christianity or whose ancestors had. Instead of requiring them to reconvert, they were reaccepted through a process they called *teshuva* (repentance). In one case, a man was apparently accepted into the *teshuva* process even though he only claimed his *father* was Jewish (among the Torah-observant, Jewish identity descends matrilineally). This accepting process, which was practiced for centuries, had a profound and positive impact on the community. I later joined another community accused of accepting poorly documented Jews. They claimed a heritage from the nearby island of Rhodes, which might have been the justification for their approach. In that case, I was happy to simply play to my ignorance and follow the Rabbi's lead.

To this day I have no idea how "inclusive" that Rabbi actually was.

To this day, I don't want to know.

RANDOMS

In life, there are two kinds of surprises. Bad surprises, which tend to come at you out of the blue. And good surprises, which you tend to have to create an opening for.

Cancer can strike at any time, but you have to buy a ticket to win the lottery.

One of my favorite illustrations of this is Norman Borlaug. In 1937, Borlaug was a graduate student. He had an undergraduate degree in Forestry and had worked as a Forest Service officer on the Middle Fork of the Salmon River - where my parents would later live and where my eldest three siblings would be raised. He'd lost his job and returned to school.

One day that year, he attended a lecture. The event itself would seem unremarkable. The lecture was given by Dr. Elvin Stakman - an expert in the identification and treatment of diseases in wheat. During that lecture, Dr. Stakman stated that "[science could] go further than has ever been possible to [end] the miseries of hunger and starvation from this earth."

With that statement, Borlaug – by all accounts a tremendously caring person – found himself drawn to a concept. A concept that *he* could impact hundreds of millions of lives. With that chance encounter, the student, the teacher, and our entire world were forever changed.

In the following decades, Dr. Borlaug revolutionized farming - particularly in the Third World. He led the Green Revolution. He saved many more lives than Hitler ever took[1].

All of this was instigated by a single, almost chance, social interaction.

You can't predict what you can learn from others, but your life and the lives of others can be transformed by those unexpected conversations.

Today, I prioritize those conversations. When I travel (and other times), I make a point of opening myself to conversation with others. My kids are chagrined, and I never *used* to do this, but nowadays I will walk through an airport lounge or a crowd at a fair and I will initiate conversations with anybody I can identify a commonality with. I don't force myself. I'm not that guy in the next seat over who won't shut up. But I give a conversation a seed and then see whether – once the ice is broken – the other party wants to encourage it.

The power of these serendipitous encounters can be incredible.

For example...

- I had a fascinating conversation with an ardently secular Israeli cognitive anthropologist who enabled me to see a whole section of Torah in a new light.

---

[1] He's controversial today for helping so many people survive and thus impacting climate change in some way.

- My willingness to write from other cultures' perspectives was supercharged by reactions to my writing from a Nigerian colleague[1] and a middle-aged black woman I met on a train[2].

- I still work with a Christian Zionist I met on another plane trip. I was seated between him and a Muslim terrorist-in-training on a flight from Luton. Shortly after that conversation, I wrote about it and shared it with many others (I've added the write-up to the end of this section.)

I go to shiva calls (visiting houses of mourning), even if I don't know the person who died or their families. I consistently ask one question: "If the deceased had one attribute, one characteristic or one action you'd want to see spread – what would it be?"

I want to learn from others and share what I've learned. It can only bring us closer together.

---

[1] I wrote a story describing a young man immigrating to Lagos by bus from a small village to the north of Nigeria. I showed it to him shortly after we met and he said, "Hey man, how long you live in Nigeria?" I'd never been to Africa, but I'd described *his* experience when he'd immigrated to Lagos from the north. He had a fascinating story. As a tiny slice of it, he was a convert from Islam to Christianity. I thought he would have converted stealthily. But... no. He and his family announced in the village square that they were converting. It offered them protection. If they were then murdered for their decision, everybody would know who did it. He remains one of my readers.

[2] Being from rural Oregon, I don't know many black Americans. I wrote a story from the perspective of a middle-aged black woman in Philly. Meeting this middle-aged black woman from Virginia, I asked her to read it. She was crying by the end of it, thanking me for describing her childhood church so perfectly.

My entire professional career has been based on being able to take a step further back than those around me in order to see and approach difficult problems or opportunities from new angles. I'm pretty good at my own "new" angles given my personal history and education. But nothing helps you grasp new perspectives more powerfully than talking to (or even about) the people who hold them.

Random conversations can change a person – or even the world as a whole –in ways that are entirely unpredictable.

A Conversation with a Terrorist in Training

I was one of the first to board the plane. It was an EasyJet flight from London to Tel Aviv and at under five hours, I considered it a reasonably short hop. My one misfortune on this flight was that I was seated in seat B. A middle seat. I almost never find myself in a middle seat.

As additional passengers began to board, I played a familiar game. I analyzed them, wondering who my seatmates would be. Would they be the kinds of people who minded their own business — the kind of people you never bother to say "hello" to? Would they engage in polite small talk before turning to a book or movie? Or would I really learn something from them — finding myself next to somebody with a fascinating background or a promising future.

This wasn't quite my normal Tel Aviv flight. In the boarding area, there had been more than a dozen Wahhabi Muslims (note, they don't like being called that — they just follow a long-deceased leader named Wahab who claimed to be restoring pure Islam).

310

These guys are distinct because of their haircuts, beards, and (most tellingly) their dress. I mean that last one almost literally. They dress in ankle-length tunics.

Oh, and while a tiny minority of Wahhabi may commit terrorist attacks, the Wahhabi are also the source of the vast majority of Sunni terrorists.

Notably, there were a few women in the group and while they were wearing the *niqab* — their *niqabs* were not black. On a spectrum then, these guys were to the left of the Islamic State, but it wasn't clear how far to the left.

So, I was sitting on the plane and I've got to admit, I was hoping to score a Wahhabi seatmate. It would make for an interesting conversation.

The first guy to show up is the guy on the aisle. He's white and dressed in conventional western clothes. Not a hit. Moments later, my window-side companion shows up and *score!*, he's got the whole get-up going on. He slides past me and then the white guy sits down, plops on some earbuds and a face mask and passes out before pushback.

The Wahhabi guy and I start talking.

He's from Manchester and he works in Finance (a customer support agent for an innovative credit card anti-fraud company, as I recall). Soon, he starts talking about the Jewish "invasion" of the Al-Aqsa Mosque. I turn the topic to the side; I'm not interested in a shouting match. So, instead, I get him to start showing me the beauty and purity of his Islam — especially when compared with Judaism. While I am no expert, he is quite surprised that I know what I know. And I have a lot of fun showing him the similarities in jurisprudence between the faiths as well as the fundamental differences in our relationships to G-d and our desired means of influencing the world.

311

Before long, it is clear he's really a beginner. He tells me that he'd only begun to learn the Koran three years earlier. He explains the sorts of mistakes newbies make in reading it (e.g., mixing in Urdu pronunciation). But although he can read the Koran, he speaks no Arabic and no Urdu. He's simply been fed (and eaten up) these standard lessons on maintaining the purity of the text and the tradition.

He and his group (they are all together) are coming to Israel for a rage trip. They are there to be given a guided tour of the suffering of the Palestinian people and to have their anger cultivated.

As the conversation continues, he confides that his uncle and aunt and parents are afraid of him. He explains that Islam is a religion of peace — and how Mohammed forbade the killing of children and women or the destruction of infrastructure. He explains the prohibition on suicide attacks.

As part of this, he tells me about another uncle, an officer in Pakistan, whose son was killed in school. The Taliban showed up, asked the children of the officers to step forward, and then machine-gunned them.

He condemns this.

But then he shares a question his teacher asked him — "If your enemy kills your loved ones, how are else you supposed to respond?"

The context is Israel.

At this point, it is clear to me that he is being trained. He is being trained to believe that *his people* are peaceful and G-d-like. Soon, he will be taught that they must, nonetheless, respond to the crimes of their enemies.

I'm sure he will soon learn, if he continues to be a good student, that this allows the crossing of certain lines.

He is being led down a path of complete radicalization. The process and the timelines match what profiles we have of past terrorists.

And so, it is clear to me that this conversation is an important one; perhaps more so for *his life* than for mine.

In response to his teacher's question, I ask him to imagine that both sides might be asking that same thing. I ask him what the outcome of that would be.

And then I show him my book, *the City on the Heights*. In particular, I share the Mohammed chapter with him — sharing how that character is radicalized by the crimes committed against him. I want him to read and begin to grasp a broader picture.

I want him to see the path of my Mohammed's life.

Thankfully, he is fascinated by the book.

He asks me about Zionism — he'd been told it was the equivalent of ISIS for Jews. I share our history with him and describe what Zionism is — a desire to return to our ancestral land. I explain that it is not exclusively religious. Many secular people are Zionist, and many religious describe themselves as anti-Zionist. The distinction among the religious is one of action: a disagreement over whether G-d returns us to our land, or whether we do it ourselves.

It is clear, as he asks me how I study, that this young man respects me.

And so, I tell him I am a Zionist.

I never say this to Jews (because it isn't a primary motivation in my life), but he needs to hear it from me.

He asks me which kind — the kind who believes G-d should return the Jews to their land or the kind who should return ourselves.

And I say, 'both.'

Soon after, he falls asleep and the white guy on my right wakes up.

That guy is a Christian Zionist who lives in Israel. Not just in Israel, he actually lived in Me'ah Shearim — the ultimate ultra-Orthodox neighborhood. I proceed to have a totally different conversation with him, as you'd imagine.

He too is quite interested in the book.

As we make our final approach, both men are awake and alert. I keep the conversations separate. I try to think of what thoughts to leave the Wahhabi Muslim with.

I prepare for our descent.

Perhaps we'll fly over my home.

But then something remarkable happens.

In all the times I've flown into Israel (which is quite a few, I live here), I've always circled over Modi'in (my home) or come in straight from the coast. But on this flight, we fly straight inland and over Tukaram. I show him how thin the country is.

And then we fly over Rawabi – the new Palestinian city – I've never flown over Rawabi. It is a gorgeous city, a striking contrast to dismal Manchester.

I tell him about it, and it shocks him.

It isn't going to be on his tour.

Finally, we land, and I share my card with both men.

I've since been in regular contact with the Christian. The Muslim never reached out to me.

HUMANITY

My exploration of relationships has slowly stepped outwards. From G-d and marriage to children, community and the random people I've met. But there is a whole world beyond even them.

I've always been struck by the pain of that world. From Hurricane Mitch and the Asian Financial Crisis to the religious wars in the Middle East, the suffering of the Uyghur people and American poverty, I've always hoped that somehow things could be better.

For a long time, my ideas about how to make things better were centered on my mother's political philosophy: religious liberalism. Religious liberalism aims for a State with a very limited *moral* footprint. The State's role is to keep the peace, protect property, streamline legal and other interactions and defend the populace. As much as possible, *moral* obligations would fall on the civic-minded and often religiously guided citizens of that State. They wouldn't have any one religion, but basic precepts of moral behavior would drive necessary acts of charity, allow different groups to define their community as they saw morally fit and ensure basic civic behavior is maintained.

It is a compelling vision. It is quite a common Conservative vision – encompassing an American ideal of heavy charitable contributions combined with tremendous individual freedom and freedom of association and religion. The wealth created by the underlying capitalist system (not crony capitalist as the State's power is limited) would combine with the civic impact of that charitable giving to create a society that is wealthy enough to take care of everybody – albeit within different moral traditions and approaches for doing so.

It is a vision I *used* to subscribe to whole-heartedly. I imagined the spread of such a vision, by whatever means, would enrich those exposed to it. My political perspectives began to change when I began to develop *my* understanding of the cycle of human fulfillment through Goodness, Holiness and ever-growing Responsibility.

This cycle can actually fit many different political and economic systems. It is all just a matter of emphasis. For Communists or Socialists, it would start with the *holiness* of a society in which poor people are freed from the ever-present awareness of evil (loss) caused by fear. It aims, in its way, for a Tahor (pure) society – one far from the loss of potential expressed by Tumah (impurity caused by exposure to evil). For a Religious Liberal like my mother, it would start with individual *Responsibility*, which she would argue can only be developed through freedom. The religious part, with its religious institutions supported by individual choice and freedom, would build on the *Holy*. For a pure atheist capitalist in the Ayn Rand tradition, it would start with the *Good* (represented by creation), proceed to *Responsibility* and expect the rising tide to address the *Holy* through an economically focused lens.

The Torah axis isn't really concerned with *the* battles between these approaches. Its primary concern is *human fulfillment*.

When comparing the Torah system with a Religious Liberal system, there are some definite deviations. While individual responsibility is certainly important in the Five Books of Moses, there are also societal obligations. Not just obligations *within* communities, but *across* communities within a geographic region. In my reading, a society that doesn't restrain the corruption of powerful individuals faces divine punishment (the Flood). Likewise, a society that has no concern for *Holiness* (charity and connection to the future) is essentially self-destroying (Sodom). Within the first major batch of laws, the Torah states that a society that mistreats the stranger, widow and orphan is punished by G-d, *as a society*. It is the only *national* punishment that exists prior to the sin of the calf[1]. It suggests a much broader moral precept that ought to apply to *all* societies[2]. It speaks to a charitable obligation that extends beyond voluntary giving.

---

[1] Which precipitated a change in the relationship with G-d and a whole new batch of national consequences.

[2] Many things do *not* apply to all societies. These include protections for the fulfillment society described. These protections are extreme in description, but the implementation is again more

Later on, the Torah has two seemingly contrary statements within a few verses of each other. One says: "there will be no poor among you." The second says: "There will always be poor in the land." You have to give charity because of those poor in the land; those poor who are *not among you*. In other words, you have to take care of the poor who are *not* part of your communities. And, of course, land is redistributed every 50 years and debts are erased every 7. There is a reset that is dramatically distinct from a society focused on the protection of property[1].

The "individual responsibility" model doesn't fit.

Of course, the mandatory redistributionist models don't quite fit either. In the Five Books of Moses, charity focuses on two core methodologies. The first is the leaving of the corners of fields and gleanings. The poor can harvest, glean and then process and prepare their own food. This isn't a cash handout. The poor person *must* engage in creative work (gathering, winnowing, grinding and baking) in order to eat[2]. The only thing they don't *do* is planting and the only thing they don't *have* is land ownership. Some part of creation is divorced from acquisition, but they still engage in as much creation as possible. They get to experience fulfillment and that experience isn't short-circuited by being given a cash or even a

---

flexible. The purpose (protecting core values) is common to every functioning society.

[1] Although, as the text makes quite clear, no humans actually own the property. It is simply granted to them on the basis of their relationship with G-d.

[2] I wrote a chapter in *The City on the Heights* based on this concept, but set in modern Iraq.

meal. The second is the limitation on debt. Just as with modern bankruptcy, there is a way out of debt. The books can be wiped clean in order to prevent evil (e.g., bad circumstances) from defining entire lives or multiple generations. Tied in with this is the timely payment of wages.

While the Five Books of Moses make a point of holding up the poor as full people with a claim to the divine relationship and holiness[1], they do not suggest they simply have a right to food or other wealth. They don't get welfare checks or even soup from a kitchen. Instead, they get the right to *participate* in the cycle of Goodness and Holiness – with the raw materials necessary for Goodness provided to those who lack them[2].

My Torah study has led me to believe that the emphasis of a social and political structure should be on enabling human fulfillment. Enabling human fulfillment is not *necessarily* dependent on Capitalism, Communism, Liberalism, Democracy or any other modern system. Yes, there *are* massive benefits to having an accountable government, but even that can take many forms. It *should* take many forms. While a free and responsible society engaging in a self-chosen fulfilling life is the ultimate goal, stepping *towards* that ideal can involve many other types of governance. The ideal, for any

---

[1] The redistribution of land is cast within this divine relationship. Land is simply an opportunity to engage in the cycle of fulfillment.

[2] While there is an encouragement to loan money to the poor interest-free, and to redeem your relatives from slavery, neither is really a total obligation. "Society" does not take your money to ensure they are fulfilled. The actual *obligations* are somewhat limited.

particular culture at any particular time, may very well *not* be an attempt at a Liberal Democratic government with a religious society.

In a way, my political and economic philosophy started with my mother's well-reasoned and thought-out philosophy of Religious Liberalism and then, through study and analysis of my own (and the shock of American failures), has led to my *father's* instinctive grasp of creation, holiness and fulfillment.

In books, podcasts and other forums, I've written, and spoken, about policy ideas based on these concepts. Policy ideas about taxation, healthcare, education, foreign policy and more. I feel as if I could help. As if my method of thinking about the world might sidestep some of the ideological loggerheads that have dominated recent *centuries*. As if *I* could influence people, just a bit, to focus not on freedom, wealth or harmony – but fulfillment. To influence people, and then politicians and governments to pivot to this perspective. Perhaps they could borrow my ideas and recast them for their own political advantages. But we've been so trained to think in terms of right and left – and react reflexively against any position that appears to belong to those we oppose – that we can't recognize another axis when it is staring us in the face[1]. Perhaps I'm wrong. Perhaps everybody sees what I see. But I

---

[1] People used to see our triplets, lined up in three capsules, and say "Look, twins!" They didn't expect triplets, so they couldn't even process they were there.

certainly feel as if I stand alone in terms of both ideology and policy.

Alone, and completely impotent.

This frustrates me deeply.

But it has not frustrated me completely.

Since very early in my life, I have sought to be a Man of G-d. My own failures have helped me realize what that actually means. I now know that to be a Man (or Woman) of G-d is to be a blessing to others. A blessing, in turn, is a growth in opportunity – whether it be material or spiritual.

In other words: a Man of G-d empowers others.

I've tried so many times to touch the world. To be a blessing. Who Can Help? lasted weeks and helped nobody, GiveDaily shriveled up without ever really growing. A computer training company I started (to help middle-aged people in the 90s learn how to think like software developers and thus be empowered in their use of computers) failed. Bible4Community attracted few users. In just the last year, I attempted to make an anonymous social network that enables groups to celebrate their achievements (theGreaterI.com). It is already dormant. Since moving to Israel, I have written nine books, counting this one. All (but the one you're reading) have sought to be entertaining fiction; a sort of back-door method of exposing people to my ideas. My best-selling book sold 170 copies – probably more than all the others combined[1].

By any metric, my attempts have been failures.

And yet... and yet people have told me how my stories and books have changed their lives.

Life is a ripple.

And so I now understand that if I can be a blessing to only a few people, if I can empower *them*, then I can be a blessing to many more. Sure, I will probably never achieve any sort of mass success. But then again, the world is rarely blessed though grand actions and massive waves of change. It is often cursed by such things. Blessing most often comes from individual acts of caring and dedication.

The world is blessed by the still, small, voice of G-d.

This approach is why I'm writing profiles in my community and why we are hosting small events focused on the theme of uplifting. They are only a *little* effort. They only take place *within* the community. They are almost entirely private. But they are also an acknowledgement that the most important

---

[1] Some of them are unpublishable – a white Jewish man is *not supposed to* write fiction from a black woman's perspective. The *Hidden Agent* would probably get me cancelled if I were more popular.

impacts are often those you *cannot measure*. Indeed, they are an acknowledgement that the most important impacts are often those you *cannot even see*.

I used to ask students interviewing to get into the University of Pennsylvania what they'd spend a million dollars on – if I were to give it to them. Almost all gave the typical "give it to charity" answer. A few dared to admit they'd keep it. I wasn't asking the question to judge their morals or honesty. I was asking because I wanted to see whether they had thought about how they'd try to change the world – given *more* power to do so.

I used to think I had my own answers to that question. I used to think I knew what I'd do. Now, I know I don't. A million dollars, or even a billion, can only do so much to change how people think[1]. A billion dollars won't spread a new moral vision and it won't empower people, except in a very superficial way.

It won't enable true fulfillment.

Cultures and communities that are uplifting must be cultivated person-by-person and bit-by-bit. Governments and economies that uplift can only follow in the wake of those cultures and communities.

---

[1] Just ask Presidential Candidate Michael Bloomberg

323

I'm no Churchill or Martin Luther King Jr. I'm no great author or business leader. I'm a Quality Assurance Manager at a small aerospace company. I'm a husband and a father. I have far more in common with that greengrocer who lived a quiet life than I do with the great Michelangelo who might have once visited his store.

And yet... and yet... just like that greengrocer, I can be a source of fundamental blessing.

We all can.

Knowing that should fill our souls with joy.

We are created in the image of G-d.
No matter who we are, our potential knows no limits.

Thank you for sharing my journey (so far),

Joseph Cox

MY OTHER BOOKS

Please, if you think this book has helped you – pay it forward. Tell others about it, leave reviews online and check out my other written and recorded content at www.JosephCox.com. If you want to read other books (apparently, none as good as this) some of my recent books include:

The Hidden Agent – the story of an FBI agent investigating an African preacher implicated in the deaths of over 30 people. This book is *also* an exploration of the nature of blessing and curse.

The City on the Heights – the story of a 16-year-old girl from Mosul who escapes with her brother after ISIS kills her parents. This book is *also* an exploration of another approach to foreign policy in areas cursed by ethnic struggle and violence.

Candidate Everyone – the U.S. elections as a reality TV show. This book is *also* an exploration of ideas on health care, education and taxation. This is a very light and fun read.

The Torah Shorts Series – a series of five books (and 58 stories) based on sections of the Torah. Stories range from intrigue in pre-Columbian Peru to relations with alien civilizations to musicians and addicts discovering new possibilities (and much more). Some are awesome, most are pretty good and some are 'meh.' I would have taken the 'meh' ones out, but some people find the stories I consider the worst to be actually be the most engaging. Whaddya' know...

Made in the USA
Middletown, DE
15 August 2022

71209110R00186